C000277265

Magic Moments

Magic Moments

LIFE-CHANGING
ENCOUNTERS WITH
BOOKS, FILMS, MUSIC ...

John Sutherland

P

PROFILE BOOKS

First published in Great Britain in 2008 by
Profile Books Ltd
3A Exmouth House
Pine Street
Exmouth Market
London EC1R 0JH
www.profilebooks.com

Copyright © John Sutherland, 2008

10 9 8 7 6 5 4 3 2 1

Text design by Sue Lamble

Typeset in Quadraat by MacGuru Ltd
info@macguru.org.uk

Printed and bound in Great Britain by
Clays, Bungay, Suffolk

The moral right of the author has been asserted.

All rights reserved. Without limiting the rights under copyright
reserved above, no part of this publication may be reproduced,
stored or introduced into a retrieval system, or transmitted, in
any form or by any means (electronic, mechanical, photocopying,
recording or otherwise), without the prior written permission
of both the copyright owner and the publisher of this book.

A CIP catalogue record for this book is available from the British Library.

ISBN 978 1 84668 078 6

The paper this book is printed on is certified by the © 1996 Forest
Stewardship Council A.C. (FSC). It is ancient-forest friendly.
The printer holds FSC chain of custody SGS-COC-2061

FSC
Mixed Sources
Product group from well-managed
forests and other controlled sources

Cert no. SGS-COC-2061
www.fsc.org
© 1996 Forest Stewardship Council

Up! up! my Friend, and quit your books!
William Wordsworth

Why?
John Sutherland

Contents

Introduction

THE IDEA BEHIND this book is simple. Coleridge puts it memorably in *Biographia Literaria*, recalling his first brush with books as a child, and the private, precociously Coleridgean wonderland those strange black marks on a white surface created for him:

> At six years old I remember to have read Belisarius, *Robinson Crusoe*, and Philip Quarll – and then I found the *Arabian Nights' Entertainments* – one tale of which (the tale of a man who was compelled to seek for a pure virgin) made so deep an impression on me (I had read it in the evening while my mother was mending stockings) that I was haunted by spectres whenever I was in the dark – and I distinctly remember the anxious and fearful eagerness with which I used to watch the window in which the books lay – and whenever the sun lay upon them, I would seize it, carry it by the wall, and bask, and read.

It would require Thesean ingenuity to track it, but there is a thread leading from that ball of maternal wool to *The Rime of the Ancient Mariner* and the laudanum flask.

In this book I've selected moments, mainly literary, which were life-changing; or, at least, mind-changing, or – at the very least – influential. The moments are arranged sequentially, through time. My *biographia literaria*. Every literate person has one, all fascinating, although I claim nothing grandly Coleridgean for mine. There is something both quaint and terrifying in the vision of that little six-year-old Sam wrestling with the military exploits of Flavius Belisarius. In the original Latin, one doesn't doubt. For me, it was Tarzan of the Apes. For today's children, many of them, Grand Theft Auto.

Looking back through the moments recorded here, I see as many different versions of me as of books. 'How queer,' mused Virginia Woolf, 'to have so many selves – how bewildering!' Obviously, I read more than what is here recorded, saw more films and plays, and heard other music. But assuming we all come into adulthood as what the Mafia call 'made men' – and private Swiss schools call 'finished' young women – these moments record what, in large part, made and finished me: my final self. Nowadays the age of majority (by which society assumes maturity) is eighteen. In my day, it was twenty-one, and this account ends shortly thereafter, in the early 1960s.

A Note on Illustration

THIS IS A book about things – things read, seen and heard. As any author will testify, illustrating books like this, with the growth of agency licensing and the inexorable tightening of copyright laws, has become, for writers of limited means (are there any others?), a nightmare. More so as the standard contract throws the cost of paying on to the author. A dozen such fees can wipe out an advance.

Meanwhile, in the cyberworld, imagery runs riot: either because out there on the Wild Web West it is impossible to enforce property rights, or (as often) because property holders have, tacitly or formally, conceded limited public domain permission (note, for example, the citations to illustration on www.wikipedia.org).

As I write (in spring 2008) there is furious debate in the British Parliament and press about 'hybridity': the mingling, that is, of embryonic human and animal DNA. It is timely to attempt something analogous in the world of literature: to mingle, that is, print and digital DNA to their mutual benefit.

Attached to this book is not the conventional *apparatus criticus*: 'end matter', 'footnotes', 'index' – typically dragged along behind a book, like Marley's chain. Instead there is a springboard to a website. On that website will be found further signposts, a mere two clicks away, to places on the web where illustration can be readily found. Illustration, that is, which will put flesh and blood on the book's bones. It's important to stress the website is a way station, not a pirate station. It does not contain proprietary material, although it points towards where useful material may be found. The site also has the kind of annotation which book purchasers rather resent paying for, but which they may be interested in glancing at.

To illustrate the illustrations point: Chapter XVII discusses the 1954 TV adaptation of George Orwell's *Nineteen Eighty-Four*. In those pre-videotape days, the BBC could not archive this sensational dramatisation. It was done 'live'. So was the repeat, a few days later, done live. This second version, however, was filmed on 35mm. It was, however, of too poor a quality to convert to DVD when, half a century later, that technology came along. The commemorative repeat of the programme in 2004 (using the 35mm copy) was 'grabbed' by enterprising viewers and put on YouTube, where it can be found at: youtube.com/watch?v=UmHVooJqSMo&feature=Pl ayList&p=AC65E19055A43295&index=14.

It would be laborious to copy that URL out, but one click from the companion website will get you there. More importantly, it will flesh out the chapter, without the need for cumbersome description. So too with the short chapter which follows, on the various versions of early rock and roll: Bill Haley, Elvis Presley, Big Mama Thornton, etc. Audio-visual snippets will, I trust, enrich that discussion. And, perhaps, convey, better than words can, what was 'magic' for me at the time. For those who may have missed the above allusion to 'Marley's chain', the website http://charlesdickenspage.com/

carol.html will make all clear. Those interested in fleshing out, in an unpleasantly literal way, the manga 120 *Days of Sodom* referred to in Chapter XX will find a signpost to it.

In the text that follows, signposting on the companion site is indicated with a discreet asterisk. Readers may jump off the springboard as they please; or not. The website is www.magicmomentbook.com.

Books, once published, are fixed things (recent revisionary book history has suggested that this aspect of the printed word was a hindrance, not a help, to the expansion of scientific knowledge in the Renaissance, overturning more heroic views of Gutenberg's revolution). The World Wide Web, by contrast, is dynamic and fluid. Nowhere is Keats's 'written in water' more true. The companion website here will be updated for as long as this book is in print, and there will be a facility for reader comment and criticism.

The title of this book echoes the title of a popular song of spring 1958, 'Magic Moments', composed by Burt Bacharach and Hal David, and crooned, to chart-topping success in the US, by Perry Como. It was 'covered' in the UK, as was usual in those times, by Ronnie Hilton. A syrupy-sweet song, with somewhat impenetrable lyrics for English listeners, it was for many years licensed, as a catchy jingle, by Rowntrees for their Quality Street advertisements. Many readers recalling it will salivate like Pavlov's dogs, I imagine.

Tarzan's Desert Mystery

(aetat. 5)

IF, AS DAVE does to Hal9oo in Stanley Kubrick's 2001: A *Space Odyssey*, you yanked out my memory banks,* one by one, till you came to the digital / neuron heart of it all – the 'Daisy, Daisy, give me your answer do' layer* – what you'd find there is fascination with the 'chase', with being hunted. It's coded deep in our DNA, I suspect, and goes back to prehistoric times and sabre-toothed things chasing us through the trees. The primeval story. Run for your life. Or die.

The most successful film director of modern times, George Lucas, grasped this fact with his iron rule for successful movie-making: five minutes' exposition, then cut to the chase; and keep things chasing madly for the next 100 minutes, pausing only to pick up a few billion at the box office.

I could see stories before I could read them. And the first narrative I recall seeing is the film *Tarzan's Desert Mystery*.* I was around five years old. I'd had my Lacanian moment, in front of my mother's dressing-table mirror. I knew I was I. Whatever that was.

All that 'I' can remember of the narrative of *Tarzan's Desert Mystery* – stored haphazardly in the basement level of my sensibility – is a handful of vivid but disconnected snapshots. One such is the pulsing-beeping RKO logo* (it carried one back, I now hypothesise, to the womb, and that life-sustaining maternal heartbeat). I had left that foetal haven just sixty months earlier. The only other residue is some scraps from the ten-minute chase scene which the makers of *Tarzan's Desert Mystery* tacked on to the end of the movie.

That, alas, is it.

The Colchester *Gazette* for that week in 1944 informs me that the film (which ran something under seventy minutes) was shown at the Hippodrome in a double bill with a cowboy film. Whether I sat through that other film, I don't recall.

The narrative of the Tarzan movie, as I have recently re-experienced it (on DVD, after an interval of six decades), is bizarre. Hollywood was at war. The jungle family (Tarzan, Jane, Boy) has, for the duration, broken up, to do its patriotic duty.

Tarzan will not miss his oats. Since there was no ceremony, any marital relationship between him and Jane was always strictly off the menu. The Hays Office would not allow it even if, in the interest of morale, the War Office did turn a blind eye. Cheeta was more likely to satisfy the apeman's apish needs. The many movies give no information on what those needs may have been, or whether there even were loins under the loincloth. For all the films divulge, Tarzan may have been as sexless as a worker bee.

There being no gooseberry bushes in the jungle, 'Boy' had literally fallen into the treehouse home from the skies, the sole survivor of a jungle plane crash in an earlier instalment in the loosely linked saga (*Tarzan Gets a Son*). It would be nice to think the plane was the legendary German Fieseler Fi 156 'Storch'.*

Obviously no recruiting office, however desperate, was going to sign on an illiterate apeman. By pedigree, in Edgar Rice Burroughs's source text, Tarzan was an English lord – something Hollywood preferred not to know about. If he wanted to join the colours, 'Greystoke' might have struck lucky with the Household Cavalry. The ability to converse with horses in their own lingo would have helped, as would the family entry in Debrett. But when the movie moguls bought the 'property' from Burroughs, MGM and RKO felt no obligation to stick with the creator's aboriginal version of events. On his part, the author pocketed the royalties, hated the movies, sneered all the way to the bank, and used his capital to buy up that vast tract of Southern California now called 'Tarzana' (whether apeman or real estate was named first is a moot point*).

To return to Colchester, its Hippodrome and the desert mystery of 1944, we learn that Jane has joined up, as a frontline nurse (in fact, the actress playing her wanted a timeout). From pre-invasion London, where she is stationed, Tarzan's mate (in name only) sends a letter back to the jungle house. Boy reads it to his illiterate guardian.

Jane, the letter tells them, urgently needs 'fever medicine'. It can be procured only in the jungle. Stricken Allied soldiers are dying like flies for lack of it. (The incidence of jungle fever was not running at epidemic levels in England in spring 1944, as I recall, but let that pass.)

To procure this wonderful drug, Boy, Cheeta and Tarzan must cross the Sahara Desert (the geography involved doesn't bear thinking about) to another, remote, jungle, where the medicinal vines grow. How Tarzan has come across his pharmacological expertise, or discovered the whereabouts of the other jungle, where foot of man never, apparently, treads, is unclear.

The apish trio make their adventurous way through Rudolph Valentino territory, complete with sheikhs, dunes and foaming stallions. They cross swords with a smirking Nazi master spy (played by Otto Kruger – a name even more German than Weissmuller, or the film's German director, Wilhelm Thiele, and its Jewish-German executive producer, Sol Lesser). They have some close shaves in Charles Boyer's casbah (while on the subject, how does Tarzan keep his chest so unsimianly hairless – razor, depilatory, tweezers, or simple loves-me-loves-me-not plucking?).

Finally, our heroes reach the far-off other jungle – infinitely less hospitable than the frondy place they call home (usually the LA Arboretum,* as it happens: Weissmuller rarely had far to travel from his mansion in Beverly Hills). It is, evidently, the 'jungle that time forgot' (to allude to another highly profitable Burroughs property). Prehistoric dinosaurs roam its treacherous glades and there is a spider so large it could swallow Tarzan without a burp and have Boy for seconds. The lad does, in fact, get caught in its deadly web.

I have no recollection of the big spider. Unsurprisingly, since that episode was almost entirely censored out for the British population as too 'horrific' if the film was to keep its 'U' certificate, allowing the five-year-old Sutherland to see it. The authorities worried about one's moral welfare in those days. The fact that, outside the picture palace, the country was under aerial bombardment from Hitler's Luftwaffe brutes, and one would daily see the most horribly mutilated war victims limping through the streets in their air-blue 'hospital' uniforms, was an irony that did not trouble the

British Board of Film Censorship. The population was not to be frightened.

All this nonsense about dinosaurs and giant spiders was stock-shot, clumsily filched from RKO's *One Million Years BC* (1940).* It was patchworked in, like the Arabian stallions, to pep up a threadbare narrative. It was Hollywood practice, especially in Westerns, thriftily to recycle chase sequences. A feeling of *déjà vu* (*vu*, *vu*, *vu*) hangs, for example, over most of the 125 film versions of Zane Grey's oaters: they would turn up, eerily familiar, in the exciting climaxes of Johnny Mack Brown, Gene Autry and Roy Rogers adventures.

What stuck in my five-year-old mind (the only thing that, as it happens, did stick) were deadly sticky Venus flytraps, whose stamens shot up, without warning, nine feet out of the ground, creating a cage with quivering snake bars in which the victim was fatally imprisoned. Cheeta, I vividly recall, escapes by outjumping the deadly stamens. The less nimble Tarzan – Venus flytrapped – is assisted in his escape by his trusty, but bored-looking, pachyderm pals, summoned from their elephant grove by the famous Weissmullerian yell.

On the question of that yodel: throughout my childhood, it was imitated as children hurled themselves, bellyfloppingly, into Colchester's municipal swimming pool, down by the River Colne (the combination of river mud and chlorine has an odd flavour, and an even odder tint). But the call remained vexingly inimitable. It was not merely the inadequacies of pre-pubescent vocal cords. According to a studio technician, the Tarzanian yell was synthesised from Weissmuller's abnormally high-pitched voice (he was prudently allowed little dialogue in the films) blended with 'the growl of a dog, the bleat of a camel, the howl of a hyena and the pick of a violin G-string'. Hard to imitate, you'll agree.*

The drug is, finally, procured. How much of it, one wonders, can Tarzan stow in his loincloth and send back to Jane? What with Dönitz's formidable submarine blockade, the transcontinental parcel service in 1943 was not entirely reliable. But, as it happened, Jane wouldn't need the damn stuff anyway. The American pharmaceutical giants Pfizer and Merck, at exactly the same period as Tarzan swung through the lianas in search of his 'fever medicine', got there first. As the Wellcome Institute's history of antibiotics records: 'By late 1943, the technology for mass production had been developed and by D-Day in June 1944 there was enough penicillin for all troops.' So Jane would have got her miracle medicine through the more orthodox channels.

Much of it, in 1943, was needed for an unglamorous fever – VD. Many soldiers, alas, fell below Tarzan's exemplary standard of celibacy. So, as it happened, did the five-times-married Weissmuller: Esther Williams – another aquatic superstar – records, in her autobiography, that she would put on an extra layer of swim-clothes when in the water with him, as protection against the inevitable underwater grope.

Tarzan's Desert Mystery is, even by the undemanding standards of the series, feeble. The film draws on astonishing ignorance about the geopolitics of the Second World War. The ignorance goes far beyond the recurrent zoological blooper of Tarzan's regular hand-to-claw combat with tigers – a species somewhat rarer than man-eating spiders in Africa. North Africa was a major theatre of war in 1943–4. Did the Great British public really think that El Alamein was next door to a jungle and that the Eighth Army had dinosaurs, as well as Rommel's Panzers, to contend with?

The plot of *Tarzan's Desert Mystery* conveys the sense of an acutely embarrassed Hollywood. 'We're,' as the heavyweight

First Max Schmeling, then Hitler

champion Joe Louis liked to proclaim, 'on God's side.' But what about the man in the loincloth? The Brown Bomber could be, and was, recruited to the war effort (although in 1943 'Negroes' were not permitted in frontline combat or 'white' units).*

The non-military status of Tarzan was rendered even more embarrassing by a Tarzan called Weissmuller – a name which positively shrieks to have an Iron Cross dangling from it. Explaining that the actor was born, part Jewish, in Hungary, to a public that credited there might be dinosaurs in Africa was hopeless.

In other circumstances, RKO would have ruthlessly anglicised their star – as they did, for example, with their matinee idol John Garfield (né Jake Garfinkle: not, in the 1940s, a name that would have been magnetic on the marquee).* But Weissmuller's name could not be changed, because it was inscribed in history and popular lore. Johnny had won five gold Olympic swimming medals for America, in the 1924 and 1928 Olympic games, establishing sixty-seven world records.* You could no more anglicise the name 'Weissmuller' ('white miller') for PR reasons than that of Eisenhower ('iron hewer') for the purposes of the land invasion of Europe (why is that *verfluchter* German killing us? many foot soldiers in the Wehrmacht must have thought).

I knew nothing of such perplexing things at the time. *Tarzan's Desert Mystery*, as I experienced and archived it in my pinched little *tabula rasa*, squirming excitedly on my one-and-ninepenny seat, was all man-eating, octopoid vegetables. Triffids *avant la lettre*.* The brain is very strange. I would carry those veggy-killers with me through life. Even now, I never look at fried calamari without thinking of them and, somewhere deep inside, shuddering.

I remember where I saw the film in more concrete detail than the flickering narrative itself. It was at the Hippodrome, in Colchester High Street. More precisely, in the downstairs stalls alongside my mother, who intended the outing as a treat for me. Her own treats at the time were more adult, and involved Americans who were carnal rather than celluloid. She, in her Colcestrian way, was a Venus flytrap.

I recall the tobacco smoke curling lazily through the projected beam. It was nasal velvet, like the plush seats with their pitted, blackened ashtrays and, if you looked carefully, the screw holes where once opera-glass holders had been.

They were archaeological relics of a previous Hippodrome. The building was originally commissioned from the maestro of Edwardian playhouse kitsch, Frank Matcham.* The structure is a budget-priced, off-the-shelf version of Matcham's magnum opus, the London Hippodrome – a

Colchester Hippodrome in the 1950s

playhouse which (true to the name) really did accommodate on-stage animal acts.

Colchester's imitation, which opened in 1905, was initially called the Grand Palace of Varieties. The pompous name was soon dropped. The building nestles alongside a genuinely grand Colcestrian palace, the baroque town hall, constructed shortly before, in 1902. The Hippodrome clearly aimed to be a worthy neighbour. The structures, as their florid decorative detail indicates, are of the same vintage as, less creditably, is the pub, the Lamb, whose building, with the pointed arch, is nearest in the photograph above (there was another pub on the other side of the Hippodrome whose name momentarily escapes me). In between the cinema and the town hall was a butcher's and a dry cleaner's. All (Colchester) life is there, as the *News of the World* would have put it.

The surprising cartouche

The Hippodrome could accommodate some 1,400 patrons in the stalls, the royal boxes, the upper circle and the stratospheric 'gods' – so far from the screen that even opera glasses wouldn't have helped. In my young day (and right through to the early 1950s) the top-level benches were favoured by schoolboys with a tanner burning a hole in their short trousers.

The gods, which I came to know well over the next ten years, were hard on the backside but gave one a close-up view of the Hippodrome's ceiling feature, a huge plaster cartouche in the shape of a shell (Colchester is famous for its oysters – something that endeared the place to the ancient Romans; 'Oysterdrome' would not, however, have worked). The decoration features two undraped neoclassical lovelies with what look like randy trolls in their laps, who seem, incredibly, to be 'copping a feel' (as we would learn to say a few years later).*

I never went to the Hippodrome without looking wonderingly at its erotic décor (and, in later years, without a little thrill of the loins – one was very hard up for such thrills in the 1950s). There were, in the back two rows, 'love seats' – tandem affairs where couples could canoodle and possibly – if the usherette's censorious torch beam did not home in – cop their own feel, in homage to the scene above them.

In the mid-1920s, with the arrival of talkies, the Hippodrome had converted from music hall to cinema palace, as part of the Gaumont circuit's keeping up with the times. As TV ate, remorselessly, into cinema attendance, and with the mild liberation of the country's gambling laws, the Hippodrome became a Top Rank bingo hall in the early 1960s. In 1985, following *Saturday Night Fever* fever, it mutated into a disco. It is now the town's premier 'club'. Doubtless, of a weekend night, more feels are copped than ever in its history.

Matcham's undraped ladies have looked down on all these changes as serenely and as statically as the maidens on Keats's Grecian Urn. And, in 1944, they looked down on me.

Henry V

(aetat. 6)

IN NOVEMBER 1944 a 'royal box' was taken at the Regal. Well named, it was the most palatial of Colchester's five cinemas and the only one which had been purpose-built for flicks.

The occasion was a children's outing, to celebrate one of their number's birthday. Which companion I cannot remember. His age must have been, like mine (a couple of weeks earlier), six. The film, Laurence Olivier's *Henry V*, I do recall: quite large chunks of it (particularly Robert Newton's over-the-top, beetroot-faced Pistol).*

The muse of fire meant, if I look back, nothing to me; nor did the patriotic, on-screen, dedication:

> To the commandos and airborne troops of Great Britain, the spirit of whose ancestors it has been humbly attempted to recapture in some ensuing scenes, this film is dedicated.*

It was the first film I recall seeing in Technicolor. In the starved world of England at that time, where vests were washed every fortnight and even the sunsets seemed grey, Olivier's film was incandescence in celluloid. It was my infantile À rebours.*

It was, of course, Olivier's 'some ensuing scenes' which were eagerly awaited in that box, as the waves of Shakespearean rhetoric washed over us. Particularly the spectacularly catastrophic (and wholly un-Shakespearean) French cavalry charge. The horses were draped, as one later discovered, with colourful tablecloths. Wartime technology had done wonders for cinema photography. That part of the film (one also learned later) was shot in Ireland, a country whose tablecloths – unpersecuted by wartime austerity – still flared as gaudily as they had in James Joyce's day.

Independent Ireland was maintaining a studious neutrality during the war (when it ended, the premier, de Valera, paid a visit of condolence to the German Embassy on the death of Hitler. Doubtless, had the Republic of Eire been in existence in the fifteenth century, they would have sent a consoling message by pigeon to the Dauphin of France after his sad reverses at Agincourt.)

In that final cavalry charge, as propagandised by Olivier, the cunning British, wearing only singlets and tights, drop out of trees to knock the comically over-armoured French aristos off their horses. As the prelude to the battle indicates, the metallic frogs are so cumbersome they would need a block and tackle to remount.

Those dropping English fighters are, of course, precursors of the 'paras' (airborne troops) saluted in Olivier's dedication. He is 'humbly attempting' in them, as he says, to reproduce British battleground triumphs: more specifically, the triumph of British hit, run and hit again tactics. As a later warrior would say, those paratroops float like butterflies, sting like bees.*

The archers, with their light weapons, quick response and mastery of tactical surprise, are forerunners of the commandos. They too hit and move, hit and move, striking like lightning where least expected.

Historically it would all be very different. Olivier's film was shot from 9 June 1943 to 12 July 1944 in Enniskerry, Eire; and at Denham and Pinewood Studios, England (the great charge was shot, out of narrative sequence, in high summer 1943 – a gloomy juncture in the conflict).

The film was released to the nation in the last week of November 1944. In between those dates (July and November) there intervened Operation Market Garden – more popularly known as 'Arnhem' (or, in barrack-room lore, 'the biggest fuck-up since Mons'). The dates of that sad episode are 17–25 September 1944.

The grand plan, as conceived by Montgomery, was to secure a series of bridges over the main rivers of Holland by dropping paratroops behind enemy lines, splitting them like an overripe tomato, allowing a lightning advance by armoured units into the German heartland.* It would shorten the war, Montgomery (now head of SHAEF) estimated, by six months. He would ride in triumph down Pall Mall in January 1945, the greatest British general since Marlborough.

The paratroops, alas, did not succeed as brilliantly as Olivier's arboreal commandos. There was (unknown to British Intelligence) a brigade of heavily armoured Waffen SS, on rest and recuperation, in the Arnhem area. The 'Red Devils' were picked off like so many clay pigeons as they fluttered down helpless from the skies.* Those who landed, untrussed themselves from their harnesses and were able to unpack their cumbersome supply canisters found that their small arms, Brens and Stens, made no impact on the entrenched Germans, with their Spandaus, fearsome 88s and Tiger tanks. The commandos could not, for all their speed of movement, tactical flexibility or great gallantry, either hold the bridges or clear the access roads for reinforcements to sweep through and on to Berlin. It was a reverse Agincourt. Heavy armour, materiel and defence in depth won. There has never been another mass airborne assault in military history since. Arnhem rewrote strategy.

Oddly, I knew an Arnhem veteran, who was dating my mother. He was one of the lucky ones to escape, with only shattered eardrums (another distant relative of mine died at Arnhem – his body was never recovered). In spite of what Adrian Mitchell alleged, Vietnam was not the first war one was lied to about, nor the one about which the worst lies were told.* Those last scenes in *Henry V* were one big lie. Or, to put it more kindly, a war myth: like the Angel of Mons.*

But, in the early 1940s, one wanted what Ibsen called life lies. The illusions that keep one going. Technicolor lies were even more welcome in that drab era. The children in the box at the Regal cheered, clapped, jumped up and down and left the cinema secure in Victory. It came, but six weary months later than Larry and Monty promised.

Wind in the Willows and Great Expectations

(aetat. 7)

BY 1946 MY POWERS of narrative control were improving apace. I could, as they say, 'follow a story'. I know why. I had been given a copy of Kenneth Grahame's *The Wind in the Willows*⋆ by some enlightened aunt. She was unrelated by blood or family – and no more an aunt than Uncle Mac, on *Children's Hour*, was my uncle. With men away during the war, every friendly woman was an honorary 'aunt' – as, in Elizabethan drama, every friend of the same age is a 'cousin', or 'coz'.

Aunt Margaret's gift was a hardback pre-war edition (none of those 'wartime regulations', which made books look like invisible ink on toilet paper, clamped between recycled cardboard). And it featured the inseparably congenial E. H. Shepard illustrations: designs which exude the content of the Edwardian period.

Years later, Shepard's pictures would merge in my mind with Philip Larkin's Edenic poem, 'MCMXIV', in which he lyricises the last true summer England would ever know:

And the shut shops, the bleached
Established names on the sunblinds,
The farthings and sovereigns,
And dark-clothed children at play
Called after kings and queens,
The tin advertisements
For cocoa and twist, and the pubs
Wide open all day.*

Or with the ending of my favourite H. G. Wells novel, *The History of Mr Polly*.* It is the story of a draper's assistant who burns his house down, fakes suicide (divorce, Edwardian style) and goes off to live by a river with a jolly, fat woman publican. The novel ends with Alf in pastoral bliss, in the garden of their inn, the buxom Flo by his side. 'It was', we are told, 'one of those evenings serenely luminous, amply and atmospherically still.' Flo and Alf talk, desultorily, about this and that. And then they lapse into contented silence, 'lost in the smooth, still quiet of the mind. A bat flitted by. "Time we was going in, O' Party," said Mr Polly, standing up. "Supper to get. It's as you say, we can't sit here forever".' Nor could Larkin's 'innocent' moment of British history last forever (no more than me, of course, did he ever personally experience it – Edwardian England, pre-both-wars England, had the status of a wonderful mirage for us both). That world would be blasted to buggery on Flanders Fields, starved to emaciation in the Great Depression and blasted to buggery again in the Second World War. But while it lasted, the Edwardian moment was the true England. One could know it, *feel* it almost, but never recover it.

There was a goodish 1949 film adaptation of *Polly*, which I saw a bit later. It starred (if that is the right word for any 1940s

British film) John Mills. All I can recall is the hero's frantic cycling – the prelude to his eventual break for freedom. I had, having just passed the eleven-plus, a 'bike' being the standard reward, acquired my 'Hercules' and was cycling hard into a fantasised future.*

Although there was a lot of countryside and riverside around Colchester (since built over), I had never knowingly seen a mole or a badger. Rats I had seen in plenty – although I couldn't have distinguished *Rattus rattus* from Grahame's watery variety. Ratty, of course (as I now know), was not a rat at all, but *Arvicola terrestris* – a water vole. 'Voley and Moley' – it might have worked.

Toads too I had seen. I recall seeing one blown up to explosion, with a straw, like an over-inflated balloon,* by a peculiarly vicious schoolfriend whose other favourite trick was to pin still-struggling dragonflies to his school blazer lapel: they would flap feebly for hours. My natural world was impoverished and more Darwinian than what Grahame depicts – where the only time a tooth or claw is reddened is when biffing the oikish stoats: lumpen proletariat that they are. Of the lower class myself, I was perversely in the camp of the biffers, not the biffed.

Clearly the ménage of Ratty and Moley (fellows in digs together – literally, since they've dug their apartment by the river) is Edwardian gay. Such, I've always suspected, was also the covert arrangement in 221B Baker Street between the moody sleuth and his doctor friend.*

Published in 1908, before either of the two wars which had shattered my family, *The Wind in the Willows* communicated a cosy, secure world, all parlour kettles on the hob, slippers and glowing hearths, tweedy jackets and money which did not have to pass through the indignity of a Friday pay packet.

Two chaps in a boat

I had never known this windy-willowy world, and never could know it, but I ached to inhabit it. It was the peace before war, which could never be recovered after war. And never was.

Black marks on a white surface (or images flashed at ten frames a second on a larger white surface) could transport one there – but not so as to stay.

Moley and Ratty must have picked up their furtive, after-lights-out buggery at public school. It passed me by, as did all the other public school Latin stuff (Dulce Domum, the pipes of Pan, etc.). What stayed were the beautifully machined comic episodes – especially those peripeties, or many downfalls, of the preposterous, poop-pooping Toad: in his gypsy caravan, his horseless carriage, on the run from prison, on the run from terrifying washerwomen, and Toad Gloriosus, reinstated as lord of Toad Hall.

If the stoats were oiks, he was the ludicrous toff. It was Badger, in his donnish set, and the ineffably upper-middle-

Toad, in full armour

class chaps, in their digs, who were admirable. That was the class where my expectations of social mobility ('raising myself in life') were directed. Not Toad Hall, or the stoaty riff-raff. My role model, in 1946, was a rat. The class subversions, and prejudices, of *The Wind in the Willows* sank into me like the purple on the indelible pencil. I still have them.

As King of the National Curriculum,* I would ordain Grahame's book as English Narrative 101. Whether for Literature or Sociology, I'm not sure. It was *The Wind in the Willows*, read and re-read (mainly in bed, at night, waiting for my mother to nip back from the Cross Keys and 'tuck me in' before nipping back out), which equipped me to come to some kind of terms with the subtleties of the British class system. More importantly if, as Gorky said, 'books are my university',* *The Wind in the Willows* was for me a primary education in how to read those books.

***

Adult literature seeped into my sensibility, before I had these reading skills, via the cinema, as I suspect, for many children today, it does through the TV screen. If I dredge through my 1946 moments, one luminous memory stands out – David Lean's *Great Expectations*, starring John Mills again and Dame Edith Evans. It ran in the Colchester Hippodrome, as the *Gazette* informs me, in November of the year.*

I had not seen the film again until a few weeks ago (as I write). But quite a lot had stuck with me; not merely fragments, as with *Tarzan's Desert Mystery* or *Henry V*, but whole, connected episodes.

It was some years before I would go on to read Dickens's novel. My introduction to *Great Expectations* was the 1946 film. There are worse gateways. Two moments stayed with me and always will. The first, unsurprisingly, was the sudden irruption of Magwitch (hammed up outrageously by Finlay Currie) leaping from behind the seven gravestones of Pip's family in the opening scene. The bloodthirsty father, rising from the tomb, recalled trauma of my own. I had recently lost a father, in the war. What remained of his charred body was interred I knew not where. Would he, too, leap out on me, murderously, the graveyard divots still sticking to him, demanding veal and ham pie? Was he angry that worthless I had survived, when worthy he (everyone told me how wonderful he was) had so much left to live for?

Did he, like Magwitch, have an alter ego, a 'young man'

in comparison with which young man I am a Angel ... That young man has a secret way pecooliar to himself, of getting at a boy, and at his heart, and at his liver. It is in wain for a

Let there be light!

boy to attempt to hide himself from that young man. A boy
may lock his door, may be warm in bed, may tuck himself
up, may draw the clothes over his head, may think himself
comfortable and safe, but that young man will softly creep
and creep his way to him and tear him open.*

Even more vividly remembered than the liver-devouring young
man (I'd already met a few like him in the school playground)
was Lean's ending. Generally faithful to Dickens's original,
the director took gross liberties with the conclusion. In the
film, Pip – John Mills – is shown madly ripping down the
curtains which exclude the tiniest beam of natural light from
Satis House: Miss Havisham's living mausoleum, erected as
a memorial to her own bitterly frustrated expectations in life.
In the film it is bright day outside. Light streams in as Pip
tears away blind after blind.

Dickens himself, as I would much later learn, had been in at least five minds how to end *Great Expectations* as it came to its serialised conclusion in his tuppenny magazine, *All the Year Round*. The characters were in his hand – but how should he dispose of them? God, doubtless, has the same dilemma. Dickensians quarrel over the variant endings, like terriers with a bone (the best place to find them laid out for inspection is in Edgar Rosenberg's Norton Critical Edition of the novel*).

In the ending most frequently published, Estella – cold as the stars she is named after – and Pip run into each other, quite fortuitously, in the long-burned-out ruins of Satis House (it was destroyed by Havisham's lunatic arson. The charred ruin is present in all of Dickens's many endings, but is signally absent in Lean's). The encounter in the rubble is unexpected, and the couple walk away together, as the sun goes down, with Pip's last words:

> I took her hand in mine, and we went out of the ruined place; and, as the morning mists had risen long ago when I first left the forge, so the evening mists were rising now, and in all the broad expanse of tranquil light they showed to me, I saw no shadow of another parting from her.

The stars are coming out and the shadows of night encroaching. Exit Pip and Estella, into the obscurity of the (un)happy ever after. Who knows which it is to be?

Dickens played with this crepuscular ending in subsequent published versions. He could not, apparently, stop himself tinkering with it. He toyed with a radically different ending in which Pip and Estella meet, years later, in the harsh hubbub of London's streets: in Piccadilly, no less. They exchange

The dark Victorian ending

some meaningless pleasantries and go their separate ways, swallowed up into the maw of the metropolitan lonely crowd. We see no shadow of another meeting in that ending.

Lean (who did the screenplay, with his long-time collaborator, Ronald Neame) clearly had some licence as he came to the end of his film. But he wrenched round his final scene 180 degrees from anything Dickens had toyed with.

'Fiat Lux' would be Lean's theme. Not for him a fade-out into the twilight, or a disappearance into seething London. In his version Satis House stands – wholly unruined. Why this drastic deviation from the Dickensian source? Because, I suspect, in 1945 there were so many burned-out houses in England already, thanks to Hitler's incendiaries (my grandmother actually discovered a dud on her doorstep, coming back from the shelter after one of the Luftwaffe's 1944 'nuisance' raids: bloody nuisance they were, too). The heart would have sunk at the notion of Pip and Estella getting it together on the bombsite of their childhood. The cinema was where the population came to get away from the debris of war. It was not until the Woodfall Films* of the late 1950s (*Saturday Night and Sunday Morning, Room at the Top, A Taste of Honey*) that 'realism' – the world outside the one-and-ninepennies – would penetrate the picture palace. We weren't ready for it in 1946. There was enough kitchen-sink drama in our kitchens, thank you very much.

Pip's tearing down the curtains and letting in the light has a wonderful, and wholly timely, 1946 resonance. It's right for the moment (which is why, I would like to think, it has stuck in my mind all these years). Lean's film symbolised the end of a hated and omnipresent fact of war, the 'blackout'. It was a kind of state-imposed blindness, blinkers on the soul. As the BBC records, since 1939:

> A nation-wide blackout was enforced and everyone rushed to buy dense black material with which to make new curtains to cover the windows and the front and back door. All the street lights were fitted with shades and their power reduced, the colourful lights in Piccadilly Circus were switched off for the duration, and vehicles had their head and side-lights masked with what looked like shallow tin lids with two three-sided triangles cut into them and the resultant flaps prised forward 90 degrees thereby reducing the glare and offering some protection from enemy aircraft.*

On VE night, the poet Stephen Spender and his wife, Natasha, walked from their house in St John's Wood to Primrose Hill, where – on the dawn of this new era – they gloried in the blaze of London lights beneath them. I too recall as a red-letter day (night, rather) in my childhood going up to Piccadilly to 'see the lights': the wonderful Bovril and cascading Schweppes illuminations (done with vast arrays of light bulbs, not neon). It was as much a national pastime as Butlin's, or Friday night at the flicks. Zoe Gail had a hit with a hopeful song of the time, 'I'm Going to Get Lit Up When the Lights Go Up Again in London'.* Ah, when though? (Three years after Miss Gail's record, as it happened.)

Great Expectations is regularly voted one of the nation's all-time favourite books. In the BBC's 'Big Read' in 2003 it came in at no. 17 (one behind The Wind in the Willows, it's pleasing to note).* Lean's Great Expectations gets good feedback from the contemporary filmblog community – along with ubiquitous complaint about the 'ludicrous Hollywood ending'. Ludicrous for Hollywood, perhaps – whose lights and tinsel were never dimmed. The darkest days of the war were never other than metaphorical on Sunset Boulevard. But Lean's ending was right on target for the Hippodrome, Colchester, in November 1946.

The Amazing Wilson

(aetat. 8)

FRIDAYS WERE A BIG DAY for eight-year-old me – comic day. The comics themselves were folio, newsprint and over-whelmingly textual: words, words, words. And never enough of them in the weekly, fourteen-page, stapled gathering.

I could barely get to sleep on Thursday nights, such was my anticipation of the feast to come. For a couple of years, I always had my nose stuck in a comic. If not a new one, then some old favourite from the huge stack piled alongside my bed.

There was a colour reproduction splashed on the front of the comic: in every other way, the 1946 product would have been entirely familiar to a late Victorian boy. And not merely the format. The contents were an age-old brew of penny-dreadful thrillerism (the thrills cost tuppence in 1946) and *Boy's Own Paper* (as published by the Religious Tract Society) upliftingness. The BOP was still going in the 1940s; I avoided it, unless desperate.*

The big four, to all of which I subscribed, were the *Wizard*,

Hotspur, *Rover* and *Champion*.★ I say 'subscribe', but they were bought for me at Hyam's the newsagent's across the street by my then family guardians. They were only too glad to shell out the weekly bob or so – the comics kept me so agreeably 'good' (i.e. quiet) for such long periods. They were not themselves 'great readers', as they would say. A hundred years earlier, more unscrupulous guardians than they might have dosed me with Godfrey's Cordial, that cocktail of opium and treacle designed to keep the unruly Victorian child ruly.★ No child, in any period, could have been more addicted than I was to my weekly fix.

All the series worked for me – even the public school nonsense (sub-Frank Richards) of the Red Circle school in the *Hotspur*. But there was one athletic superhero about whom I fantasised endlessly. Namely the Amazing Wilson, whose exploits on track, road, field and mountain peak (he'd done Everest of course – Hillary and Sherpa Tenzing would find a note in a bottle, under a Union Jack, commemorating their failure) were chronicled, week by week, in the *Wizard*.

Wilson exploded on to the pages of the *Wizard* in the darkest days of the war – on 24 July 1943, as the comic-book historians (those precise connoisseurs of ephemera) inform us. He was the embodiment of British underdoggery; which was, of course, topdoggery – so top, indeed, that it didn't even need to preen, as lesser nations and races did when they won something.

The cult of Wilson can be tracked to *Guy Livingstone*, that epitome of the Muscular School, pioneered by the Victorian novelist G. A. Lawrence in the aftermath of the Crimean War.★ The superbly athletic, ineffably arrogant, hard-living, chain-smoking Livingstone regards it as 'ungentlemanly' to 'train'.

One wins because, simply, one is superior. One wins, more simply, because one is English.

Wilson, for example, would appear, from nowhere, at the peak of a gruelling climb in the Tour de France on a roadster – wearing cycle clips round his turn-ups – and win, leaving the bemused continentals in his wake, eating English rubber. Wilson would challenge the year's Derby winner to a 100-yard dash – and show the nag a clean pair of heels (remarkably clean – since the amazing one ran without shoes).

Our hero's background was regularly explained, as newly literate readers (eight-year olds, like me, in 1946) came on board, pennies in hand, and needed to be filled in. Young William Wilson, such new recruits would learn, had been born in far-off 1795. A hermit, on Ambleside Moor, had entrusted him with the elixir of life – and a lifelong (very long) propensity to anchoritic solitude. This together with an amazing physique and a recurrent need to show it off to the world.

Wilson, as the record books recorded (the *Wizard*'s record books, that is), had arrived on the British athletic scene in 1938 by coming from nowhere to run a three-minute mile at a major meet. Paavo Nurmi, the 'Flying Finn',* was, at the time, struggling to get within panting distance of four minutes. No struggle for Wilson. He simply vaulted the spectators' fence, wearing his usual outdoor togs, to streak, barefoot, past all the other lumbering 'milers'.

During the war Wilson gave up his loner life on the moors to join the RAF. In his Spitfire he effortlessly chalked up twenty-five kills. For others in airforce blue it may have been *per ardua ad astra* – for him it was easy-peasy. In the run up to the 1948 Olympic Games in London, the *Wizard*-buying youth of the nation, me among them, were extremely relieved to learn that Wilson *was training the British team*. Doubtless he would take a back seat during the competition itself, out of politeness to the visitors. Bad form to win all the gold when lesser folk had come so far only to make do with silver and bronze. I loved Wilson. The *modesty* of the man – like Sherlock Holmes, he was the incarnation of British amateurism. And British racial superiority.

Wilson's various athletic feats were followed, and narrated, by Frank Ducker – his Boswell. In a typical 1946 episode Ducker is found lying in bed, at seven in the morning, sipping tea and listening to the news on the radio, in his London flat. A bulletin startles him: 'Wilson, the British athlete, has arrived in Philadelphia to take part in the Decathlon starting tomorrow.'

A longish quotation will indicate, among much else (inveterate scorn of 'Yanks', for example), the commendable level of literacy expected of a juvenile reader in 1946:

> Ducker's cup of tea splashed all over the bed. He flung the clothes aside and in his pyjamas, dashed to the phone. He dialled hastily and eventually got through. 'Is that the Trans-Atlantic Airways?' he roared. 'Listen, I want to go to America today. What's that? My only chance is to be at the airport in case anyone cancels a reservation at the last minute?' Ducker was fortunate. Two hours after hearing the radio announcement he was airborne. Twenty-four hours after leaving London, Ducker sat in a taxi-cab that was whirling him along a concrete highway towards the vast stadium at Philadelphia. A newspaper lay across his knees. His gaze scanned the big headline: 'Wilson Here As Gino Finn Challenger' ... Frank put on a pair of sunglasses as he paid off the taxi and entered the stadium ... The crowd were rooting for their favourites, but loudest

of all was the cry of 'Gino! Gino!' In glistening white, except for the golden eagle on the front of his singlet, Gino Finn looked like a lord of the sun with his fair hair, piercing blue eyes and magnificent bronzed body. Pete Purdo, dark and grim, had a torso like the trunk of a tree. Joe Legume walked lightly with the inturned toes of his race. Cal Lee, the Flying Yank, moved with a long loping stride. Wilson, hardly heeded in the excitement, appeared last, shuffling along in his old black costume and canvas shoes that he had not bothered to lace up. There were to be three heats for the hundred metres (one hundred and nine yards 1 foot 1 inch) sprint, the first two in each heat to run in the final. Wilson kicked off his shoes and walked bare-footed to the line when his name was called ... Wilson, despite a puzzled stare from the starter, just stood waiting with his arms hanging loosely. Ducker held his breath in excitement and anxiety. The gun cracked and Wilson flowed into movement. Before the crouchers had hit their fast stride he was in front of the lot of them. It was astonishing to see the heads of the spectators turning to follow his course. So tearaway was his speed, so big a lead did he gain that he could have finished walking, but he crossed the line like a flash and was carried on by his impetus for another ten yards. The voice that announced that Wilson had run one hundred metres in nine seconds was harsh with amazement.

He then clears the high-jump bar, set at a world-record six feet seven inches, with an effortless backward somersault. Wilson goes on to leap so far in the long jump that he lands outside the sandpit, in the grass beyond. Philadelphia is dumb-struck:

A tape measure had to be fetched and then a spluttering

announcer stated that Wilson had jumped twenty-eight feet. Wilson sat down again and chewed at a blade of grass, while the other places were decided. Gino Finn actually jumped twenty-six feet nine inches, but the crowd were too busy discussing Wilson to take much heed.

The writer, Gilbert Dalton★ as I now know (stories in the comics were, of course, unsigned in 1946), maintains a cracking pace in his narrative. And he has the short-storyteller's knack of packing in information – some of it, like the conversion of feet to metres, or actual world records, of considerable use to a lad. About Joe Legume's 'inturned toes of his race' I'm not so sure. When comics went pictorial in the 1950s (a sad day, it was, for youthful English literacy) Dalton went on to create Alf Tupper – a cartoon version of Wilson, if more proletarian. I had no time for Tupper, with his Charles Atlas physique and plumber's bag.★

Alas, the Wilson stories were at odds with the brute facts of post-war international sporting competition. At the Olympic Games in 1948, the US swept the board with thirty-eight gold medals, Sweden won thirty-four, and France (France!) twenty-nine. Great Britain came twelfth in the table, with just three.★ At Helsinki, four years later, we won just one – in the last hours of the games: and that medal was essentially won by a horse, 'Foxhunter' – ridden, for tattered British pride, over the jumps, hurdles and fences by Colonel Llewellyn.★ When he died, in 1999, the Colonel had his ashes sprinkled on the grave of his gallant steed. It was a gesture Wizard readers of 1946 would have appreciated.

Wilson articulated, for a young schoolboy at a sporty school, the time's acutely frustrated sense of imperial triumphalism and all-too-evident humiliation in every kind of international contest. We invented these sports, we wrote the rule books – we *owned* them. But the Australians came over and skittled us out at cricket (the 'Invincibles', the British press ruefully called the Ozzies on their 1948 tour); Moscow Dynamo were invited to tour in 1946 and shot balls into the back of our net at will (in one game, against a first-class British side, the Muscovites won 10–1);* the Argentinians trounced us at polo; there had been no British champion at Wimbledon since Fred Perry; and no English boxer could stay upright against an American opponent for more than three minutes. Bruce Woodcock, given his performance in the ring, might as well have represented his country at diving.* Not that we won any medals there.

But at least we had Wilson. Or the *Wizard* readers of 1946 did.

Lorna Doone

(aetat. 8)

I MUST HAVE first come across *Lorna Doone* in a young reader's edition. I may even first have encountered it as a Classic Comic – I certainly first came across Kingsley's *Westward Ho!* in that form. If I close my eyes, I can see the illustration of that climactic moment in which, denied his revenge on the Spaniard who has blighted his life, Amyas curses God (the Deity who has just 'blown' and destroyed the Armada) and is struck by lightning and blinded.

The Classic Comic *Lorna Doone*, I see, Hollywoodises the scene by Wizard's Slough (with rather more display of breast by the heroine than the Blackmore novel sanctions).*

The year I read the text proper of Blackmore's novel I am absolutely certain of: 1947. That year's winter, from January to March, was cruelly bitter and tediously prolonged.* Were these cruellest months the 'Victory' for which I had loyally waved my thrupenny paper flag, in the great VE parade through Colchester's High Street, in May 1945? It felt more like Stalingrad. This image would be inaccessible to me for a

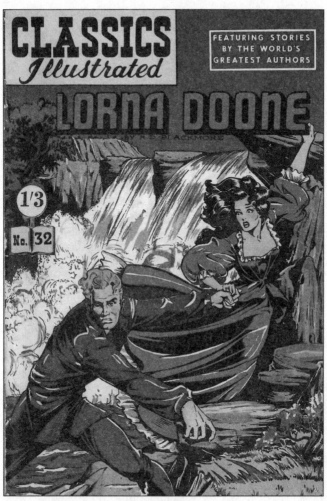

Not quite Blackmore

few years. I came across Theodor Plievier's novel, when it was published in hardback translation, in 1953.* I was riveted to *Stalingrad*'s narrative from the opening paragraph, describing German soldiers' trousers stiff as drainpipes with frozen faeces. Things, I stoically realised, could have been worse.

When I read that clunkily translated book, my mind – as it always does when cold is the subject – flashed back to February 1947: call it post-thermal stress syndrome. There were, in the early months of that year, fuel shortages, 'power cuts', and rationing which reduced the weekly meat allowance to the size of an Oxo-cube and sweets to something the size of a sugar cube (assuming anything other than loathsome 'cocoanut squares' were in stock).

The biting cold was compounded by malnutrition and foodstuffs as unappetising as the huge wayside drifts of dirty snow, 'permafilth', lining the streets. Dried eggs, Spam, snoek, margarine, which could double as axle-grease (with which substance it shared much of its chemical composition). One ate bread and dripping with relish. And looking back, one was lucky to have even those short commons. In Europe, particularly Germany, hundreds of thousands died in the 'Hungerwinter'.*

Somehow, in this awful cold season, I had come across a full-text copy of *Lorna Doone* – the real thing. There wasn't much else to do but read. By candlelight, sometimes, when the 'cuts' came in and the radio went off. I was particularly taken with Chapter 52, 'The Great Winter'. A representative passage indicates its timeliness. Cometh the season, cometh the chill, cometh the novel:

> That night such a frost ensued as we had never dreamed of, neither read in ancient books, or histories of Frobisher.

The kettle by the fire froze, and the crock upon the hearth-cheeks; many men were killed, and cattle rigid in their head-ropes. Then I heard that fearful sound, which never I had heard before, neither since have heard (except during that same winter), the sharp yet solemn sound of trees burst open by the frost-blow. Our great walnut lost three branches, and has been dying ever since; though growing meanwhile, as the soul does. And the ancient oak at the cross was rent, and many score of ash trees. But why should I tell all this? the people who have not seen it (as I have) will only make faces, and disbelieve; till such another frost comes; which perhaps may never be.*

That next frost-blow, as far as one young reader of *Lorna Doone* was concerned, came in 1947. But the fact is, if the history books are to be believed, it was nothing compared to John Ridd's in 1683–4.* In that winter belts of sea ice three miles wide floated along the Channel coast. A celebrated frost fair was held on the deep-frozen Thames. John Evelyn described it thus:

Coaches plied from Westminster to the Temple, and from several other stairs to and fro, as in the streets, sleds, sliding with skates, bull-baiting, horse and coach races, puppet plays and interludes, cooks, tippling and other lewd places, so that it seemed to be a bacchanalian triumph, or carnival on the water.

Orlando (which I read aged sixteen – it remains my favourite of Woolf's novels, for its descriptive writing) has a hyperbolic recycling of Evelyn and the winter of 1683–4. It still refrigerates, vividly:

The Great Frost was, historians tell us, the most severe that has ever visited these islands. Birds froze in mid-air and fell like stones to the ground. At Norwich a young countrywoman started to cross the road in her usual robust health and was seen by the onlookers to turn visibly to powder and be blown in a puff of dust over the roofs as the icy blast struck her at the street corner.

Reviewing my memoir, The Boy who Loved Books, in 2007, the Telegraph observed that the author's heart (my cardiac plumbing, that is) was 'icy cold'. The boy could, evidently, love books; but not people. I'd like to think the reviewer was wrong. But if there is an icicle where my heart should be, blame 1947.

I have always been abnormally sensitised to the literature of cold. There is a deep-freeze cabinet in my mental library. In it are such frigidising masterpieces as Jack London's 'To Build a Fire'* (Lenin's favourite story, apparently – the winters are colder than even 1947 in St Petersburg), the final scenes of the 1948 film Scott of the Antarctic,* the Adirondack chapters of The Master of Ballantrae, the final, Himalayan, chapters of Lost Horizon. And Robert W. Service.*

Service was born in Scotland, threw up his respectable clerking job and took off for the Yukon. Like Jack London, he discovered there was more gold to be found writing about the Klondike than digging it. He died in 1958. He was not a respected figure in literary circles, although he made a fortune . from his verse.

I was familiar with Service's doggerel in my childhood. 'The Shooting of Dan McGrew' was as popular among the literate working classes in which I was brought up as its bawdy travesty, 'Eskimo Nell',* was among the rugby-playing classes. Intellectual snob that I became in my teens, I grew to despise Service, with the knowing sneer of one who boasted T. S. Eliot on his bookshelf.

Nonetheless, I retained a soft spot for one of Service's more poignant ballads, 'The Cremation of Sam McGee'. Two pals are out on the frozen trail – one, Sam, is dying of cold. He asks the other, Cap, to cremate his corpse; burn it, boil it – do anything, so long as heat is applied:

> On a Christmas Day we were mushing our way
> Over the Dawson trail.
> Talk of your cold! through the parka's fold
> It stabbed like a driven nail.
> If our eyes we'd close, then the lashes froze
> Till sometimes we couldn't see;
> It wasn't much fun, but the only one
> To whimper was Sam McGee.
>
> And that very night, as we lay packed tight
> In our robes beneath the snow,
> And the dogs were fed, and the stars o'erhead
> Were dancing heel and toe,
> He turned to me, and 'Cap,' says he,
> 'I'll cash in this trip, I guess;
> And if I do, I'm asking that you
> Won't refuse my last request.'
>
> Well, he seemed so low that I couldn't say no;
> Then he says with a sort of moan:
> 'It's the cursed cold, and it's got right hold
> Till I'm chilled clean through to the bone.

> Yet 'tain't being dead – it's my awful dread
> Of the icy grave that pains;
> So I want you to swear that, foul or fair,
> You'll cremate my last remains.'

Cap does as instructed. Sam's spirit, at least, is warmed, as it mushes onward, to the great goldstrike in the sky.

In Derek Humphry's 'assisted death' manual, *Final Exit*,★ one is told that a favourite Japanese mode of suicide is to wander out into the snows (ideally of Fuji), lie down and wait for final peace. The terminal sensations, reportedly, are of numbing warmth, not chill. I can't believe it, any more than did Sam McGee. I would rather, like Matthew Arnold's Empedocles,★ hurl myself into the burning mouth of the volcano: one scalding shock. Then nothing. But no cold, thank God.

Noyes + Noyes

(aetat. 9)

AS THE PRECEDING REMARKS about Service may have suggested, I have no ear for poetry (for a university teacher, this is like a surgeon with a phobia of blood). But I was struck in December 2007 when an Ofsted Report recorded Alfred Noyes's 'The Highwayman'* as topping the list of ten poems that all eleven- to fourteen-year-olds should read (Ofsted loves numerical precision – it gives them the illusory sense that they are in control).

So it had been, sixty years earlier. Noyes's highwayman galloped tall in the saddle then as, apparently, he still gallops. The only difference – which may well measure a decline in school standards – is that in 1947 it was nine-year-olds who were prescribed 'The Highwayman'.

In my primary school, Noyes's abysmal poem, immortalised in one of Palgrave's many golden treasuries,* was forced down one's throat like the cod-liver oil which, it was promised, would make a growing child healthy, wealthy and wise. Worse still, it was forced out of one's throat. My personal loathing of 'The Highwayman' was forged by being required to read it aloud, *con espressione*, to my class in summer 1947 (a season as hot as the winter before had been cold). I stumbled, horribly. A most unmagical moment.

The quality of Noyes's verse is conveyed by the opening stanza. It's not merely the corny sub-romantic diction (Coleridge's 'Frost at Midnight' is there somewhere), or the grotesque metaphors, but the spavined prosody. I can see now, but could not see then, that, for the purpose of recitation, the first two lines can only be managed with lengthy caesurae after 'darkness' and 'galleon'. Try it:

> The wind was a torrent of darkness among the gusty
> trees,
> The moon was a ghostly galleon tossed upon cloudy
> seas,
> The road was a ribbon of moonlight over the purple
> moor,
> And the highwayman came riding—
> Riding—riding—
> The highwayman came riding, up to the old inn-door.

The handsome freebooter has ridden pell-mell across the moor this turbulent night, his French cocked hat on his forehead, a bunch of lace at his chin, to keep a lover's tryst with Bess, the raven-haired innkeeper's daughter.

The ostler Tim ('his hair like mouldy hay') lusts after Bess and has betrayed the highwayman to King George's redcoats. They lay a trap, tying up Bess with a musket pointed to her breast. Should she so much as tremble, she dies. Brave Bess deliberately moves, to warn her love of the ambush, and her heart is blasted to pulp. Hearing the fatal shot, the highwayman spurs off, as one demented, but is himself shot down, like a dog. To this day the lovers' ghosts haunt the inn on windy nights, as the moon tosses about, galleon-like, on cloudy seas.

My infantile sensibility (and unready mouth) resisted Noyes's doggerel. 'The Highwayman' is, however one looks at it, a crummy poem; not even nostalgia can condone that lunar galleon bouncing around like a maddened Goodyear blimp in a force 10. Nonetheless, there the poem remains festeringly and immovably in my sensibility. It's become, much as I resent it, part of my literary hardwiring. So too, one gathers, for every British child to this day.

Noyes's path would, four decades later, again criss-cross with mine. In 1983 I went to work at the California Institute of Technology. Caltech is micro-small and mega-rich. It has 800 undergraduates and a budget larger than that of London University, with its 30,000 students. Caltech (via its subsidiary arm, the Jet Propulsion Laboratory) puts men on the moon, rovers on Mars, and explores the rim of the universe.

The institute, located in Pasadena, in the lee of the San Gabriel mountains, was the brainchild of George Ellery Hale.* At the turn of the twentieth century, Hale had a vision. He would build the world's first 100-inch telescope on nearby Mount Wilson (madness). He would create the world's finest science school (hubris). And he would set up the world's finest humanities library and art gallery alongside his laboratories and observatories (true madness). Hale had a vision of big brains and refined sensibilities – artists, musicians, scientists, architects, poets – mingling in the great collective clubhouse, which he grandly called 'the Athenaeum'. It would be a crucible of all the genius of man (Hale took that last word seriously: there were to be no whitecoated women at Caltech – they distracted a fellow from his work).

To an amazing extent, Hale succeeded in creating his Athens (his men-only Athos, one might add) of the Southwest. The telescope (since dwarfed by astronomic mirrors many times larger) still scours the skies from Mount Wilson. The Huntington gardens, galleries, museum and library (all Hale's brain children) are world-class. And Caltech has, for its size, more Nobellists on its faculty roster than any institution in the world (and, thanks to the ideal of 'humanised science', the occasional Nobellist-novelist – Saul Bellow,* for example). Since 1975, there have even been women.

The venerated tradition of Hale's breed of young scientists who can read literature, listen intelligently to music and respond to good art was what brought me, in 1983, to Caltech, at a salary four times what London was then paying me. I have been there, on and off, ever since. A literary man in science-land.

Which brings one back to that other literary man, Alfred Noyes. Hale had been entranced, as an undergraduate, by 'The Highwayman'. And, like all scientists, he was fascinated by symmetries. And there was an interesting one where Noyes was concerned.

Caltech was shaped by three great scientists: Hale (who shook the necessary millions from the pockets of local millionaires), Robert Millikan (the most brilliant physicist of his time) and Arthur Noyes.* This other A. Noyes was a chemist, and a comrade of Hale's, from undergraduate Princeton days. In 1913 (as work started on the great 100-inch telescope) Hale recruited his friend Arthur from MIT, where he was President. This Noyes it was who later designed Caltech's 'core curriculum': the foundational knowledge which any scientist needs. A grand portrait of the trio, Hale, Millikan and Noyes (called by the reverent 'the three graces' and the irreverent 'the three stooges') dominates the Athenaeum.*

As the great telescope grew on Mount Wilson's peak, Hale had another inspiration. Why not 'Noyes + Noyes = True Genius'? There was, surely, room for a fourth grace on the Athenaeum wall – a Homer *de nos jours*? Alfred Noyes, the great poet, was duly invited, for a lavishly paid visiting year, as the largest telescope in the world reached completion, in 1917.

On 2 November, there was 'first light': the ceremonial opening of the observatory. Hale noted, cryptically, in his diary: 'Friday, November 2, 1917 – With Alfred Noyes to Mountain. First observations with 100 – Jupiter, Moon, Saturn.' The first observations, in the bright sunny afternoon, did not work. But that night, the images were perfect. And the Noyes who was with Hale at that epochal moment was, as he says, Alfred not Arthur.

It was, momentously, a poet's eye that was privileged to be among the first to scan the universe with this amazing instrument (did he, one wonders, see 'galleons' up there in the skies?). Alas, however, Hales's great Noyesian conjunction fell through. Arthur stayed, Alfred went off to pastures new after his year-long visit. But he left, as testimony to that night on the mountain, an epic poem. Published, after much creative struggle, in 1922 (the year of *The Waste Land*), it is called *Watchers of the Sky*. It opens with a prose prologue, recalling the poet's trip with Hale up the ten miles of winding Mount Wilson toll road (so called because automobiles were charged fifty cents), that memorable day in 1917. It then breaks into verse, describing the observatory dome:

At noon, upon the mountain's purple height,
Above the pine-woods and the clouds it shone
No larger than the small white dome of shell
Left by the fledgling wren when wings are born.
By night it joined the company of heaven,
And, with its constant light, became a star.

    Up there, I knew
The explorers of the sky, the pioneers
Of science, now made ready to attack
That darkness once again, and win new worlds.

I myself hiked the 6,000 feet up to Mount Wilson many times – along the same broad, sun-baked trail which Noyes and Hale had followed in 1917. It was one of my favourite

Hale on trail

walks (graded 'strenuous' by the estimable John Robinson in his *Trails of the Angeles: 100 Hikes in the San Gabriels*).* On 2 November 1987 – infused by a sense of sentimental loyalty to Caltech and dim memories of 'The Highwayman' – I took a text of *Watchers of the Sky** with me and posted myself at the observatory looking in the direction of Caltech (on whose campus there is a bust of Hale, forever gazing, with the eye of a conqueror, on Mount Wilson).

It was nightfall: the scent of sage and resin was strong in my nostrils. The whippoorwills called – with their distinctive melancholy twilight trill. The lights of the San Gabriel valley glimmered beneath me, through the arid air. A carpet of stars. I was alone. I began (torch in hand) to read out Noyes's poem.

I stopped reading. The poem is appalling.

Horizontal Heavyweights

(aetat. 10)

BOXING, particularly 'big fights' between a British hopeful and an American champ, was one of the few things that clustered my then chaotically disparate family into something resembling a nucleus round the living-room radio.

The whiff of paraffin can still bring those moments back to me – although the scent is only found nowadays at airports. Then, long before universal central heating, kerosene was a main source of household warmth. What little warmth there was to be had.

'The big fight' was both a pleasing and a depressing ritual. Since the contests usually ran late, I would be in my pyjamas and dressing gown, Horlicks in hand (it protected against 'sleep starvation'). And overexcited – at least, until the opening bell. Thereafter, excitement inevitably dribbled away. The British gladiator always bit the dust – 'Fainting Phils', the Americans called them: 'Limey dive bombers', 'canvas-kissers', 'horizontal heavyweights'.

There would be BBC commentary by the fluent Canadian

Stewart Macpherson* and inter-round summary by Tommy Farr (who, as we knew, had *really* won that 1937 fight against Joe Louis, but was robbed by the US referee and judges: Americans mildly pointed out that the Brown Bomber was fighting, from the second round, with a broken hand).*

Macpherson had a nice, and often baroque, turn of phrase. When not commentating, he chaired one of the funniest of the BBC's comedy programmes, *Ignorance is Bliss* (launched, with exquisite timing, on April Fool's Day 1946). I remember him ruminating, during one of Freddie (the 'fairground battler') Mills's* fights, as the gutsy boxer missed by a mile with one of his haymakers, 'If that had connected, Joe would have gone right out of the roof, and found himself in the street outside, waiting for a cab to the airport.' They never did connect. Joe Baksi's jabs to the head did.* And so did Macpherson's jests. If only he hadn't had a North American accent (Eamonn Andrews* later took over the commentator's mike – but he was Southern Irish).

We listened, as one might to casualty lists in a peculiarly unlucky military campaign (the mass surrender at Singapore, for example, or Arnhem), to Bruce Woodcock toppling like timber to Lee Savold, Mills being bloodily pulped fight after fight. Jack Gardner, a British heavyweight champion, girded with a Lonsdale belt with medals the size of dinner plates, was as immobile in the ring as a Belisha beacon. Gardner, a handsome ex-guardsman, had one punch – a straight left. He would advance with it held out, like a jousting knight's lance.* His opponent simply walked round it, to whop Jack in his moustached face. He retired, wisely, to run a pub, surrounded by pictures of himself in his prime.

One by one, like ninepins, British champions tumbled against any third-ranked pug who crossed the Atlantic

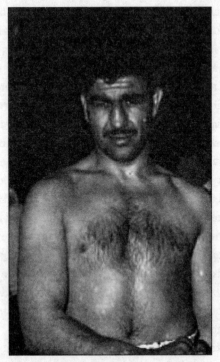

Warrior Jack

to boost his career KO score. There was one exception: a glorious few weeks, when Randolph Turpin took the middle-weight world title from Sugar Ray Robinson at Wembley, on 10 July 1951, only to lose it in the rematch at the Polo Grounds in New York, two months later.*

Turpin – ruined by the excesses of his moment at the top of the slippery pole – eventually committed suicide by gunshot (as did Mills), after a series of failed comebacks. In Turpin's case, the moral weakness was attributed to what was then coarsely called the 'touch of the tar brush': despite the highwaymanish surname (his brother, also a boxer, was called 'Dick'), he wasn't one of us. Not in 1951. Boxing now seems to me as brutal as cockfighting, as pointless as bingo and as class exploitative as almost everything in British life in the 1940s and 1950s.

There are great films about boxing (the greatest being *Raging Bull* – although Clifford Odets's *Golden Boy*★ and *When We Were Kings*★ run it close). But there are no great novels. There are some cracking short stories: Ring Lardner's 'Champion', Hemingway's 'Fifty Grand' and Jack London's 'A Piece of Steak', for example. And literary people – from Arthur Conan Doyle and George Bernard Shaw, through Norman Mailer, to Joyce Carol Oates – are fascinated by the noble art.

It represents action: something that literary people fantasise about but rarely participate in. Pens are not mightier than swords. Words cannot, like sticks and stones, break bones. However pugnacious a critic may be, the literary recipient of the violence will never need gumshield, headguard and (most important) testicle protector.

A bookish child, I joined a boxing club, the King George V on East Stockwell Street, aged eleven, in 1949. My guardians thought it would 'get me out of myself'. I was willing to be got out. 'Benny the Backstreet Battler' was a comic-book hero I admired; along with the Amazing Wilson, Baldy Hogan and Rockfist Rogan. Shockfist Sutherland was in prospect.

What I discovered was that the Bennys of the world could take me apart, no contest. Backstreet battlers, like blacks (or, in lower divisions, Mexicans, and in the nineteenth century Jews) always had the edge over any toff unwise enough to discard his class protections and enter the ring. They were the hungry fighters, we were the food. Not, of course, that I was a toff. But I read books and avoided the worst excesses of the Essex accent (the ugliest in all the regions of the kingdom).

So it was, presumably, right the way back to the first gladiators in Camulodunum, Roman Colchester.

I might have acquitted myself better. But I was always rather frightened to really hurt my opponent. It seemed wrong, somehow. They (who lived with hurt and whose class destiny was a lot more hurt) could dish it out, as well as take it. They loved the fray. It simplified the situation of their lives into hit or be hit.

I took the Stewart Macpherson route. My life would be commentary, not action. But I loved to watch the hitting. Laurence Olivier, in his autobiography, recalls that as a child he wanted – like other children – to be a railway engine driver, a warrior, an archbishop. But then, at a crucial moment in his growth, he realised he didn't have to *be* them, he could *play* them.

About the same time of life, I realised that I didn't have to risk my profile, my uncauliflowered (but irritatingly 'Clark Gable'*) ears, my retina or my neurons. I could *read* the battle of life. It was easier, and much safer, than living it.

This Gun for Hire

(aetat. 11)

I MUST HAVE FIRST encountered Graham Greene via the 1942 noir classic *This Gun for Hire*. The film is based on Greene's 'entertainment' (as he called such thrillers), *A Gun for Sale* – the title was too ambiguous for America, where there were more gun shops than movie theatres.* Greene was using the term metonymically, for 'gunman', of course.

I saw the film years after it was made, in 1948, as I now calculate. Cinemas used to have special matinees on Sunday afternoons, when they would show old films. There was some provision under the Sunday Observance laws that allowed them to interrupt the otherwise universal Sabbath gloom. I was always terrified that I would be seen by some church-going friend (or, horrible thought, by a teacher) queuing up outside. I knew that Sunday films were shameful, although perversely that added to the pleasure. The salt on the KP nut, so to speak.

My mother took me to see the film. She was interested – in a purely cosmetic way – in the star, Veronica Lake. My mother had modelled her appearance on Lake. I thought she (my mother) was the more beautiful of the two.

I have little connected recollection of the film. The presiding memory is of the impassive, frigid mask of Alan Ladd's face and the voice, so much larger than him, which boomed out from his small, trench-coated frame.*

Greene's 1930s narrative is wrenched somewhat and relocated to wartime America. It centres on a sociopathic contract assassin, Philip Raven, played, of course, by Ladd – whose reputation was made by the movie.

A stone killer, Raven is contracted to assassinate a chemist, who has discovered a mysterious formula. Having executed his task (and his victim) with his customary efficiency, Raven is double-crossed by his tycoon employer (a filthy capitalist in the novel, a dirty fifth-columnist in the movie). He exacts revenge. In the process, he falls in with a moll, Ellen Graham, played by the actress Raymond Chandler rather spitefully called 'Moronica Lake'.* Moronic or not, Ladd liked her because she was smaller than he: a feature not shared with 90 per cent of the female population and somewhat more of the male. Raven and Graham bond, and he is humanised by her benign influence. Or perhaps not. The movie, which is extraordinarily nihilistic, played out my fantasy life with my Lake-like mother. Slouched in the stalls of Regal (as I recall), I could imagine myself as fascinating to her as Raven clearly is to Graham.

I was not the only young person to be impressed by This Gun for Hire. Martin Scorsese (b. 1942) took (among much else) Ladd's cold 'You talkin' to me?' from the movie as the hallmark line for Taxi Driver.*

I was a more intelligent viewer of films when I saw The Third Man, on its release, at the Playhouse, a year later in 1949.

Greene's hand lies heavily on this movie, in whose making he was directly involved and which was a screenplay before it was a novella. *The Third Man* is Greeneland on celluloid.

I can still visualise, as it struck me then, the extraordinary opening (always thrilling moments). Anton Karas's fingers were shown darting over the plangent zither strings, plucking that dinka-dinka-dong-a-ding theme music.* The bomb-wrecked city, the shortages of every luxury, the crushing bureaucracy (papers, ration books, passes) were all familiar. But somehow Vienna made them exotic: like the zither (what would George Formby's banjo have done with it?).

The scene which stuck in my mind then, and always has, was that in which Harry Lime rises from the grave (the Viennese sewers, to be precise) for a rendezvous with his old schoolfriend, now his baffled pursuer, Holly Martins (the school at which those two were once mates must have been stranger than Hogwarts).

They are in circular motion, on a giant Ferris wheel, the *Riesenrad* – a forlorn relic of Vienna's imperial days, now a symbol of the ups and downs of world history. In 1846, capital of the Austro-Hungarian empire and a centre of world culture. In 1946 a bombsite, occupied by philistine armies. Beneath the two men is a war-torn city – more and more of which they can see as they rise. As they reach the highest point, 64.75 metres above ground level, Harry ruminates:

> 'Look down there. Would you really feel any pity if one of those dots stopped moving for ever? If I offered you £20,000 for every dot that stopped, would you really, old man, tell me to keep my money? Or would you calculate how many dots you could afford to spare?'*

Face to face, what Harry coolly suggests (extermination for profit) would be unthinkable. Himmler vomited when, just once in his ghastly career, he witnessed what *Endlösung* actually meant to those at the receiving end of his 'solution'. At Minsk 100 people were shot on the edge of an open grave as a demonstration for him. The Theatre of Holocaust.* In the sanitary seclusion of his office, the SS monster was happy enough to sign away millions of lives. He went back and carried on serenely churning out death orders. He didn't require any £20,000s for the dots he eliminated.

Why should 'closeness to the event' make that much difference to rational human beings? It's something with which *Star Trek*'s Spock constantly wrestles, inconclusively, in the cold, cerebral chamber of his Vulcanite mind. He'll never know.

The scene was also perplexing for me. Aged eleven, I was able to take on board moral problems, and even wrestle with them, in my infantile way. And this particular problem was close to home. All too obviously, the scene on the *Riesenrad*, high above Vienna, allegorises the damage visited on European cities by aircraft – from altitudes even higher than the great wheel can reach. That point at which humanity is flies to wanton boys.

My father had died in Bomber Command.* I myself had been bombed, and very unpleasant it was. Orwell's opening line in 'The Lion and the Unicorn', 'As I write this, highly civilized human beings are flying overhead, trying to kill me', has always raised the hair on the back of my neck.

What, *The Third Man* pauses to ask, is the morality of remote killing? The war itself asked the same question. The uneasiness one felt was collective. It extended from a (wholly unwanton) boy in Colchester to Downing Street. Despite their horrific losses (among whom was my father), Bomber Command was denied an active service medal. There was no statue raised to Bomber Harris, the commander, until 1992, when it was promptly vandalised by those whom some 50,000 aircrew had given their lives to defend – as the aircrew believed.* The British had a national sense of guilt which they dealt with, typically, by not thinking about it.

Moral judgement starts in perplexity. I never now fly into a major city without, as I fasten my seat belt, posing somewhere in my mind Harry Lime's Mephistophelean question.

Peter Ibbetson

(aetat. 12)

THE BIGGEST LITERARY FACT in my adult life is
Victorian fiction. And that rich literary seam – one of the
glories of the human mind – has been in my life from the
earliest period of my literacy. My first brush with the genre
was in 1945, via an idle schoolteacher, averse to the tedious
toil of teaching. He passed his hours of classroom confine-
ment by reading aloud, chapter by chapter, Harrison Ainsworth's *Old St Paul's*.* A gothic best-seller of the 1840s, it is
based, as I would later discover, on Hugo's similarly topo-
graphic *Notre-Dame de Paris*.

Ainsworth's tale of plague and the Great Fire (and, with
deference to the blush-prone maiden's cheek, the libertine
delinquencies of the Earl of Rochester) shamelessly recycles
Defoe's account of the plague year, which in turn recycled
documents of a century earlier. Little fleas have smaller fleas
– and so on ad infinitum.

I was particularly taken, and can still shudderingly recall,
the patient-killing and corpse-robbing nurse and undertaker,

Old St Paul's burns

Judith and Chowles, doing their *danse macabre* in the cathedral vaults around their ill-gotten gold, before being engulfed in the stream of molten lead from the burning roof.

I was seven. And, thanks to Hermann Goering, I had a clear idea of what it would be like to expire under crashing roofs and burning timbers.

The first Victorian novel I read at school with my own eyes (the way having been opened by *Lorna Doone* and the film of *Great Expectations*) was *Masterman Ready*, by Captain Marryat. I was ten.

The book was considerably older – around fifty years older, as I recall – with a long list of previous readers scratched into its flyleaf label, extending back well past my parents' generation. Some of those names might now be inscribed on the town's majestic war memorial (reckoned by locals as the most majestic in the country⋆). It was a relic of pre-war 'improving'

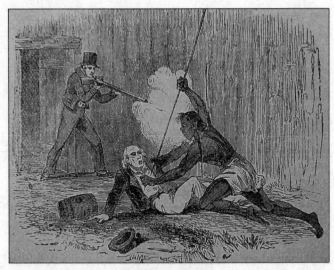

Masterman Ready dies

reading and antique educational optimisms. Good books make good boys.

My *Masterman Ready* was school issue. New supplies of books for the classroom – never generous in the depressed 1930s – had been wholly paralysed during the war-torn 1940s. There were better things for a country in a fight to the death to do with its scarce paper than waste it on children's education.

Like other bibliophiles, I have always found 'pre-owned' books an aid to pleasure. The ghostly company of former readers around one adds to the enjoyment. A kind of spectral reading group, in twenty-first-century terms.

Marryat's novel is a parable on what Thomas Carlyle called 'servantship' – knowing your place in life and keeping to it.* Victorians had a fondness for the idea. In Marryat's tale, the wise old seaman takes care of the Seagrave family (father, invalid mother, four children), shipwrecked, as they all find themselves, on a desert island. They are his master, he is their man. More specifically, Masterman is their butler, their gamekeeper, their nanny, their cook. Pretty soon, he has the island running like a well-conducted boarding house in 1940s Margate. Masterman never forgets his station in life. He dies with the word 'sir' on his lips, a cannibal assegai in his guts, sorry only that he cannot continue to serve 'his' family. There will, they may be sure, be clean linen robes and well-tuned harps awaiting them when the Seagraves join him in that better England in the skies.★

Lumps of *Masterman Ready* detach themselves to resurface in such far-off places as the stockade siege in *Treasure Island*, and even faintly reverberate in *Lord of the Flies* (with Piggy as a kind of parodically unready Masterman). When were novelists ever observers of other novelists' property? Marryat himself wrote *Masterman Ready* as a old sea-dog's corrective to the innumerable 'nautical errors' in *The Swiss Family Robinson*★ and, while correcting that work, nicked chunks of Wyss's narrative (not least the basic plot).

I read a lot of sub-Marryat later, via Percy F. Westerman★ (e.g. *Andy All-Alone* – a rattling Robinsoniad) and at an early age I knew the difference between being marooned and being shipwrecked (Ben Gunn is one, Robinson the other) and why there need be no sand on a 'desert' island. I toyed with the idea of joining the Sea Scouts (a movement routinely advertised in Westerman's flyleaves) but was put off by all the toggles and reef-knot stuff.

The first Victorian novel I owned, as my own property, no one else's bespittled or ink-stained fingers having turned its pages, was *Peter Ibbetson*, by George du Maurier.★ I myself did not procure it. I did not buy or, in any wilful sense, choose it. Books drifted up on my foreshore, like Crusoe's flotsam, before the age of eleven – when I had access to the public library and some freedom of choice.

For a reason I never fathomed, my mother bought a small job lot of books from a publisher's warehouse sale. This was also in my twelfth year. Among the purchases was an omnibus volume of George du Maurier's three novels: *Peter Ibbetson*, *Trilby* and *The Martian*. The greatest *Punch* cartoonist of his age, du Maurier turned to fiction, on the advice of Henry James, no less, when his eyes began to fail, making his close-up pictorial work difficult.*

The plump volume my mother bought for me, a Pilot Press edition, had been published in 1947, and had hung around in the warehouse for a couple of years before being remaindered. It contained (I write in the past tense, but the volume is on the desk before me as I write) the writer-artist's original illustrations. It was reproduced on poor-quality wartime regulation paper, but was, in its way, a thing for an eleven-year-old boy to value, if no *edition de luxe*.

Trilby never much interested me. There was too much French *argot* and *vie de Bohème*. Cigars and *vin rouge* meant nothing to me at that age. I associated France with the misery of irregular verbs. Nor did *The Martian* grip me (although it contains a sensitive account of du Maurier's terror of incipient blindness.) *Peter Ibbetson*, by contrast, gripped me by the throat. It still has me in its grasp.

First published in 1891, it is a subtler 'scientific romance'* than anything published by H. G. Wells in that decade, when science fiction (but not the name for it) was born. Du Maurier was fifty-five, and, as he said, 'in the afternoon of his existence'. Had he but known it, he was rather closer to nightfall. He would die four years later, cutting short a promising career in fiction.

The story takes the form of a prison confession of Gogo Pasquier, the son of an English mother and a French father. The opening section of the narrative covers his idyllic but motherless childhood in Passy. His beloved father dies and he returns to England, which he hates, to be brought up by a relative (an uncle who is no uncle) he distrusts and is renamed Peter Ibbetson.

He grows up a successful architect. While carrying out an expensive commission for an aristocratic client, he meets a striking society beauty, the Duchess of Towers. Coincidentally she is revealed to be a childhood acquaintance from Passy days. Then an ugly duckling ('Mimsey'), now she is ravishing.

The Duchess it is who introduces Peter to the practice of 'dreaming true'. By putting oneself in a certain configuration at the moment of sleep (on your back, with hands intricately crossed behind the head) the adept can actually *use* dream to voyage back into their own past. That past is stored in all the detail which conscious memory forgets:

> Evidently our brain contains something akin both to a photographic plate and a phonographic cylinder, and many other things of the same kind not yet discovered; not a sight or a sound or a smell is lost; not a taste or a feeling or an emotion. Unconscious memory records them all, without our even heeding what goes on around us beyond the things that attract our immediate interest or attention.

Heady stuff.

It is not merely mental tourism of the past which the practice allows. True dreamers can meet and interact with others who have mastered the technique. There is, du Maurier speculates, a whole world beyond the pillow (interestingly, in Vienna, a young Dr Freud was conducting his investigations into the sleep life of his patients, with as sensational conclusions, at exactly this period. *Die Traumdeutung – The Interpretation of Dreams* – would be published in 1899*).

Is it plausible? There's a sly authentication of the true-dreaming business. Christians (du Maurier's novel is sophisticatedly agnostic about religion) argue that clasping the hands in front of the face gives the believer a hot line to God. Why should other manual postures not work likewise?

Peter's induction into the true dreamworld follows a night of conversation with the Duchess:

> I got back to my hotel in the *Rue de la Michodière* ... [With] that haunting, beloved face with its ineffable smile still printed on the retina of my closed eyes, I fell asleep.
>
> And then I dreamed a dream, and the first phase of my real, inner life began!
>
> All the events of the day, distorted and exaggerated and jumbled together after the usual manner of dreams, wove themselves into a kind of nightmare and oppression. I was on my way to my old abode: everything that I met or saw was grotesque and impossible, yet had now the strange, vague charm of association and reminiscence, now the distressing sense of change and loss and desolation ...
>
> I knew perfectly who I was and what I was, and remembered all the events of the previous day. I was conscious that my real body, undressed and in bed, now lay fast asleep in a small room on the fourth floor of an *hôtel garni* in the *Rue de la Michodière*. I knew this perfectly; and yet here was my body, too, just as substantial, with

all my clothes on; my boots rather dusty, my shirt-collar damp with the heat, for it was hot. With my disengaged hand I felt in my trousers-pocket; there were my London latch-keys, my purse, my penknife; my handkerchief in the breastpocket of my coat, and in its tail-pockets my gloves and pipe-case, and the little water-colour box I had bought that morning. I looked at my watch; it was going, and marked eleven. I pinched myself, I coughed, I did all one usually does under the pressure of some immense surprise, to assure myself that I was awake; and I *was*, and yet here I stood.

Later, Peter argues violently with his rogue of a guardian (who may, it transpires, be his father). He beats him to death with a poker, after the swine has cast aspersions on Peter's mother. The parricide Ibbetson is sentenced to hang. His sentence is subsequently commuted, thanks to the Duchess's friends in high places. He will spend the remainder of his life in the relative ease of a hospital for the criminally insane. Hovering enigmatically over the whole text is the suspicion that the narrator may be stark staring mad. He may belong in the bin (as I then would have called it, and now never would dare).

By 'dreaming true', Peter can continue the relationship with his true love, the Duchess, as they gambol happily through the land of their childhood past, forever in their late twenties, creating an alternative present for themselves. They have an affair, consummated in (true) dreamland. They see their childhood selves as their children. Every morning (every night, that is, in the drab 'outer' life) they start their dream-day with superb coffee, croissants and cigarettes (only a prisoner in an English jail, Peter observes, can truly appreciate these French amenities – I felt much the same when I visited France, for the first time, five years later).

Excitingly, the lovers discover that true dreaming is an instrument whereby they can explore 'antenatal' history. Following their connected genetic chain (they're cousins), they journey back through time to the prehistoric era, where Peter – easel set up and palette in hand – sketches woolly mammoths and pterodactyls.

After twenty-five years of this idyllic dream marriage, and nocturnal tourism, the Duchess dies. She returns in a vision to Peter, promising an even richer life together after death. They will, it seems, not merely dream true, but die true.

Peter Ibbetson was a huge best-seller, to the genteel chagrin of Henry James, who never enjoyed that success. But best-sellers, like fashions in clothes, are short-lived things. Their freshness, as John Mortimer sardonically put it, is somewhere between that of milk and yoghurt. Why, half a century on, was du Maurier's romance magical for me in 1950? A boy, that is, for whom wet dreaming would shortly be a more pressing issue than true dreaming and whose environment was as alien to du Maurier's France as the Red Planet.

The answer has nothing to do with the daring ('for the time') sex which sold *Peter Ibbetson* in the 1890s, a decade when anything French was exciting, from 'letters', through 'naughty postcards', to the turgidities of Zola.

There were clear-cut congruences between Ibbetson's life and my own. My childhood was disrupted, my father killed in war, and I was – unwillingly – 'evacuated' to places I hated, with uncles and aunts whom I feared and disliked. I could 'identify', as they say in AA groups when 'sharing' life experiences. More importantly, du Maurier's novel allegorised my relationship with books, more particularly, Victorian fiction. I could travel there: as myself and not myself. Reading the stuff, by day, was my dreaming true.

Echos du Temps passé

Peter Ibbetson is exquisitely illustrated by the author; the faint, nebulous presences of Gogo and the Duchess, hovering over themselves in childhood, are haunting. I don't know if even in France twelve-year-olds read Proust avidly. Perhaps Sartre and de Beauvoir did. But there is a particularly fine, full-page illustration of the Duchess, arms crossed, standing in front of a montage of her childhood, with the caption *Echos du Temps passé*. Had Proust, when he began *À la recherche du temps perdu* in 1909, read *Peter Ibbetson*? I was in no intellectual shape to take on Proust in 1950. But, scaled down to what I could take on, du Maurier introduced me to something of what I would later encounter in the subtler novelist. Namely, the extraordinary potency of memory – and the ways in which it can be used to make sense of life.

Of course, furtively, like thousands of 1890s readers of *Peter Ibbetson*, I placed my arms as instructed, fell asleep and got nothing other than sore shoulders the next morning. But, even when night-time experiment failed, Victorian fiction continued to be my other country. My escape from the solitary prison of the here and now. My cell.

Du Maurier's novel has a curious after-history. It was filmed, in 1935, starring (of all stars) Gary Cooper. This was, in fact, the second film adaptation: a silent *Peter Ibbetson* had come out in 1921. Both versions were (unusually for Hollywood) moderately faithful to the original.*

The 1935 film and the book of the film were, in the same period, 'discovered' by the surrealist Paul Éluard. He had followed a woman he did not know but who caught his lecherous eye into a cinema. Once inside, his artist's eye distracted him from his sexual prey. The film showing on the screen was *Peter Ibbetson*. Éluard subsequently enthused, passionately, about the movie to André Breton.* The surrealists duly enshrined *Peter Ibbetson* 'as the cinematic embodiment of their magnificent obsession with *l'amour fou* – the love that transcends all known obstacles'. It was, said Breton, 'a triumph of surrealist thought'. Dreaming true was up there with the slashed eyeball in Buñuel's *Un chien andalou* or Dalí's floppy watches.*

It's not clear that the surrealist crew registered that a fellow artist, Parisian-trained, was the procreator of this Hollywoodised 'triumph'. For them it was enough that *Peter Ibbetson* endorsed the primacy of dream over fact. The royal road, as Freud called it. For me, du Maurier was the royal road into Victorian fiction.

Svengali

(aetat. 12)

TRILBY NEVER AFFECTED me as powerfully as *Peter Ibbetson*. One detail, however, did stick adhesively: du Maurier's pen-and-pencil depictions of his villain, Svengali. It's hard to see how it couldn't. The face, all grease-shagged hair and hooked nose, fused in my (twelve-year-old) mind's eye with Alec Guinness's Fagin,* which I saw at the same time. Oddly, neither merged with the *Nacht und Nebel* images which were also current after the 'Belsen' films, shown to the adult population in 1945.*

It was many years, and much corrective introspection, before I could purge my mind of the ingrained anti-Semitism inherited from my wholly unenlightened social background. Before, that is, I could read *Trilby* at all critically and, as I would now think, properly (Elaine Showalter's 1995 edition of the novel was immensely helpful: it came out, ironically, in an OUP series under my general editorship – creating some odd chronological reverberations in my mind).

My first real understanding of the vileness of the camps

Svengali

was conveyed, inevitably, by a novel: Erich Maria Remarque's
Spark of Life,* which I picked up later (with recollections of
All Quiet on the Western Front) from Colchester's public library
('Why', I recall thinking, as I decided whether to expend one
of my two tickets on it, 'does he have a woman's name?').

It's a powerful novel – Remarque had an axe to grind
against the Nazis, literally. As an act of spite, the Third Reich,
unable to touch the refugee author in America, had arrested
his sister on a trumped-up charge and beheaded her.*

Spark of Life is a better novel than its best-selling predecessor. But I had a lot happening in my reading life in 1951
and its impact – though beneficial – was merely arresting and
thought-provoking, not life-changing.

Such Power is Dangerous

(aetat. 12)

BETWEEN TEN AND THIRTEEN, bookish children can be observed experiencing reading rages. They grind their eyes and push their noses savagely against the page. They hoover up, obsessively, everything by their favourite authors they can lay hands on. They slow their furious pace down as they near the end, so as to savour the last, delicious drops of narrative. At no stage in life is reading more intense.

Even those whose profession is books rarely re-experience in later years that raging pre-pubescent lust for print. Dr Johnson records that the only work which, as an adult, he could bring himself to get up early for (he was an incorrigible slugabed) was Burton's *The Anatomy of Melancholy*. Otherwise the mattress won every time. It does for most of us. The alarm clock rarely rings for literature.

Dr Johnson wrote his only work of fiction, *Rasselas*, in two weeks, to defray the cost of his mother's funeral.* (I bought a fine edition of the exemplary tale of the Abyssinian Prince in Doncaster's Bookshop on North Hill around this time and enjoyed reading it.*) That (the fortnight's composition, for family emergency), to forge an improbable link, is all the Great Cham has in common with his fellow novelist Dennis Wheatley.

Wheatley and Rider Haggard* were two of the story-tellers I favoured most in my own reading-rage years. Both authors were amply represented on Colchester's public library shelves – although some of the Haggard titles had to be hunted down in the children's annexe, where, to be honest, a self-respecting twelve-year-old did not like to be seen. Wheatley's novels – which always contained one daring 'hot' scene (you could locate it easily; the book always fell open at those much relished pages) – were strictly adult fare.

The 'Prince of Thrillers', as he liked to style himself, Wheatley was a self-anointed heir to the 'King of the Thrillers', Edgar Wallace* (Wallace had died in 1932, during the making of the film King Kong, the only work of his which has any resonance with the general public nowadays – appropriate, given his own aspirations to kingship).

Wheatley, a bon viveur and London wine merchant (in that order), turned to fiction in 1932, when the Slump wiped out his luxury lines of work. A resourceful man, he opted for one of life's little sweeteners that was actually thriving in the Depression: popular fiction (the relevant volume of his autobiography is wittily entitled Drink and Ink).

An astute merchandiser of consumables, whether in bottles, cases or hard covers, Wheatley 'pushed' his first novel, Forbidden Territory, by means of 20,000 advertising postcards. In current terminology, he invented the mailshot. It had worked for Beaujolais nouveau, and it damn well worked for thrillers.

Later on Wheatley, the most inventive of writers, would

pioneer the 'Crime Dossier' detective novel,* in which physical 'clues' were boxed up with loose leaves of narrative in pseudo-documentary form. They were the forerunner of Bill Burroughs's and B. S. Johnson's 'cut-up'* experiments – not that they could be argued to be, in any sense, the inspiration for those drearily high-minded things. If you can get hold of the crime dossiers, they remain impressively ingenious and fun to solve / read.

Forbidden Territory is a disciple's updating of Wallace's *Four Just Men* (itself an update of Dumas's famous three*). It introduced a crime-fighting, Commie-bashing quartet headed by the aristocratic Duc de Richleau – the drawling embodiment of cosmopolitan (wine-bibbing) cool.

It's a pity that the long-running series that sprouted from this hugely successful first novel (propelled by Wheatley's postcards, it hurtled through seven printings in seven weeks in 1932) was so successful. It has overshadowed some (marginally) better things which he did. A late exploit of the fearsome four, *The Devil Rides Out*, was picked up by Hammer Films* in 1968, with Christopher Lee as a superbly OTT Richleau, and a script by Richard Matheson (author of *I am Legend*, source-text for the 2007 film). *The Devil Rides Out* was a huge hit in British cinemas, and the Hammer adaptations kicked off a Wheatley cult – including, along with the diabolist nonsense, the wonderfully preposterous *The Lost Continent* (it's made of seaweed, floats in the Sargasso Sea, and is infested with monstrous crustaceans and cannibalistic descendants of marooned pirates. The studio ran out of money halfway through and had to do desperate things with papier mâché).*

Wheatley's satanic romances are, in terms of craft ('art' is entirely the wrong word), far inferior to his quieter *The*

Haunting of Toby Jugg, which features a paraplegic Second World War fighter pilot, living alone in a country house, who is malevolently tormented by a warlock in a kind of *Whatever Happened to Baby Jane?* scenario.

I read Wheatley's rattling yarns, as I read Haggard, for the rattle, principally: the brain could take the stuff in as fast as the finger could turn the page. But some of the yarns (like *Jugg*, which I loved) have left a residue, long after they washed over one.

Buoyed up by the debut success of *Forbidden Territory*, Wheatley had resolved to dash out his second thriller in a week, as Wallace boasted he routinely did. The Prince duly borrowed a friend's secluded cottage for his challenge to the lately deceased King of the genre. In the event, *Such Power is Dangerous* took Wheatley two weeks to write. Just like *Rasselas*. And, like Dr Johnson's fortnightly effort, it sold reassuringly. Wheatley used the revenues not to bury his mother, but to pay off his first, divorced, wife. He then went on to make a fortune for himself and his next spouse. *Autres temps, autres moeurs*, as the Duc would say.

The 1933 novel itself may or may not be Wheatley's best – if such assessments make any sense with this most unambitious of literary practitioners – but *Such Power is Dangerous* was certainly effective on me in 1951. The central idea is gripping and original. A sinister British tycoon, Lord Gavin Fortescue, and a ruthless Hollywood mogul, Jos Hinckman, conspire to establish a 'Combine' of all the film studios in the English-speaking world. This alliance will give them not merely dangerous power – but world dominion. 'Our revenues', predicts Fortescue,

'will be greater than the budget of any but a first-class

state. The wealth of Ford and Rockefeller would not compare with ours. Again, our sphere of influence would be unbounded. By the type of film we chose to produce we could influence the mass psychology of nations. Fashions, morals, customs, could be propagated by our will – we should be able if it suited us to fill a whole people with a mad desire to make war on their neighbour – or if we considered that a universal language would lead to world peace we could induce the children of all nations to learn English, by a decision that our talking pictures should be made in no other tongue. We should have power to do either endless good ... or boundless evil. No king or emperor would have had such power in the world before.'

This, one reminds oneself, is AD 1933, many decades PM (Pre-Murdoch, that is).

What Wheatley fantasises, all too plausibly, is totalitarian control of the world not by jackboot, or by KGB surveillance and the Lubianka, but by the opium of the masses: the movies. It's more prescient and worldly wise than Aldous Huxley* (who, in a pinch, would you trust? A man-of-the-world London wine merchant or a myopic Oxford intellectual?). Populations sleepwalk into tyranny, Wheatley perceived, with a cinema ticket (or, latterly, a remote control) in their hands.

The villains in Such Power is Dangerous are foiled by a feisty (and upper-class) British star, Avril Bamborough, and a handsome young son of Hollywood, Nelson Druce. Nelson has invented a device – the X-Projector (a kind of 3D) – which will revolutionise the industry (this, with Technicolor on the horizon, is similarly prescient). The plot is mechanical but, like other machinery of the time (wind-up alarm clocks, for example), efficient – if occasionally clunky. Clunkiest of all is the dialogue. At this period in his life Wheatley had never actually been to the West Coast of America. His ear for American vernacular is less than tin.

The 'hot scene' in *Such Power is Dangerous*, for example, involves a Chicago gunman, Angelo Donelli. Crazed with wop lust for the fragrant English rose, Avril, he breaks into her bedroom and pinions her, with the instruction, 'Do not maka da noise.' Then the trousers droppa and the chloroform bottle comes outa. Avril's blue blood boils – but in vain does the maiden writhe against the loathed embrace:

> The vile little beast. Avril sobbed with rage and pain, and loathing. He meant to dope her, did he? – she'd heard of such things, read of them in books, or awful cases in the papers. It had never entered her mind that such a horror should happen to her ... He whipped a handkerchief from his pocket and uncorked the bottle with his strong white teeth – then he held them both high out of reach of Avril's head.
>
> 'Ef you not careful,' he panted, 'da chloroform, it spill, burna your lovely face, eh? Angelo not wanta hurt you, but he lova you, yes.'
>
> Avril lay frantic beneath his grip, nothing should serve to suffer this awful thing.

As the ravisher's hand slips between Avril's virginally clamped thighs and the chloroform pad hovers over her crimson lips, the Yank Tarquin is felled – and killed – by 'who knows who?' (this is not a question for which the alert reader will need any crime dossier-style clues: manly Nelson, of course).

Reading the novel in 1951 changed me – or, more precisely, it complicated my outlook on some important things in my life. *Such Power is Dangerous* introduced the idea that films were made, they didn't just happen in cinemas. More significantly, that films were, in a sense, *making* me. And why were so many of them American? And what – other than my one-and-ninepence – were the motives, ulterior and proclaimed, of the makers of those films?

Such Power is Dangerous made me healthily suspicious of what I consumed. Other, better novels and movies (Budd Schulberg's *The Disenchanted*,* Clifford Odets's *The Big Knife**) would complicate the suspicion still further. But the seed was sown with Wheatley's thriller. Scepticism is where criticism starts.

Re-reading *Such Power is Dangerous* (still the undemanding labour of only an hour or so), I was struck by aspects which wholly passed me by in 1951. The introduction into the action, for example, of a director called 'Alfred Titchcock', who is hot to make a film called *The Forbidden Territory* (Hitchcock was a friend of Wheatley's and did indeed hope he could make a film of that novel – the 'titchy cock' joke is, knowing Wheatley, deliberate). There is also a rather unlikeable star of the silent era who made his name playing a comic tramp, now a mogul, 'Percy Piplin'. Wheatley clearly found Charley Chaplin 'common'. East Street Market urchin and West End wine merchant never shall meet.

A whole chapter in *Such Power is Dangerous* is devoted to a hilarious description of what Hollywood does to the highbrow book of the year before – Huxley's *Brave New World* (1932). Wheatley has great fun trashing the great novelist. Huxley, of course, was the intellectuals' intellectual – Bodleian, not tuppenny library stuff. Hollywood, as Wheatley fantasises, brings the big-brain novelist down to earth:

Much had been made of the Native Reservation Scene, but

not unnaturally, the Hollywood producer had felt Mexico
to be totally inadequate. He preferred Africa, in order that
he might more fittingly bring in lions, tigers, elephants,
and every other animal that he could lay his hands on.

The novel is riddled with similar libellous in-jokes that, half
a century later, the publisher's lawyers would have sternly
legalled out. It makes for a yeasty mischievousness which
even now renders *Such Power is Dangerous* a jolly reading experience. It is rarely read, however. My London Library volume
records the last borrowing as four years ago and the once
extensive presence of Wheatley on the library shelf has been
winnowed down to two or three titles. *Such Power is Dangerous*
will be lucky to escape the next purge, as old volumes are
tossed out to make room for new.

XII

The Cruel Sea

(aetat. 13)

NICHOLAS MONSARRAT'S *The Cruel Sea* was published in 1951 and reportedly (there being no accurate best-seller statistics at that time) was read by four million Britons between its publication and the release of the film, two years later, in 1953. It too broke records and was seen by tens of millions.*

The country was ready for a novel like Monsarrat's which – in James Jones's phrase – 'blew the lid off the war'. As with Jones's novel *From Here to Eternity* (1951, filmed 1953 – with a similar double success in the US*), it wasn't just the anti-heroic depiction of the war ('the *bloody* war', as Jack Hawkins memorably called it in the British film) but the sexual explicitness which opened millions of pockets. And, in my case, eyes. It also opened ears; the expletive 'bloody' was high on the lexicon of BBFC banned words: it was only sanctioned in this case by the manifest earnestness, and high-mindedness, of the film-makers. And, of course, the fact that we won the bloody war.

One of those many million copies of *The Cruel Sea* came the way of my best friend at the time. His parents had left it lying around, after devouring it. It was a literary treasure trove for thirteen-year-olds. One's chances of getting a copy from the public library, where, if not in the poison cabinet, there would be a reserve list months long, were remote to non-existent. And twelve shillings and sixpence (£30 in current valuation) was far beyond the schoolboy pocket. Most adult pockets would experience pain stretching that far in 1951, where many more books were loaned than bought, and £20 per week was considered an enviable professional salary.

The odd persistence of the expensive hardback (called in the book trade the 'library edition') was that its durable covers made it good for, as librarians calculated, some 150 readings. If my experience was anything to go by, so intensively was *The Cruel Sea* read, particularly the narrative's racier sections, that I doubt every copy in Cassell's hardback edition made it to double, let alone treble figures.

In a last spasm of cultural Podsnappery, Cassell also put out what was preposterously called a 'cadet' version – costing half a crown less – which had the most interesting (to me and other readers of cadet age) passages bowdlerised, or excised.

My pal Mick, exercising his first-dip *droit de seigneur* on his parents' book, whetted my appetite by describing the more arousing, and horrifying, scenes. When I finally got my hands on *The Cruel Sea*, Monsarrat did not disappoint. Dredging back for my most vivid first impression, it was, unsurprisingly, the marine *danse macabre* of a ring of skeletons, long after their ship was torpedoed, roped together in the water, bobbing their bony craniums and grinning toothily at each other, as if they were at an Old Time Dance evening. About the same time I was wrestling (hopelessly) with Eliot's *The Waste Land*, and Monsarrat's imagery fused, irritatingly, with Section IV of that poem, 'Death by Water':

> Phlebas the Phoenician, a fortnight dead,
> Forgot the cry of gulls, and the deep sea swell
> And the profit and loss.
>> A current under sea
> Picked his bones in whispers. As he rose and fell
> He passes the stages of his age and youth
> Entering the whirlpool.

More vivid yet were the pages describing the torpedoing of the corvette on which the principal characters serve, and the deaths of most of the crew. Monsarrat describes in harrowing detail those who 'died well', and the larger number of those who 'died badly'.

Among the bad deaths is a junior officer, Sub-Lieutenant Baker. Obsessed by sex, the desperately virginal young teenager, inflamed to recklessness by overheard bawdy sailor talk, 'dipped his wick' with a prostitute on his last shore leave. His inexperience, and desperate lust, as Monsarrat describes it, was all too real to a 1950s adolescent:

> This leave, he *must* do it. The time for dreaming was past. Everyone else slept with women, and talked about it, and took it for granted. He had overheard a mess-deck phrase which pricked his imagination: 'She gave me a slice on the mat.' He wanted a slice on the mat ... How did you pick up a woman? What did you *do*? How did you tell a prostitute from an ordinary woman anyway? And then, did you give them the money first, or did you say nothing and leave it on the dressing-table afterwards? Would it be expensive?

Did they tell you how much it was, before you started? Did they understand how not to have babies? Could you be arrested if they found you doing it? What was it like, how did you begin, how long did it go on for?

He does 'it'. A few weeks later, he dies – badly, unvirginally and poxed:

> Baker ... found no terror in death that he had not already suffered in full measure, during the past week. Ever since *Compass Rose* sailed he had been wandering round the ship under a morbid load of guilt, alone with a shameful fear which the passing days had disgustingly confirmed. He knew nothing about venereal infection, and he had no one to turn to; indeed, he was only guessing when he diagnosed the swollen and painful organs, and the soiled underwear, as symptoms of what, in the happy past, he had learned to call a 'dose' – the cheerful joke of the cheerful man of the world .... The icy cold water was agreeably numbing ... He had begun to welcome the increasing cold as it ate into his groin, and the feeling that this loathsome and hated part of his body was at last being brought under control.

The film was cleaned up – if not quite to cadet standards, then to an officially acceptable high-mindedness. No soiled underwear. Eric Ambler, who did the film's script, was a more distinguished novelist than Monsarrat and skilfully carved the sprawling narrative into shapely form. He also gave it a kind of Miltonic 'they also serve' upliftingness, at odds with the source text, but necessary. The power of the film was more dangerous than that of the library book and needed to be curbed in.

Local government officials in Colchester (my mother was

a council employee at the time) were hauled off to see the film. The cinema was hired for a matinee performance. The only other film paid that compliment was the 1948 epic *Scott of the Antarctic*. My mother was unimpressed by both. She had her own views about the war which had both widowed and liberated her.

The big scene in both versions of *The Cruel Sea* is the depth-charging of British sailors, hooraying as they mistakenly assume that *Compass Rose* is steaming forward to pluck them out of the water, when the captain, as mistakenly, thinks there is a submarine beneath them and has decided that they are expendable. In the novel, the details are horrific:

> One freak item of the horror impressed itself on the memory. As the tormented water leapt upwards in a solid grey cloud, the single figure of a man was tossed high on the very plume of the fountain, a puppet figure of whirling arms and legs seeming to make, in death, wild gestures of anger and reproach. It appeared to hang a long time in the air, cursing them all, before falling back into the boiling sea.

The film tactfully averts its lens from the cartwheeling matelot – wonderfully cinematic as, in other ways, the image would have been (a sailor is shown looking from the explosion, skyward).* 'Bloody murderer!' an insubordinate sailor screams at the officers' bridge.

Captain Ericson, played throatily by Hawkins, gets drunk and in the film (not the novel) later comes out with his agonised groan: 'It's the war, it's the *bloody* war.' He does not mean war is gory (although it's certainly that) but that it's bloody awful. And probably bloody pointless.

The impact of *The Cruel Sea* on me was not merely its opening of cabinets marked 'sex' and 'death' usually closed to the 'cadet'. Monsarrat's novel, based on the author's personal service (something one could feel in the narrative), wrenched around one's sense of what the war actually was. My father was killed in the war, all my nearest male relatives had fought Hitler. My grandfather had fought the Kaiser. No one talked about it – my idea of conflict was enshrined in the huge memorial, outside Colchester's Castle Park, with its green-copper-tarnished, sword-wielding, winged angel of righteous victory. 'Glory' was the theme word.

Heroes had laid down their lives for others. It was noble. Nothing was nobler. Like other children of air-force officers who had 'fallen', I was taken to Westminster Abbey for a memorial service, where I saw the King (his face looked orange – I realised, much later, that the tiny mannequin who looked so manly in the colourised portraits was wearing Max Factor No. 8 greasepaint). Had my father – trapped in his burning bomber – died 'well' or 'badly'? It was not a question I would have dared to ask myself, pre-Monsarrat. And it was, for me, an important question to which I still have no straight answer.

Monsarrat's war was grimly unheroic. Little is achieved by the hero Ericson's tiny corvette. Seven years were taken out of the lives of those who survived the Battle of the Atlantic; all their remaining years from the many who didn't survive. More importantly, Monsarrat questioned whether England and the English – those who kept the home fires burning – were worth those years and lives.

Relevant to this question, a reflective moment from the novel stuck in my mind; and still does. During a Liverpool refit for *Compass Rose*, regarding the dockworkers rampantly skiving, cutting corners and striking whenever the whim takes them, Ericson thinks: 'These were among the people whom sailors fought and died for; at close quarters, they hardly seem to deserve it.' The sentiment is echoed throughout the narrative. Ericson ends the war not jubilant, but weary and exhausted. His last words, and the last words of the novel, are, 'I'm damned tired.'

In an apparently unpublishable manuscript novel which was doing the rounds of publishers in the early 1950s, William Golding (another wartime sailor) allegorised his uncompromising view that, right or wrong, the Second World War had secreted moral exhaustion, as a bee secretes honey – and that the poison would be in England for ever.* Subtler, and better art by far, as *Lord of the Flies* is, there are congruences with *The Cruel Sea*.

My opinions about 'the war', the biggest geopolitical fact of my life, were shaken by Monsarrat. More importantly, I apprehended that a novel and, to a lesser extent, a movie could do that shaking. They could, in a sense, change history. One's own history.

The Puppet Masters

(aetat. 13)

TUPPENNY OR 'CORNER SHOP' libraries* enjoyed their high era in the 1930s. For those who could not afford the big circulating libraries* (Smith's, Boots's, Mudie's), or were too socially humble to browse high street ('carriage trade') bookshops, the tuppenies served a necessary function. They were cheap, they were unfrightening and they purveyed unabashedly 'popular' literary ware. Fiction, typically, without a single improving motive.

Until the Roberts Act of 1959, with its injunction that local public libraries must provide the whole population a 'full and comprehensive' service, 'books on the rates' (as they were called) were self-righteously parsimonious as regards fiction. Novels were, as Victorian evangelists said, 'spiritual gin'. And even after 1959, although 75 per cent of the public library loans were novels, only 25 per cent of the annual acquisition budget was allocated to new fiction. The custodians of the nation's reading believed in improving literature and put their (our) money where their belief was.

Lord Reith and his apostles were doing the same thing on the BBC.*

There were, throughout the 1940s and 1950s (until the paperback revolution of the 1960s), sporadic attempts to revive the tuppenny libraries, via corner shops. Hyam's the newsagent's was just across the road from the run-down flat I lived in (when pressed, our crazed landlord, who lived downstairs, would nip over in his dressing gown – to universal shock and awe. Aunt Ivy, currently my guardian, would no more have done that than venture across East Street without her false teeth).

Hyam's went, tentatively, into books for loan (a tanner a go) in the very early 1950s. The stock was a couple of rows of garish, plastic-wrapped hardbacks. It was all new fiction, all genre: romance, 'tecs, westerns predominating. There was also the odd 'hot' item, of the *Forever Amber** kind (for the ladies) and the *I, the Jury* kind (for the men). There may even have been a Hank Janson* or two under the counter: *very* hot items. No young person would be loaned them.

There was also a sprinkling of science fiction. Respect for the genre in Britain had been pioneered by Victor Gollancz.* Other self-respecting publishers snootily despised it as 'tuppenny library stuff' – all ray guns and little green men.

I was on friendly terms with the man who ran Hyam's. Something less than a manager and more than a counter assistant, he and his family lived in a tied house next door to us. The shop was a goldmine. It could not help but be, in a country addicted to tobacco, sweets and racing results, with an appetite for bad fiction as well. The corner-shop lending-library experiment failed in general, but not for me. I acquired from Hyam's (and never, to my shame, returned) the first edition of Robert A. Heinlein's *The Puppet Masters*.*

The book was not published by Gollancz until later in the decade. Somehow (probably via a publisher's job lot) Hyam's had acquired a Doubleday, American, 1952 copy. It opens, explosively.

> Were they truly intelligent? By themselves, that is? I don't know and I don't know how we can ever find out.
> If they were not truly intelligent, I hope I never live to see us tangle with anything at all like them which is truly intelligent. I know who will lose. Me. You. The so-called human race.

'Me'? That required a big leap of the imagination. In the novel, it is July 2007. Everyone (every American one, that is) has a mobile phone and a saloon car (Cadillac by preference) that can vault over traffic jams. Everyone pops amphetamines and has regular cosmetic makeovers which totally change appearance, as currently preferred. Otherwise it's recognisably Eisenhower's America – excepting, of course, for 'them'.

The hero-narrator in *The Puppet Masters* is Sam Nivens – a top operative in a semi-freelance band of secret agents. Their outfit reports directly to the president. A good thing too, since Washington is full of namby-pamby wimps; men (so mis-called) unable to appreciate that their country is in peril. The politicos just don't get it – freedom entails constant war. For Orwell, the party slogan 'Peace is War' was horrific. For Heinlein, it's the first fact of life. About this time I was an enthusiastic plane-spotter, entering laboriously in notebooks the aircraft seen, day by day. There were a lot of them, it being the height of the Cold War and Orwell's Oceania being the West's biggest aircraft carrier (and, as far as America was

Preserving the peace

concerned, bugger all else than a convenient airstrip). On one glorious day I was taken on a tour of the USAF base at Wethersfield* to sit in the pilot's seat of a nuclear-capable F84 Thunderjet (wonderful name).* But, young as I was, I recall being perplexed by the huge sign at the entrance to the base – 'Peace is our Profession'.

In Heinlein's narrative, Sam's partner, Mary, is red-haired, tough as nails, walks tall and, with her spectacular mammary frontage, has men around her react like iron filings in the presence of a magnet. Heinlein liked women who were all women. So does Sam.

The 'outfit' is run by the 'Old Man' – a tough old bird who, rather surprisingly, turns out to be Sam's dad. 'They' have landed in flying saucers. The US is, of course, their prime target – as in every alien invasion in film and fiction of the 1950s (how do they *know*, out there in Tau Centauri, or wherever, which is the top-dog nation? Time was, as in Wells, they landed on Horsell Common in Surrey).

'They', it emerges, when they slither out of their transport vessels, are large slugs which attach themselves, limpet-like, to the backs of honest Americans, taking them over – but so sneakily that the en-slugged 'puppets' are invisible to any but the trained eye. There is, for 1951, a lot of sex in the novel (the uncut, 30,000-word-longer version, published after Heinlein's death, makes clear his original text had a lot more – he was always straining against the ingrained Puritanism of his genre).

Earth, led by the Old Man's intrepid unit, fights back.

Total nakedness (excitingly) is one line of defence. The president duly issues a 'bareback decree'. But, given American winters, only Southern California and Florida can take that precaution year-round. Biological warfare – infecting the hosts with diseases that kill the slugs faster than humans – is a second line of defence. Interestingly, this was a period in which the US was being accused of germ warfare in Korea (conflict broke out in June 1950).* As far as Heinlein is concerned, anything that kills the enemy is OK. The only good slug is a dead slug. Geneva Conventions are for Swiss wimps.

The novel ends with a situation of continual warfare, Earth holding its own. Just. 'We're going have to live with this horror,' Sam concludes, 'the way we had to learn to live with the atom bomb.' And what does that mean? Living with the irremovable fact that life may end, if one's guard is lowered for a second, with only four minutes warning.

In the last paragraph, Sam and Mary are setting out, in the rocket ship *Avenger*, to launch a pre-emptive strike on the slugs' 'nest', in far-off Titan, a moon of Jupiter.

I feel exhilarated. Puppet-masters – the free men are coming to kill you!

Death and Destruction!

Before re-reading *The Puppet Masters* for this book, I dredged up what I remembered from that first encounter, fifty-five years earlier. Two things surfaced. Most vividly it was semi-naked adults, fondling each other's buttocks to assure themselves of sluglessness. There was little physical contact in my family circle – it would have taken something even more momentous than an invasion from outer space to change that.

The other primal recollection was the infectiously paranoid mood of the novel. The enemy, the nameless 'they', were everywhere. And invisible. They were, in the phrase current in the 1950s, 'the enemy within'. Who knows, perhaps one had oneself been taken over, but was unaware of it.

I'd unknowingly brushed against elements of the Heinleinian philosophy a bit earlier in the 1950 movie *Destination Moon** (the Hippodrome, again). Heinlein did the story for the film. It is surprisingly accurate in foretelling the actual 1969 Apollo landings – with one major difference. The film, as I recall (I haven't reseen it), opens with a government-built rocket exploding on the launch pad and a visionary scientist (determined to get the US to the moon before the Russians) concluding that the mission can only be accomplished by free enterprise. By capitalist ingenuity and know-how, not by Washington bureaucracy. Damn wimps and traitors, all of them. In the event it was, of course, NASA, not Wal-Mart, which enabled Neil Armstrong to make his one small step for man two decades later. Heinlein was wrong about that.

What struck the 1950s British reader about Heinlein was not merely his full-blooded, and if necessary blood-

spattering, allegiance to the American way (later immortalised as his motto TANSTAAFL – 'There ain't no such thing
as a free lunch', a favourite acronym of the Reaganites*). It
was the ability of science fiction, *as a literary genre*, to articulate, domesticate and (for the unformed mind) make sense of
complex ideas, moods and facts of the time. 'Brainwashing',
for example (a word invented during the Korean War).* The
slugs made much more sense to a ten-year-old boy than
Pavlov, conditioned reflexes and the intricacies of the behavioural psychology, as fictionalised in that most tedious of
romans à these, B. F. Skinner's *Walden Two* (1948).*

There were other confusions Heinlein helped crystallise.
Why, in April 1951, were British soldiers (a whole regiment,
virtually, of the Glorious Gloucesters*) dying in the Republic
of Korea – which, even more than Czechoslovakia in 1938,
was a country far off, of which we knew little? Forget ideology,
Heinlein urged. Battle was the only way to preserve our way of
life. It *was* life. And it was, unavoidably, the future. You fought
them at the Imjin river rather than wait till you had to fight
them at Gravesend.

In 1952, surveys revealed that a majority of the British
population, and most of the Conservative administration,
believed that a Third World War was inevitable at some point
over the next five years. That fear subsided, in the mid-1950s,
with Khrushchevian 'thaw' and visions of peaceful coexistence.* But it was running white-hot at the beginning of the
decade. *Death and Destruction!* That was the cry.

Heinlein's ultra-Darwinistic and Adam Smith (run-wild)
doctrines were an antidote to the cradle-to-grave welfare
state, with its bureaucratic finger in every pie, however small
(up in Jura, Orwell was furious that he could not even kill one
of his own pigs without permission from Whitehall). 'Attlee

= Austerity' (i.e. two eggs a week) was the equation in most people's minds. There were few regrets when the Tories took over in 1951: 'You've never had it so good' was just over the horizon.

Above all, there was, in the early 1950s, the McCarthyite paranoia about the Red Menace.* Communism could take over your mind, rendering you a tool of Muscovite international domination. But it did it so subtly, so insidiously, so sneakily, that not even your nearest and dearest would know. In Britain the Labour Party was popularly suspected of being led by Moscow stooges. The stigma that there was an invisible slug between their shoulderblades hung over Hugh Gaitskell, Harold Wilson, Nye Bevan and every trade union leader in the land, bar none.

A few years later, it was a tamed-down version of Heinlein which went on to achieve classic status – as written (ripped off, as purists insist) by Jack Finney (*The Body Snatchers*, 1955) and filmed by Don Siegel (*Invasion of the Body Snatchers*, 1956).* Finney/Siegel achieved a more spine-chilling effect by making the invaders (pods, who create perfect vegetable simulacra of their hosts) invincible. The slugs/pods win.

It is not merely the Red Menace but the *Gleichschaltung* of Eisenhower's America which the Finney/Siegel satire targeted with such uncanny precision – and more wit than Heinlein ever aspired to. The film location, Sierra Madre (on the outskirts of Pasadena) was both the American heartland and 1950s American dreamland; two cars in every family garage. I saw the film. But that depiction of America, glutted on its own affluence, was as alien to me then as the Sixth Moon of Saturn. In *Rebel without a Cause* (1955) – also set in Los Angeles suburbia – the schoolkid, James Dean, went to school in his open-topped limousine!* In English terms that made as much sense as a sixth-former having his own aircraft carrier.

Thirty years later in life, Pasadena would be my own home (on arrival, I toyed with buying something in Sierra Madre – the schools are excellent – but the prices were too rich for my blood). I never drove the I-210, in one of the three cars in my garage, past the Santa Anita turn-off (where Kevin McCarthy desperately, and vainly, tries to flag down the passing traffic and warn them of impending doom) without recalling the film.* Sometimes, as a private joke, I would even fondle the base of my spine.

The Feather Merchants

(aetat. 14)

'THE WAR' was by far the biggest thing in my early life – although I felt strangely alienated from it. I was, at one point in the conflict, an 'evacuee'. The truth was I always felt evacuated from where the war was actually happening, central as its repercussions were to my unimportant existence. Impinged on as I was by it, I thought a lot about the Second World War, and those thoughts rebounded off what I was reading, and drove what books I chose to read.

In 2007 the History Channel ran a programme on the D-Day landing on Omaha Beach.* That particular theatre of the invasion had been a veritable slaughterhouse. Someone, as usual in great military operations, had blundered. A grizzled veteran, his eyes welling up, recalled the surreal oddities of the carnage: things that, for those who were there, rendered the gung-ho melodrama of (say) *Saving Private Ryan* or *The Longest Day* wholly beside the point. It had been strangely different.

A man lay dying, the vet recalled. He knew, or must have

suspected, it was all over for him. From his trouser side-pocket he removed an ASE (American Services Editions) copy of Betty Smith's *A Tree Grows in Brooklyn*.* As his life ebbed away, he read the novel: the bullets and shells whizzing overhead, the dead, dying and soon to die all around him. 'It was so strange; so strange.'*

My mother (widowed earlier in the war) was dating American air-force officers in 1944. One of them (his name was Russell, the inscription said) left behind a copy of *A Tree Grows in Brooklyn*. It was the same edition of Betty Smith's book that the unknown warrior took to the killing fields of France with him and died reading.

Smith's novel is a *bildungsroman*: the life-story, from the early years of the century, of a New York Irish girl, Francie Nolan. The daughter of a charming, feckless 'singing waiter', Francie is brought up in the vibrant but impoverished world of the Brooklyn tenements (in a later mutation, these would be the 'projects' which Hubert Selby Jr writes about, a circle of urban hell, in *Last Exit to Brooklyn*.*). In that polluted quarter of the city, only one tree grows, the Norway maple. It symbolises the indomitable human spirit. Francie calls the tree which grows in front of their building 'the Tree of Heaven'.

Smith's narrative shows the clear influence of American realists James T. Farrell and Thomas Wolfe – with a touch of Edna Ferber's epic sweep. The American realist school still had some time to run. It would generate two last masters, Herman Wouk and Irwin Shaw; neither of whom, to my mind, has received his critical deserts.

Smith's novel, which my mother, needless to say, never returned (Russell, evidently, was not demanding about reading matter), knocked about the various houses we flitted to – 'furnishing rooms', as books were thought to do, even in

our sub-literary station in life. I read it without great enthu-
siasm, but some interest. There was quite a lot of sex in it.
One later discovered that there had been a lot more sex, much
of which was cut out so as not to inhibit sales among the large
Catholic reading public in cities such as Boston, where the
pulpit was a stronger influence on book purchase than a rave
review in the *Globe*. I remember being struck, vividly, by such
scenes as that in which a savage hue and cry hunts down a
paedophile; another in which the fourteen-year-old Francie
is groped on the rush-hour subway; and a third in which,
during a whirlwind, forty-eight-hour romance, Francie (now
adult) has eve-of-departure sex with a marine, Lee, about to
be shipped overseas to war (the First World War, that is).
Would a fellow, I wondered, have to risk his life for a taste of
that premarital *summum bonum*? If so, how would I ever make
out?

A best-seller on its publication, in 1943, Smith's book
would sell a phenomenal three million copies in two years.
Only *Gone with the Wind* had done better. And oddly, for
reasons which are hard to explain, the ASE edition of *A Tree
Grows in Brooklyn* went down extraordinarily well with the US
armed forces abroad. So popular was it that a second edition
of 97,000 copies was issued in July 1944. It was the first ASE
book to go into a second printing.

One of those thousands ended up in 13 Long Wyre Street,
Colchester. I seriously read Smith's novel, now a familiar
object, in the late 1940s and dipped into it again from time
to time, as one does with old bookshelf friends, relishing
favourite passages. I went to the trouble of getting hold of
and reading Smith's second novel, *Tomorrow Will Be Better*
(1947), which Colchester public library had acquired. It has
a male protagonist and is less good than its predecessor.

Like Margaret Mitchell, Smith was destined to be a one-book author.

Another novel, left in Long Wyre Street by the never-now-to-be-known Russell (bless him: I hope he lived and thrived), made a more favourable impression on me. This was Max Shulman's *The Feather Merchants*.* Published in 1944, it remains one of the funniest books I have ever read, and in its day it must have been one of the most seditious.

Russell left behind a first edition, published in the US by Doubleday. It would have come via the Officers' Club, not the concessionary (PX) store from which ASE volumes were distributed. It was a handsome volume. Unlike their British counterparts, American publishers were not constrained by 'wartime regulations' which made books look as if they were printed on bog paper. *The Feather Merchants* was a fine book to handle.

Shulman had been drafted into the USAAF and published the novel as a serving man. How he got clearance to do so, if he ever applied for it (which, given the mischievous quality of the book, I doubt), is mysterious. In the countries Shulman was fighting, it would have been a bullet in the back of the neck for an author as insolent as him. Incredibly (to me) in 1945 *The Feather Merchants* was actually reissued in an ASE edition.

The novel recounts the adventures of USAAF Sergeant Daniel Miller, who returns on furlough to his home town in Minnesota in 1943 (Sergeant Shulman, in the same arm of the military, originated in that state). Intending, on recruitment, to be a war hero and fall gallantly on the field of battle, the heavily bespectacled Daniel was assigned instead to clerking work. 'Some minor technicality, about how I couldn't see,' he wryly notes. His girlfriend, Estherlee, who surrendered her virginity to him, like Francie Nolan, on the eve of his departure, and has been bravely awaiting the dreaded War Office telegram ever since, is unamused.

Comic misadventures ensue. They centre round two hilarious burlesques of wartime fiction and film. Daniel and his Machiavellian (best) friend, Sam, get drunk in a bar. College graduates both, they spoof the final, bridge-blowing scene of Hemingway's *For Whom the Bell Tolls*. The Spanish Civil War novel had been sentimentally filmed (as a Hollywood counterblast against Fascism) in 1943 Technicolor, picking up a slew of Oscar nominations. It was a good year to be anti-Fascist in Los Angeles.*

Gary Cooper played the American hero, Robert Jordan, showing the Republicans how to fight a war. Ingrid Bergman played the luscious (and Fascist gang-raped) peasant girl, Maria, who surrenders her body to Robert the night before he, in turn, gives his life to the cause. Pablo, the doomed and drunken leader of the guerrilla band charged with destroying the bridge to hold back Franco's hordes was played by Akim Tamiroff, an actor as un-Spanish as his name implies. The thought of drawing on the already large Hispanic community in Southern California for even the walk-on Spanish parts did not, apparently, strike Paramount Pictures as a good idea.

The film's dialogue – which the audience is meant to assume is demotic Spanish – is done, as was common in the time, in super-stilted English, with lots of thees and thous.

Riding high on their generous intake of deadly 'sty stingers' at the Sty (a strip club on the edge of town), Daniel – egged on by the villainous Sam – does his Gary Cooper imitation, unaware that a local reporter, John Smith, is listening and taking notes:

I could hear them coming up the road. 'Thee must pull the wire, Anselmo,' I said, 'if they reach the bridge.' 'Nay,' he said, 'not while thou arst on it.' 'It is of no consequence,' I said. 'Thee must pull the wire.'

'Jeez, what a story!' exclaimed John Smith. 'They can't keep me on classified ads after this one.'

'She came to me as I lay in the sleeping bag,' I said, 'get in, little rabbit,' I said. 'Thee must show me what to do,' she said. 'I will learn and I will be thy woman.' 'Yes,' I said fiercely, 'yes, yes.'

'What's all this?' asked John Smith.

'Nay,' said Sam. 'Tell them of the bridge ...'

There are two things rendering this even more hilarious (and subversive) in 1944. What Shulman guys, with all that Spanglish, is scarcely less ludicrous than what the film presents, with the straightest and most grave of faces (Hemingway hated the movie – it offended his ear). Secondly, the film of *For Whom the Bell Tolls* enjoyed the status of a sacred text in civilian America, in the year of its triumph. Serving men, like the book's author, Max Shulman, evidently thought less well of Cooper's heroics and Bergman's erotics.

Sergeant Daniel Miller wakes with a crippling hangover next morning to discover that he is a local hero. The townspeople believe that he is Robert Jordan – or, at least, a real American warrior who has virtually won the war by blowing up bridges in North Africa. Hail!

Daniel, in a Kafkaesque parody of what many serving soldiers on leave felt, finds himself cast in a heroic role he cannot escape, but which he must play through. A small consolation is that the delectable Estherlee is his again ('Yes, yes' – Shulman had obviously read James Joyce in his years, like Miller, at the University of Minnesota).

The other burlesque in *The Feather Merchants* (the term, incidentally, is a contemptuous military term for civilians) is a fictitious movie called *Murder the Bastards*. 'Because of the patriotic nature of its subject, the Hays office had blinked at the title'. The film is a transparent, and again hilarious, spoof of such screen hits as *Destination Tokyo* (1943), *Across the Pacific* (1944), *Thirty Seconds over Tokyo* (1944), celebrating the heroism of American's bomber crews.

The hero of *Murder the Bastards*, Omar (a cartoon Bogart), and a stowaway half-caste beauty on his flying fortress, Philomene, are captured when their B17 crashes after a spectacularly successful raid on mainland Japan. They are interrogated by a 'Jap colonel, played by Sidney Fatstreet, eating grapes off the tip of a dagger'. (The massively corpulent Sydney Greenstreet was the villain, opposite Humphrey Bogart, in *Across the Pacific**). 'When will you democratic fools learn,' sneers the yellow fat one, 'that your system of government is decadent.' 'Oh yeah,' replies Omar:

> 'Democracy is the right to boo the Dodgers. Democracy is the smell of popcorn, the golden wheat fields rippling in the western breezes, the Sunday movie, the corner drugstore, the mailman's whistle, the shucking bee and the quilting party, the letters to the editor, the torchlight parade, the new gleaming forests, the kid on the bike. Democracy is the right of every man to stand up and speak his mind, just as I am doing now.'

Having spoken his speech, Omar is taken off to be tortured on screen and Philomene to be raped, decently off screen ('the bastards!' mutters Omar, as she is dragged back, looking violated). The joke goes on in the same broad vein, just this side of slapstick.

What's extraordinary is that this novel was written by a young serving man, at a period of extreme national emergency, 1944. Democracy, one deduced, was the privilege of mocking even what one was fighting for, and while one was fighting for it. One of the first things the Nazis did, of course, was to shut the Berlin cabarets – exit Kurt Weill, exit Bertolt Brecht. No satire for the men in black. It was anti-Nazi and degenerate.* While *The Feather Merchants* was being chortled over, and while Shulman was writing, US fighting men were dying – thousands a day, some days.

Russell, who gave the novel to my mother, who left it around for me, may himself have died flying over Germany, being less immune to bullets than Omar (or Humphrey Bogart). The casualty rate among Flying Fortresses based at nearby Boxted was fearsome. Or perhaps, like Shulman's hero (and Shulman himself), he was a desk-bound soldier, keeping the planes in the air.

What *The Feather Merchants* communicates was the subversive sense that, catastrophic as war might be, the false consciousness it generated could be mocked into something more sober, propaganda-free and worth genuinely fighting and dying for. A kind of smart-arse irony was good political medicine. Burlesque was a better defence of democracy than the shucking bee, the quilting party or the Nuremberg Rally. Irony beats Blood and Iron every time.

A friend better read (or just more superficially sophisticated) than me borrowed my copy of Shulman and returned it with the belittling verdict that it was all very well – but by no means as subtle in its comedy as James Thurber. He, Thurber, was a great American writer, not a literary clown.* That may well have been correct. But Shulman did things for me that Thurber's *My Life and Hard Times* never did.

I read *The Feather Merchants*, with relish, at a period when the British film-going public was, every week it seemed, blitzed (metaphorically) by ultra-patriotic, self-glorifying war films. The earlier – *Seconds over Tokyo* – wave had been 'How we're winning the war'. This next wave was 'How we won the war'. Notable blockbusters in this wave were *Angels One-Five* (1952), *The Dam Busters* (1954)* and *The Colditz Story* (1955).

The Feather Merchants was a welcome antidote. Necessary, even, at least for me.

Lady Chatterley's Lover

(aetat. 15)

I FIRST READ *Lady Chatterley's Lover*, perched on a dormitory bed, in Paris, aged fifteen and a half. It was my first trip abroad. A school trip, in April, to hone up oral skills for forthcoming exams. My first impression, as we de-bussed in the dusky capital, was nasal. Paris *smelled* different. It was Gauloises, coffee that didn't come from a jar – and fascinating decadence. 'You may not,' we were sternly instructed, 'go to Montmartre.' 'Algerians,' it was darkly explained. 'White slavery' was euphemistically, hinted at. I did go there, with a similarly wayward *copain*, to see the film *Jammin' the Blues*.* Wild boys we were. The film's superb opening shot of Lester Young enwreathed in tobacco smoke remains the most powerful jazz image I know.

Historically, France was going through a bad patch. The franc was in freefall. The government was offering crazy bonuses to any family prepared to have children. Few were. The defeat at Dien Bien Phu had confirmed the sense that the country was finished.*

There was a new prime minister, it seemed, every other week. Pierre Mendès-France,[*] the 143rd premier (143!), was briefly in power during my, almost as brief, sojourn in his capital. He sealed his fate by launching a *santé-sobriété* campaign. He wanted to take away the last sweetener of their existence that the French had left. Advertisements in the Paris Métro warned one that 'even a litre of wine a day can be bad for your health'.[*] Another world. That was the kind of sobriety I would come to favour. Amazingly, they served us schoolboys near-beer with coarse, black bread at the refectory, and what we xenophobically suspected was horse meat. *La vie*.

The Olympia Press volume of *Lady Chatterley's Lover* was bought communally from a Seine-side *bouquiniste*[*] (wearily familiar with English schoolboys' needs) and passed around. It was much fingered, and, one had to suspect, furtively wanked over in the reeking lavatory, by the time I got my turn.

I, like the others, gobbled down D. H. Lawrence's 'hot' scenes with what the makers of Viagra would call erectile functionality. Even the idea of flowers would, days after, by association, excite me, in recollection of the (ludicrous now) scene in which Mellors garlands his true love's pudenda.

> With quiet fingers he threaded a few forget-me-not flowers in the fine brown fleece of the mound of Venus.
>
> 'There!' he said. 'There's forget-me-nots in the right place!'
>
> She looked down at the milky odd little flowers among the brown maiden-hair at the lower tip of her body.
>
> 'Doesn't it look pretty!' she said.
>
> 'Pretty as life,' he replied.
>
> And he stuck a pink campion-bud among the hair.
>
> 'There! That's me where you won't forget me! That's Moses in the bull-rushes.'

'Phallic hunting out', I thought, filling in those huge and reverberating Lawrentian blanks with fantasies of my own peculiar making, as to where the hunt might lead (into very dark places, as the critic John Sparrow indignantly pointed out, in a devastatingly sour article, in *Encounter*, after the novel's acquittal in 1960*).

Oddly enough, the only thing that affronted me, perched on my Parisian cot – among the veritable blitz of familiar-everywhere-but-in-print 'four-letter words' – was the occasional excremental stuff Lawrence throws in. Especially that scene (in the same Chapter 15 as the twee floral stuff) in which Mellors declares, as evidence of his unconditional love (touching the 'two secret openings of her body'):

> 'An' if tha shits an' if tha pisses, I'm glad. I don't want a woman as couldna shit nor piss.'
> Connie could not help a sudden snort of astonished laughter, but he went on unmoved.
> 'Tha'rt real, tha art! Tha'art real, even a bit of a bitch. Here tha shits an' here tha pisses: an' I lay my hand on 'em both an' like thee for it. I like thee for it. Tha's got a proper, woman's arse, proud of itself. It's none ashamed of itself this isna.'

The reason for my being affronted (then) is easily deduced. I knew nothing about sex other than private, and grotesquely inaccurate, mental imagery – I pictured Connie, mid-copulation, as being like something from the cover of *Reveille*,* or *Tit-Bits*, without the two-piece *cache-sexe*. Shit and piss I did know about; and, given the worse than Victorian sanitary arrangements of my early childhood, hated. Whatever else, I did not want those things adorning my dream lover. Wild flowers bedecking liberated genitals were OK. But the last layer to be stripped away from the English puritan person-ality is toilet training. When I read *Lady Chatterley's Lover*, I was very much of Yeats's indignation that love should pitch his mansion 'in the place of excrement'.

Even that deep-seated *pudeur* fades with time. Half a century on, I had lived to hear *Lady Chatterley's Lover* as a BBC book at bedtime: as unerotic as the nocturnal cocoa and biscuits. I was as likely to be sexually aroused by the shipping forecast. I still admired the book, but as a eunuch might admire the female form. Or Mr Spock everything originating on mad planet Earth. Why should they ban *Lady Chat* in 1954 and laugh themselves sick at Catherine Tate's anal-intercourse jokes and four-letter-word blitzing in 2007?*

I would, later on, write a whole book about the 1960 acquittal of *Lady Chatterley's Lover*. It was called *Offensive Litera-ture*. But in 1982, when I wrote it, I was no longer offended. Or aroused. April in Paris was a long way past. Nonetheless the quality of *offence* seems to me important, and worth retaining, at least at the cutting edge of our cultural lives.

Lady Chatterley's Lover, as first experienced, confirmed to me the ideal outlawry of reading. A tag of Nietzsche's (along with the inevitable 'God is Dead') was much bandied about in my adolescence: 'Live in danger. Build your cities on the slopes of Vesuvius.' In 1955, sitting on the bed in Paris, I was on that slope; and very thrilling it was.

On the Waterfront

(aetat. 16)

MARTIN SCORSESE TESTIFIES that, after seeing Elia Kazan's *On the Waterfront* – more specifically Marlon Brando's *On the Waterfront* – 'I was never the same person again.'* *Raging Bull*, Scorsese's mid-career masterpiece, ends with frank homage: a much battered, world-weary Jake La Motta (De Niro) looking into the bulbed mirror of his nightclub changing room (himself rather bulbous nowadays), rehearsing Terry Malloy's famous 'I coulda been a contendah' routine.*

Scorsese was twelve years old when *On the Waterfront* came out in 1954; I was a few months under sixteen. I saw the film, with a well-meaning uncle (since it was an 'A', I needed to be accompanied by an adult) in Colchester's Regal picture house.* And I, like young Martin, was changed utterly: at least, for a while I was changed.

It wasn't the director, Elia Kazan, or the scriptwriter, Budd Schulberg, who worked the magic on me (and, as he recalls, on twelve-year-old Scorsese, in far-off Queens, NY). It was

Tormented Marlon

the star, Brando. Never was the trade term more appropriate. I hitched my little Colcestrian wagon to that star.

After viewing *On the Waterfront*, I mumbled mimetically for days – entranced by Marlon's 'method'. I spent a hard-saved four quid at Millets for a high-collared windcheater, in homage to the one Terry Malloy wears in the movie. It hung as unflatteringly as a fur boa on a clothes horse.

The term applied to the adolescents of the time was 'crazy mixed-up kid'. Brando was an unadolescent thirty years old at the time (playing twenty-seven) but, if no kid, Marlon personified 'mixed up'. And so what about the age? Salinger was a cool thirty-two when he published *Catcher*, and James Dean, the archetypal CMUK, was twenty-four when he played the schoolkid Jim Stark in *Rebel without a Cause*.

One gloried in the image of introverted angst.

A month or so after seeing the film, the initial magic faded and the glorying stalled. It wasn't merely the impossibility of projecting Brandoesque intensities in the English provinces. 'Stand up *straight*,' my mother would snarl, on those occasions when she deigned to notice me, 'and stop *mumbling*, for God's sake.' She had never been a bobbysoxer, but she had a soft spot for American crooners and would have been happier, I suspect, had the movie-makers gone along with their first choice for Malloy, Frank Sinatra.

There were, over time, other disillusioning factors. The 'facts of the case', for example. These were more likely to be found inscribed on the page than projected on to the screen. Boots the high-street chemist (like Smith's the newsagent's) ran a circulating library in those days. I didn't subscribe. But discard volumes could be picked up for pennies. Heavily bound in brown fabric, the Boots volumes had a prominent boot lace hole in the spine. A nice touch.

Six months after my film epiphany, I came across Budd Schulberg's *Waterfront** on Boots's bargain shelves. The story, as written and filmed, is straightforward. In the New York docks, the workers are exploited by their corrupt union – a 'local' branch of the ILA, or International Longshoremen's Association (never identified by name in the movie. Even bad guys have libel lawyers).

The rampant criminality of the mob-dominated locals had been exposed in a Pulitzer-winning series of articles by Malcolm Johnson, published in the *New York Sun*, in late 1948, called 'Crime on the Waterfront'.* In the film Terry Malloy, a washed-up pug and low-level henchman of the local, unwittingly sets up the murder of a childhood friend, Joey Doyle. Doyle was threatening to testify – 'sing' – to a state commission investigating corruption. The local, under its mob boss, Johnny Friendly, has a short way with canaries.

Romantic involvement with Doyle's sister and the painful growth of conscience induce Terry himself to testify. In the novel, he is, inevitably, rubbed out by the mob. He's a 'wart on the ass of progress', as Friendly puts it. And, on the printed page, after the minor irritation of the investigating commission the local re-establishes its corrupt rule. In the book, Terry is not the Christ figure Brando portrayed, just a 'pretty tough kid', no more capable of changing history than any other wart.

In the film the outlook is much sunnier. Terry lives – united with his true love. The local is overthrown, Friendly himself is tossed into the Hudson river.* Perhaps, we hope, an honest longshoremen's union will come into being; or no union at all. All will now be peace and fraternity on the waterfront. (In fact, what was coming was containerisation, which would render the longshoremen truly a wart on the ass of progress.)

Kazan had imposed a similarly upbeat ending on his other
Brando-starring movie, A Streetcar Named Desire. In Tennessee
Williams's play, Stanley Kowalski – by sheer loin power –
repossesses Stella. He wins. The raped Blanche, her feminine
wiles come to naught, loses. In the film, by contrast, the brute
is kicked out. It is he who loses. No oats for Stanley.

The audiences of the day demanded such moral sweeteners before leaving the dream house. The 1950s could not
bear too much reality. Enough of that in the real world; you
paid your one-and-ninepence to escape for a couple of dark,
velvety, smoke-laden, choc-ice-eating hours.

But, with the book in hand, a question mark hovered
over the movie. And there were other complications to foul
up one's first, dreamhouse, impressions. Johnson's articles
had been a major source for On the Waterfront. The other, more
immediate, source for the film's makers was 3,000 miles
away, on the West Coast. There, too, the burning issue was
whether to 'sing like a canary' or 'stand pat'; say nothing,
whatever the consequences.

For both Kazan and Schulberg, it was a painful and
acutely personal dilemma. Schulberg's earlier novel What
Makes Sammy Run? (1941) had, along with its biting satire on
1930s Hollywood, recorded in some detail the founding of
the Writers' Guild of America: a trade union for people like
Budd Schulberg (the WG is on strike now, as I write, in early
2008).*

John Wayne, and other Hollywood right-wingers, still
regarded Schulberg, on the basis of What Makes Sammy Run?
and the founding of the union its author clearly endorsed, as
a died-in-the-wool 'Red'.* He was, the hardliners believed,
up to his neck in a 'Communist plot' to take over Hollywood.
Schulberg, who had been 'named', was, inevitably, hauled

in front of the House UnAmerican Activities Committee, in 1951, and sang. No canary sang more sweetly for Senator McCarthy's eager henchmen on HUAC. Yes, he had been a Communist in the 1930s. And yes, he would name names. He had been an UnAmerican, but now he recanted. He was as American as Duke Wayne himself. Schulberg was the friendliest of 'friendly witnesses'.

Kazan sang as well. He too had been a Communist, like other theatrical people, in the 1930s. During the Great Depression, it had been quite respectable. In the Cold War, it was not. He too was called before HUAC.* He too was a friendly witness. He too named names. And then he and Schulberg glorified their acquiescence through Marlon Brando.

Nowadays I can barely watch *On the Waterfront*. Forget the mumbles. I hear the canary's trill. I smell the whitewash. Nor, in the 1950s, did one feel much sympathy for dockers (British 'longshoremen'). In the country's great ports their selfish wildcat and official strikes crippled Attlee's reforming government. The same dockers went to war against Churchill's 1950s administration (with even greater ferocity, since he was the politician who had once sent troops with loaded rifles against strikers at Tonypandy in 1910*). It was only too easy to believe dockers were a load of petty criminals run by Moscow, determined to ruin their country. Or, failing that, the not-worth-dying-for 'docker' bastards Monsarrat had portrayed a few years before in *The Cruel Sea*.

Time has worn many holes in that once dazzling fabric of the film. In the famous 'I coulda been a contendah' exchange, I now see – quite clearly – that Brando couldn't be bothered to do the whole scene with Steiger, who at key moments was obliged to talk to the wall. And the legend that Brando, brilliantly, improvised his 'contendah' riff is angrily contradicted by Schulberg. He may have added a 'mumble or two', but he was following a script written for him. Certainly, phrases like 'one way ticket to Palookaville' bear the writer's, rather than the player's, mark.

On the Waterfront focuses, sharply, the perplexity at the heart of any thinking person's reading career. Which is 'right' – that early overwhelming experience after which one 'was never the same person', or later complicating analysis?

We murder to dissect, said Wordsworth. The fact is, we don't have to. Time does the murdering for us. It is a wonderful film, until you think about it.

Nineteen Eighty-Four

(aetat. 16)

AT THE CLIMAX of the most studied novella in the twentieth century, the central character Kurtz utters, on his deathbed, the words, 'The horror! The horror!' Oddly, for a man who is, nationally and racially, a mongrel ('all Europe had gone into his making') he chooses the English language for his last words. Or perhaps his author, Conrad, chose it for him as the dominant dialect of European racism.

At an early stage in the narrative of *Heart of Darkness*, the hero-narrator, Marlow, bobbing on his little boat at the mouth of the Thames, looks back at England and observes, portentously, 'This, too, has been one of the dark places of the earth.'

The observation was never more literally true than in wartime and immediately post-war England – darkness ranged from the physical blackout to the unimaginable moral darkness of *Nacht und Nebel*, the camps and the chronic fuel and electricity cuts. All those living through the decade – even the newly literate young – were connoisseurs of horror and darkness. It was not until 1949 that the lights were switched back on in Piccadilly Circus, after twelve years' dimness.* I went up to see them – on the newly nationalised British Rail.

The universal sense of horror was longer dissipating than the gloom. It is, I think, to the credit of the 1950s that the British could still feel horror as keenly as they did. Fifty years later, we have lost that capacity to feel. Is it insensitivity, moral toughness, a mastery of Brechtian *Verfremdung* or emotional depravity that allows audiences to sit through *Saw IV* and giggle excitedly?

Whatever the explanation, the coarsening/hardening of national sensibility can be measured in a changed response to *Nineteen Eighty-Four*. Orwell's last, gloomy novel (a satire on the Attlee government, *au fond* – despite the author's firm denials) was published on 8 June 1949, in an edition of 25,000, by Secker and Warburg.

The book was respectfully, but less than ecstatically, received: it was powerful, but generally thought to be 'crude'. Orwell could write better. By 1954, Secker had printed some 50,000 copies in the twelve-and-six hardback form. That year, the novel was 'Penguined'. With Attlee and his 'Party' gone, in 1951, the novel might have been thought to have done its satirical work and have had its day. After John Wyndham arrived (*The Day of the Triffids*, 1951; *The Kraken Wakes*, 1953) the SF element in Orwell's novel, clearly more a reflection of 1948 than a prophecy of 1984, looked passé. An austerity-era grump by a dying man. Ray Bradbury's sleek vision of tyranny by TV ('telescreen') and 'affluence' in *Fahrenheit 451* (1953) looked more plausible than the horrors of Room 101.*

In autumn 1954, Secker's sixth 'library' edition (they were reprinting 1,000 copies of the novel at a time) had slowed to around 150 a month: a figure just sufficient to keep the work in print, but hardly to cheer the publisher. All this was changed overnight with the televising of Nigel Kneale's* 'horror' adaptation, put out by the BBC on Sunday evening, 12 December 1954 (school term ended the following Friday).

In the five days following the transmission, as Secker's record reveals, 1,000 hard and 10,000 paperback copies were sold, and Orwell's last novel (he himself had died in 1951) was boosted into the posthumous super-sellerdom which it has enjoyed ever since.

My family home didn't have a 'goggle-box' – as we, without them, contemptuously called the sets. It was not, as it is among cultural contrarians today, something to be proud about. There were, newspapers gleefully reported, houses (particularly on council estates) which – to preserve their standing in the community – had the huge 'H' aerials on the roof, but no TV in the living room below.

I missed out on the first BBC broadcast of *Nineteen Eighty-Four*, but – inflamed by playground gossip (rats, eyeballs!) – I was careful to book a place, with a better-off friend, to see the repeat a week later. It wasn't actually a repeat in the modern sense, there being no video technology. The cast went through the whole thing live again, like the second night in a theatre.

At the time there was just one TV channel, the BBC, which closed at ten – with 'the Queen' (one still hadn't got quite used to the gender). The production starred Peter Cushing* as Winston Smith. Cushing's constipated, pinched-cheek look would be carried over into his portrayals of arch-agents of light versus darkness in innumerable Hammer Horror films of the 1960s. He always reminded me of Charles Wheeler, without the skyscraper hair.*

It opened with the heavy clanging overture (based on Holst's 'Mars') and the monitory voice-over, 'This is *one man's* vision of the future' (not, of course, Lord Reith's view – too much Orwellian satire on TV). There followed a Wagnerian montage of atomic explosions before the opening scene in Victory Mansions.

André Morell played a sinisterly suave O'Brien – with a clear overtone of SS officer. The dominating icon, 'Big Brother', was heavily moustached. Orwell intended the allusion to Stalin. 'Uncle Joe', that reassuring presence in the early 1940s was, ten years on, the West's bogeyman. There was a disconcerting resemblance to Gilbert Harding, the mustachioed grump on the *What's My Line?* panel, renowned as the 'rudest man in Britain'* (and a classics scholar – the two often go together).

The BBC anticipated ruffled feathers and angry squawks. Twice, on both evenings, they issued the solemn warning that the upcoming *Nineteen Eighty-Four* was 'unsuitable for children or those with weak nerves'. This had the entirely predictable effect of gluing even the most susceptible (including, of course, sixteen-year-old schoolchildren like myself) to the screen, their nerves pinging like overwound violin strings.*

There was at least one fatal result. As the *Daily Express* on 14 December delightedly reported, under the headline 1984: WIFE DIES AS SHE WATCHES:

A forty-year-old mother of two children collapsed and died while watching the TV horror play 1984, it was disclosed last night. She was Mrs Beryl Kathleen Mirfin. Mrs Mirfin, a local beauty queen of 1936, was watching the play on Sunday night at her home in Carlton-hill, Herne Bay. With her was her husband who is an estate agent and two friends. In the early part of George Orwell's nightmarish fantasy of a Police State future – Mrs Mirfin collapsed. A doctor who was called asked at once: 'Was she watching the TV play?'

Even those who survived the horror might be marked for life. In the *News Chronicle*, 13 December, Mrs Edna Burgess was reported as saying:

'I trembled with fear as I watched: it was not fit for ordinary human beings. It was not fit for ordinary decent-minded human beings. It was nothing but unoriginal bits of horror put together.'

Excitement about the 'H-Play' (as the *Daily Mirror* promptly labelled it) spilled over into Parliament. On 15 December a critical motion was put down by five Conservative MPs, deploring 'the tendency evident in recent BBC programmes, notably on Sunday evening, to pander to sexual and sadistic tastes'. It must be stopped.

Nineteen Eighty-Four became instantly unstoppable. 'Big Brother is watching you', 'doublethink', the 'two minute hate' were everywhere – catchphrases as suddenly current as Bluebottle's 'you dirty rotten swine' or Hercules Grytpype-Thynne's 'silly twisted boy'. Indeed, two weeks later *The Goon Show* did a programme-long spoof, 1985, which provided yet another parrot refrain, the moronic Eccles's 'It's good to be *aloive*, in Noineteen Eighty-Foive!' The programme opened with the sublimely ominous warning, from the much-mocked 'announcer', Wallace Greenslade:

The BBC would like to caution parents this programme is unsuitable for the very young, the very old, the middle-aged, those just going off, those on the turn, young dogs and Alderman John Snagge.

Good-naturedly, Snagge, the most respected of announcers, voice-overed the announcement in the February repeat of the show. Elsewhere on the service, a waggish BBC TV weatherman began his bulletin on 13 December with the barked announcement, 'Stand by your sets, citizens, bad news coming up!'

The furore diffused into high places. The 'irresponsibility' of the BBC, serving up this 'horror', fed into the debate on the ending of the BBC's monopoly. And over the following years *Nineteen Eighty-Four* was adopted as a set book, for sixth-formers. It's now as canonical as the Qur'an in a Pakistan madrasa. My current sense of the novel is overlaid by innumerable interviews with university entrants, primed to parrot out the staff line on the contrasting dystopian vision of Huxley's *Brave New World* and Orwell.

At the time, in 1954, it was not ideology which was at issue. As for the luckless Mrs Mirfin, it was Room 101 ('the worst thing in the world, Winston') and the eyeball-gnawing rats. Kneale's script recycled at some length O'Brien's ruminatively donnish speech on the nature of the torture ('It was a common punishment in Imperial China ... sometimes they go for the eyes first. Sometimes they burrow into the cheeks.') Fingering the apparatus (manifestly mocked up from a studio vacuum cleaner), he pedantically explains how the rodents – taken from the streets two weeks ago and starved – will shoot down the plastic tube, to feast on their victim's face. The scene can be revisited, with the whole of the adaptation (so blasé is our age about it) on YouTube. There is no warning to the young, or the weak of nerves. (The YouTube version, incidentally, is the repeat, caught on 35mm film. It was judged insufficiently good quality to consign to DVD and all one can now see is an off-air TV grab of a 2004 BBC unrecorded transmission.)

'Horror' is what made *Nineteen Eighty-Four* so over-whelming an experience in 1954. More specifically, it was the nation's hypersensitivity about horror. For a number of other reasons, 1954 was an 'H-year'. The word had manifold current resonances. When, for example, the *Daily Mirror* used the tabloid shorthand 'H-play', it was alluding to the film classifications of 'U' (universal), 'A' (adult only) and 'H' (horror!). There was, until the 1950s, no 'X' – sex on screen being unthinkable.

The 'H' certificate was imposed by the British Board of Film Censors in 1932 – as a direct response to the 1930s American horror films *Dracula* and *Frankenstein*. They, too, had curdled blood in their day.*

'H' was, literally, a radioactive letter. On 1 March 1954, the US Army had set off, on Bikini Atoll, the largest man-made explosion in the planet's history. It might, indeed, end that history. This was the 'H-bomb' (H for 'hydrogen', but with inescapable echoes of the horrors perpetrated in Dr Frank-enstein's laboratory). The H-bomb, the world apprehended, was the weapon which could destroy not merely cities, like Hiroshima, but humanity. It was the horror bomb. The Doomsday Weapon.*

On still another front in this H-year, the campaign against American so-called 'horror comics' was gathering irresistible force, driven by the child psychologist Frederic Wertham's 1954 polemic, *The Seduction of the Innocent*.* Wertham's argument was twofold. On the surface, comic books such as William Gaines's E.C. ('Entertaining Comics') series, launched in 1950 (with titles such as *Crypt of Terror* and *Vault of Terror*),* desensitised the juvenile reader. 'Subliminally' (here Wertham got a bit crazy) the cunning artists in these publica-tions had inserted vile imagery – the knowing eye could, for example, pick up vaginas in the background: enfolded into an innocent-looking armpit, or the bark on a tree. Horror comics were, indeed, strong stuff.

The comics had a formative effect on one juvenile reader, Stephen King, who – aged twelve – came across a cache in his family attic. Thus was the King of Horror born. In an interview (on the launch of his novel *Christine* in 1983) King was asked, 'Do the horror aspects of your writing come from having read E.C. comics and that type of thing?' The novelist replied, 'Oh, God knows! Some of it has to, sure, because those comics really grossed me out when I was a kid, and they also fired my imagination'.

George Romero (b. 1940) was also, as a child, both grossed out and imaginatively fired. In later life, he and King would pay homage to E.C. comics in their collaborative movie *Creepshow*. The two artists, in their different media, turned juvenile horror into style. Were they corrupted – or, by the mysterious alchemy of art, inspired?*

These were subtleties to which 1954 was wholly indifferent. Spurred by the (to their mind) clearly deleterious effects of horror comics, the Conservative government rushed into law the 'Children and Young Persons (Harmful Publications) Act'. It came into force in 1955 and, with hindsight, seems as inane an official response to a non-emergency as John Major's Cones Hotline.*

Why was 'horror' so burning an issue in 1954 – why this epidemic 'Mirfinism'? Because, one might plausibly hypothesise, the nation was still genuinely horrified, to the roots of its being, by the real horror of the age – the British Army films of Bergen-Belsen which had been shown to the population in the last days of the war.

America was largely spared the awful privilege of seeing what the British troops breaking into Bergen-Belsen had seen. All the adults in my family circle saw the film. Children's eyes were spared – the more literate among them had to make do with the illustrations (horrible enough) in Lord Russell of Liverpool's *The Scourge of the Swastika* (1954).*

The British bruise was still acutely tender. And remained so, for the best part of a decade. How else can one explain, for example, the film *Abbott and Costello Meet Dr. Jekyll and Mr. Hyde* being given an 'H' certificate in 1953, in the UK? (In the US, it was H for Hilarious.*) By that year, I had outgrown an earlier fondness for the comic duo. But if one compares that absurdly unhorrific film with, say, *Saw IV* (the latest instalment as I write – the series looks good for half a dozen more sawfests) chalk and cheese does not come into it. Much has changed.*

We have, in our new century, lost much of our capacity to be horrified. At least, horrified in the way in which the British population so clearly could be in 1954. Even four years later, the first *Dracula* horror movie, in what would be a long-running Hammer franchise, could only creep into general release by cutting a whole section out of the last scene, where the face of the Prince of Darkness (Christopher Lee) turns to Gorgonzola, as he's struck by a shaft of the morning sun, and he claws off his rotting flesh.*

One's first reaction is to laugh at the weak-kneed early 1950s. Abbot and Costello! As with the lachrymose Victorian deathbed-in-literature, one would need a heart of stone not to laugh. But, myself, I admire those quivering 1950s knees. The primary function of the novel, as George Eliot defined it, was the 'extension of sympathy' – feeling the pain of others.

I would rather live in an age capable of being horrified than one where London buses are placarded with advertisements reading: 'Saw IV: You didn't Think it Could get Worse!'

Herman Wouk's *Marjorie Morningstar* made a strong impression on me when I read the novel in 1956.* There's a scene in it where the hero asserts that only a Jew like himself can really enjoy a ham sandwich. Because only a Jew has guilt – as well as ketchup and mustard – as relish with the thing.

I feel much the same about fiction. Only a reader capable of whole-body response – a sensitivity to horror and moral shock – can really enjoy fiction. If your eyes don't moisten in *Bleak House* at the death of Jo, or you don't shudder at the death of Krook, you don't get it.

Modern readers, particularly undergraduate readers, as I've observed, are made of tougher stuff. Good for them. Or bad for them. On the whole, I think 'bad'.

'Shake Rattle and Roll'

(aetat. 16)

WHEN IKE TURNER DIED, in December 2007, there was argument about whether his 'Rocket 88' was the first rock and roll record.* The dissipated, violent, misogynistic guitarist was history (the coroner's verdict was, unsurprisingly, cocaine overdose: he left this life rocket-driven, as he'd shot through it). But was Turner 'historical'? Was he indeed the Stout Cortes of rock?*

The question was solemnly debated in places – *The Times*, for example, which in the early 1950s regarded the likes of Ike Turner and other 'caterwaulers' as cultural slime creatures. Whatever its inception, rock had become respectable by 2007, which, purists might think, was something of a comedown. 'Repressive tolerance,' Marcusians (among whose number I briefly was in the 1960s) would sneer.*

For those coming of age in the mid-1950s, in middle England, the top nominee for primal rock and roller would more likely have been Bill Haley, his Comets and the 78rpm disc 'Shake Rattle and Roll'. The Decca label record was released in 1954, to revolve, at eye-blurring velocity and feeble half-amp volume, on innumerable Dansettes in teenage rooms round the country.

I was already well up enough on blues and jazz to realise that Haley was ersatz and, after a little research in the discographies and *Melody Maker*, self-righteously ordered the echt version from Mann's music store in the High Street. It was by the black Kansas City blues shouter Big Joe Turner and had been released a little earlier in 1954. The song 'Shake Rattle and Roll' was the composition of Jesse Stone,* another black musician. Like Turner, Stone was someone who, in the argot of today's rappers, could 'play it real'.

Haley – tubby, clad in tartan (reminiscent of those American absurdities 'Bermuda shorts'), middle-aged with a ludicrous kiss curl and – above all – *white*, did not play it real.*

The respective versions by Haley and Turner can be sampled by the contemporary listener on YouTube (a world away from the wind-up acoustic gramophone on which I first heard them – I scorned Dansettes).*

It was not immediately clear, on first hearing either of those versions of half a century ago, what the song's narrative was actually chronicling. As best one could put it together, a regular working guy (black or white, according to which record you were listening to) was waiting for his breakfast. Impatiently, it seemed. His 'woman' (how wonderful it would be to have one of those) was not serving up his chow on time this morning. She was in bed (a lubricious detail) in Turner's version (not in Haley's) and dilatory in rattling them pots and pans.

Turner is specific about his woman's physical attractions: 'you make me roll my eyes, baby make me grit my teeth' and 'you wear those dresses, the sun comes shining through', etc. These details are coyly deleted in Haley's version. Both versions, however, contain the mysterious – but clearly sexually supercharged – declaration that the bellowing, frustrated, breakfastless singer is like 'a one-eyed cat peepin' in a seafood store'. Imagination ran riot. Everything from kippers to the dark gratifications of what Freud calls the 'renifleur' ('one who is sexually excited by odours') was provoked by that enigmatic line. Some people, somewhere, knew what it meant; but not me.

Haley (who was indeed one-eyed, although it looked like a bad squint) had begun professional life as a country singer, fronting Bill Haley and the Saddlemen. His fortunes had barely prospered, until he astutely shifted styles, adding a bit more black urgency to his music, with a cover version of (what else?) 'Rocket 88' in 1951. Then, in 1954, came his breakthrough.

'Shake Rattle and Roll' posed a niggling aesthetic dilemma for the thoughtful adolescent in 1954. The same song, sounding not all that different, could be both echt and falsch, real and unreal. It was the same in jazz. Hugues Panassié, the stern French mandarin theorist of jazz vrai, decreed that if you liked Johnny Dodds* you couldn't like the wholly synthetic Artie Shaw.* Your cultural duty was always to revere the authentic, and scorn the inauthentic. But what if, like me, you liked the clarinet work of both the New Orleans Dodds (who carried his instrument around wrapped in newspaper) and the swing maestro Shaw (who dated, and serially married, the most beautiful women in America)? What if, in your heart of hearts, you actually preferred 'Begin the Beguine' to Dodds's solo on 'Potato Head Blues'?*

Categories became even more slippery with the arrival

of Elvis Presley on the scene. He too did a version of 'Shake Rattle and Roll', in 1966, drawing principally on Turner. Presley, at least at the moment of his mid-1950s irruption into popular music, was, it seemed, that messianic hybrid: a white man who (authentically) sang like a black man. Also, unlike Haley, who even at his zenith was an ole-cowpoke-looking kind of guy, scarcely sexier than Gabby Hayes, Presley was hip. Hips were in fact prominent in the performances of Elvis the Pelvis, so much so that he was banned from gyrating on TV. No need to issue such a prohibition on Haley. Presley really, as the song said, knew how to shake that thing. 'The Pelvis' exactly fitted that cultural role of white Negro, as it was defined in 1957 by Norman Mailer in his wildly polemic essay. The white Negro (later to be lampooned as the 'wigger') was one of a

> new breed of adventurers, urban adventurers who drifted out at night looking for action with a black man's code to fit their facts. The hipster had absorbed the existentialist synopses of the Negro, and for practical purposes could be considered a white Negro.

I read the essay when it became available in paperback and wrestled with the inner meaning of 'the existentialist synopses of the Negro' – should it have been 'synapses'? I see the passage still marked, quizzically, in fading pencil, on my beat-up copy of *Advertisements for Myself* (emblazoned, with sublime irrelevance, by the icon of the Queen's favourite pooch).

Of course, Presley was not *authentic*. He was higher kitsch. But he raised inauthenticity to an art form, to where such questions became, mysteriously, irrelevant. He could, as his subsequent career indicated, be whatever the moment

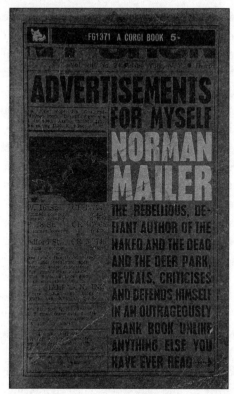

Mailer and a small dog

required. This was evident when he sang gospel or – incredibly – took 'O Sole Mio' – and made it a no. 1 hit.*

It wasn't the music, one finally realised, it was the performance. As Thom Gunn put it, in 'Elvis Presley' – the most popular Movement poem of 1957:

> Distorting hackneyed words in hackneyed songs
> He turns revolt into a style, prolongs
> The impulse to a habit of the time.

129

But again, what did turning revolt into style actually mean? What, more particularly, did it mean for someone at the time? One foundered in a mire of insoluble perplexity. How, one forlornly wondered, could one turn one's own revolt into style? Colchester was not propitious.

The Presley problem became even more tormenting with his massive 1956 hit 'Hound Dog'. This, as the discographies inform one, was a twelve-bar blues, composed by Jerry Leiber and Mike Stoller* (two talented Jewish songwriters), originally recorded by Willa Mae 'Big Mama' Thornton in 1952. Leiber and Stoller (although no one in my circle had any awareness of this at the time) were kids who had grown up and hung out together in Los Angeles. They had a passion for the blues and a quite noble desire to dedicate themselves to the form, bringing to it whatever two Jewish kids from the San Fernando valley could bring. The young composers' first hit, aged (incredibly) seventeen, was 'Real Ugly Woman', which they wrote for the blues-shouter Jimmy Witherspoon (black, of course).*

The composers went on to write 'Hound Dog' before they were twenty and they would later do a string of other platinum-sale Presley songs – notably 'Jailhouse Rock'. They had a formative influence on Phil Spector, who worked with them in the early 1960s. L&S were not predatory, like those notorious entrepreneurs who slapped their names on compositions by Little Richard and Chuck Berry, scooping up the royalties that properly belonged to the artists. L&S represented an artistic fusion between the two dominant ethnic groups in American pop music. At the same time, Jews and blacks were also shoulder to shoulder in the Civil Rights movement.

'Hound Dog' was first performed in 1952. One of the

many versions Big Mama Thornton recorded may be sampled on YouTube.* The original record became a hit, even in Colchester, Essex, not as she belted it out, but with Elvis Presley's ultra-sleek 1956 (slightly bowdlerised) version.

As with 'Shake Rattle and Roll', one was flummoxed by what the lyrics actually meant. This is how they go:

> Ya, they said you was high classed,
> well, that was just a lie.
> Ya, they said you was high classed,
> well, that was just a lie.
> You ain't never caught a rabbit
> and you ain't no friend of mine.

The hound dog in question is quite clearly, a man. And 'hound dog' in this context seems to have overtones of 'tom cat'. Was 'catching rabbits', like that mysterious business in the 'seafood store', code for some interesting sexual shenanigans? Or should one understand, rather, that the man, in this big black woman's life, is a no-good layabout? He didn't cut the mustard (whatever that meant: mustard surely came in yellow Colman's packets and you mixed it).

One thing was crystal clear. This was a righteous woman upbraiding a delinquent man. So when Presley came along and did 'Hound Dog', it was equivalent to Frank Sinatra singing, 'Some day he'll come along, the man I love', or Perry Como doing 'He's just my Bill.' Had it been, 'You ain't nuthin' but a spaniel bitch', the sex relationship would have been more orthodox. But the hit potential would have been sadly diminished.

The mix in 'Hound Dog' as offered by Presley (not all ingredients detectable to the adolescent in the mid-1950s – but dimly apprehended) is Jewish, black, Southern Baptist and alternately straight and gay. Where was any authenticity to be discerned in this strange brew, even by the most discerning young listener? The only way out was not to think about it: to suspend all critical faculties. And to do that was therapeutic. At last there was a music which demanded the stark alternative: switch off your brain or switch off the gramophone.

George Melly – then a jazz singer, who had in his repertoire a very good Joe Turner pastiche – put it well in the book he named after Gunn's poem, *Revolt into Style*: 'The whole point of Rock 'n' Roll depended on its lack of subtlety. It was music to be used rather than listened to.'*

He may have been the epitome of uncool, but Bill Haley was, as history records, a genuinely nice man, and entirely without vanity. He helped out Joe Turner when the veteran bluesman, who had enriched him, fell on hard times in the 1970s. And, whatever the pop-musicologists finally determine about who cut the first R&R record, Bill Haley can confidently claim another title. He was the first no. 1 rocker to die, peacefully and prosperously, in an old folk's home, aged fifty-six.

Ulysses

(aetat. 16)

WITH THE SENSE of hearing the tolling of a nearby funeral bell, I read in the *Independent* on 31 December 2007 (ominously terminal day) that 'at least' forty public libraries had been closed over the year. Not coincidentally, perhaps, three weeks later the same paper reported that a quarter of the British population had not read a single book over 2007. Ask not for whom it tolls. It tolls for Gutenberg.

Colchester's public library, a fine custom-built brick structure, erected in the high confidence of the post-war welfare state, was – as I said earlier – central to my early reading life. Generous as it was in its provision of reading matter, however, there was always a brooding thought-policing in the place. An eye over one's shoulder, watching. Someone, you knew, had chosen the books you were allowed to choose.

Colchester's library probably had a 'poison cabinet': books they felt obliged to acquire but equally obliged to withhold from their (vulnerable) clientele. Most such institutions did – and very strange their contents could be (anything from

Norman Mailer's *The Naked and the Dead* to Eustace Chesser's sex manual, *Love without Fear*). My guess is they also under-ordered books such as *The Cruel Sea*, which contained 'filth', on the grounds of civic sanitation.

But 'literature' posed an acute problem for the watchers. James Joyce's *Ulysses*, after the landmark Woolsey ruling in the US, was a legal commodity in 1950s Britain. And Joyce was, as the best judges testified, a great writer. *Ulysses*, notoriously, contained 'four-letter' words and passages of the deepest blue. It was all very well for some distant American jurist to pronounce Joyce's naughtiness 'emetic' rather than 'aphrodisiac'. 'Fuck', 'cunt', and 'shit' damn well wouldn't do in Colchester, AD 1955. They went beyond the emetic into the wholly impermissible. They belonged in the public lavatory, not the public library.

The Colchester librarian(s) came up with an elegant solution. The top storey of their building contained an extensive Reference Library. *Ulysses* (the only work of modern fiction so relocated) was shelved there – alongside 'Literary Criticism'. If the literary critics thought it was a great work, let them have *Ulysses* as their next-door neighbour, and leave decent people alone.

The Reference Library solution appealed for a number of reasons. Principally, of course, it was well out of the way. Ordinary browsing patrons tended not to go there unless they were looking up something specific: like the train times to London. Readers who were seated there were supervised. There was always an assistant, on a platformed desk, watching the users. Pure Panopticon.* Thirdly, if *Ulysses* was technically available – albeit inconveniently so – no one could accuse the library of censorship, and make a fuss about it in the *Essex County Standard*.

The British Museum Reading Room, at the same period, had its 'desk of shame', in the North Library. If you asked for any volume with the PC ('private case') shelf mark – say *Lolita* (before 1959*) – you were obliged to read it under the beady eye of an assistant librarian. It wasn't required that you keep your hands on the table, but that was the implication. No hanky-panky.

The librarians at Colchester had taken a further precaution. A single page, from the 'Penelope' section of *Ulysses*, had been razored out of the Reference Library copy. How, one wonders, was that particular page located? Was there a directive from Central Office – or was some dogsbody librarian deputed to plough through the text, obscenity-meter ticking Geiger-style in hand?

I did not find out about the missing page until later. I had, like any schoolboy with his wits about him, come across references to *Ulysses*, and knew it was an interestingly dangerous book. The idea of it was potent: iron filings and magnets again. I was desperate to read the thing. There was, as it happened, a copy of the Bodley Head hardback in W. H. Smith's in the High Street (they did serious books in those days). I could not afford to buy it – nor would I have had the courage to brazen out the purchase. I nonetheless picked the volume up every time I went there. I would glance through it with studied indifference, as if it had just that minute caught my eye.

As these cursory skims indicated, *Ulysses* was not a book which would yield up its treasure to a mere browser. It would need to be broken into, like a locked safe. I used to do my homework in the Colchester Reference Library (there was no desk, or table, available to me at home; and nowhere outside of the blare of the Light Programme). The atmosphere was conducive to study. And literary malfeasance.

With the nervousness of Yves Montand carrying a flask of TNT in *Le salaire de la peur*★ (1953, wonderful film), I would carry the library *Ulysses* to my desk, along with a precautionary bundle of less nocuous volumes. It was not, I noticed, much thumbed. The librarians' strategy had clearly worked.

It was after many baffled hours, over a succession of evenings (the 'Reference' stayed open till eight), that I came to the tantalising lacuna. The missing page. It was, to be precise, page 622. Having homed in on it, it was easy, next time I was in Smith's, simply to turn to the passage in question and, with a mute 'Eureka!', complete my *Ulysses* experience.

Predictably, the offence, that had attracted the censorious Blue Gillette★ was analingus. Molly's sleepy resolution:

> If he wants to kiss my bottom I'll drag open my drawers
> and bulge it right out in his face as large as life he can
> stick his tongue seven miles up my hole.

It wasn't, as it happened, a bad choice, assuming one had – given the cultural situation in the English provinces in 1955 – to sacrifice one page of *Ulysses* pro bono publico. Publico library, in this case. 'Rimming', as it would later be called (in the enlightened, and more adventurous 1970s), has always been one of the more conventionally distasteful sexual preferences – and in Colchester, at that time, would have seemed as unnatural as sexual conversation with goldfish.

On the other hand, the choice of that page could be taken to indicate a commendable inwardness with Joyce the man. Many years later, Richard Ellmann would reveal the author's penchant for coprophilia, along with the 'dirty letters' to Nora.★ Whether or not the anonymous, razor-wielding librarian was a prescient critic, the fact is that many other pages could have been removed. I suspect that single page was selected, arbitrarily, to demonstrate to the library user who was in charge. If the library user (say me) vandalised a library book, they'd quite likely find themselves up in front of the beak – like Joe Orton and Kenneth Halliwell. Those two were sent to prison, in 1962, for 'defacing' (in fact, decorating) Islington library books.* The eye over the shoulder was always there, and could turn quite nasty.

Unsurprisingly, I hadn't to this point studied *Ulysses* as a text. Nor had I read the library copy with the respect that one should bring to Great Literature. I had speed-read the thing, looking for an illicit thrill. I was a smut hound in full cry, not an ephebe, or an embryonic Joycean. But literature has many entrances. One such door is marked 'Scatology'. And, at a certain age, that way in is more attractive, I would argue, than that marked 'National Curriculum', or the one alongside, 'Set Texts: Lit 101'.

What gets the youthful reader reading? Many young Muslims, wholly good and dutiful British citizens, have, I would warrant, gone to huge efforts to read the *Mujahadeen Poisons Book* (very easily downloadable from the web – but, as the case of Samina Malik in December 2007 confirmed, very dangerous when found downloaded in a British citizen's possession). They will have read it not because they want to end up in Guantanamo, or the Old Bailey, or martyrs in Paradise, but for the simple reason that the book lies on the other side of a door marked 'Keep Out: Trespassers Will Be Prosecuted'. For that same reason I took the risk (not, admittedly, criminal) of reading *Lady Chatterley's Lover*, and the whole of *Ulysses*.

With reference to the word 'brave', there is another conclusion I would draw from my hunt for the missing page of *Ulysses*. Namely that brushes with books are often as influential as the close study of them. When I read the 1963 (Corgi, five shillings) paperback of Norman Mailer's *Advertisements for Myself*, I was comforted to find a writer I admired proclaim, without shame:

> Like many of you who will read this, I have read perhaps half of *Ulysses* and fragments from *Finnegans Wake* – but then it is not necessary to read all of Joyce in order to feel, or not feel, the meaning of his language and the reach of his genius. He is after all the only genius of the twentieth century who has written in the English language.

I'm not entirely sure what that last, uncompromising sentence means. But that Mailer should not merely confess his delinquency but *advertise* it was immensely liberating. There was a lot of liberation around in 1963, and it was not, as for Philip Larkin, 'too late for me'.* I had a few anni mirabili to come.

The 120 Days of Sodom

(aetat. 17)

THE MISSING PAGE of *Ulysses* was hunted down. None-theless, there was a category of books which eluded my sleuthing. One work of literature, in particular, was forever visible, but tantalisingly inaccessible, in the mid-1950s. Even further away from a schoolboy's grasp than Connie Chat-terley. I knew the book. I knew quite a lot about it. But I could never get hold of the thing; at least, not then, when I was most curious about it.

The book was de Sade's *The 120 Days of Sodom*. Being French, it was banned in France – unlike *Lady Chatterley's Lover* (the French do not care what the English read) – and not easily come by even in Paris. Certainly not in English translation.

I kept finding tormenting references to *The 120 Days* in other English books which were very much in my orbit. I was, for example, excited by references in Aldous Huxley's *After Many a Summer*.* That writer's reputation has sunk over the years, but in the 1950s he was regarded as the real thing for aspiring would-be intellectual adolescents like myself. It was a subplot in the 1939 novel, about the elusive de Sadeian masterpiece, which principally pricked my curiosity.

An ingenuous English scholar, Jeremy Pordage (a mock self-portrait of the novelist), is commissioned to come to Southern California to catalogue the library of Jo Stoyte, a vulgar, severely thanatophobic tycoon (based on William Randolph Hearst: aka Citizen Kane*). The 'Hauberk Collection' has been purchased from a British aristocratic family fallen on hard times. All the British family silver (Aldous Huxley/Jeremy Pordage included) is up for sale. The vulgar dollar rules. Rummaging through the trunks, Pordage discovers – clapped inside a faux prayer book – a clandestine copy of Les Cent-vingt journées, 'that rarest of all works of the Divine Marquis'.

Pordage puts the treasure on one side for his evening pleasures. Those pleasures are entirely onanistic, and literary (as, to be honest, were John Sutherland's in 1956). Alas, the degenerate scientist recruited by Stoyte to work on the elixir of life, Dr Obispo, seizes the treasure. He intends, more practically, to work through the 120 formulae of the book with Stoyte's pretty young thing of a concubine (based on Marion Davies*). He duly corrupts her with the manual, day by day: 'though how on earth the man who wrote the book was going to keep it up for a hundred and twenty days she didn't know!' – but, evidently, she finds out. Huxley is infuriatingly unspecific on the details.

What really cemented my idée fixe about the Divine Marquis and his bad book into something close to obsession was a critical work, The Romantic Agony, by Mario Praz. Praz's monograph was published in 1933 in the author's native Italy as La carne, la morte, e il diavolo nella letteratura romantica. A sexier title by far than what the English publishers came up with.*

Nonetheless, the translation was hugely popular, and widely circulated in Britain – much more so than a treatise on European Romanticism would strictly warrant. If you trawled Soho bookshops in the mid-1950s the reason was clear enough. There would be a copy of *The Romantic Agony* nestling among the Hank Jansons and 'Crisp Tales from the French'.

The main contention of Praz's book is that Romanticism originated in what he melodramatically termed 'a ferment of the blood'. Romanticism, according to Praz, is an intellectual structure founded on deviant sex, fetishism and moral degeneracy. It crystallises in 'the beauty of the Medusa, metamorphoses of Satan, *la belle dame sans merci*, Byzantium, Swinburne and *le vice anglais*'.

Living, as one had no alternative but to live, in a spectacularly viceless Essex backwater, this was heady stuff. And the black heart of Romanticism, according to Praz (his own name, even, was itself whiffy with degeneracy) was de Sade. And the de Sadeian magnum opus, of course, was *The 120 Days*.

It was a bit of a stretch to see 'the shadow of the divine Marquis' darkening, say, Wordsworth's Lucy poems, which I was grinding away at for A-level. But how would I know? Quite possibly what had brought Lucy to her premature grave was '*le vice anglais*' (I wasn't quite sure what my national predilection might be, and had some inflamed hypotheses about it: wholly wrong, as I later discovered).

I could read every single one of the writers Praz prated about so Italianly, except one. And that one, he solemnly assured us, was the most important if we were to understand all the others. Why couldn't I read de Sade? Because those who had my best interests at heart were determined that

I should not be 'corrupted and depraved' (as the obscenity legislation of the time put it) by reading it. Even if I desperately wanted – needed even – some corruption and depravity in my straitened existence. 'But of the tree of the knowledge of good and evil, thou shalt not eat of it,' as the great librarian in the sky put.

'Must we burn de Sade?' asked Simone de Beauvoir, portentously, in a much discussed essay of 1953.* How on earth would I know? I retorted mentally. No one would let me have a copy to burn. Or not. I read de Beauvoir (in French) in the hope of some examples of what a fellow should do. It was very slim pickings. There was a lot about 'ennui'. I had enough of that in my life without a degenerate French marquis supplying another tranche.

The Moors Murderer Ian Brady, an exact contemporary of mine (we were both born in 1938), was also, later events revealed, eager to lay his hands on de Sade's writings. Despite the *Lady Chatterley* acquittal, in November 1960, there had been considerable nervousness in the British book trade about taking on the Marquis. The first 'complete and unexpurgated' translation of one of his least offensive works, *Justine*, was published in a high-price hardback edition (the usual way of testing the waters), with owlish annotation, in 1964.

When it was clearly seen not to excite the DPP's wrath, the mass-market paperback firm Four Square reprinted it in 1965. It went through half a dozen editions in a year. There was clearly a market.

Brady had bought the hardback copy and placed it on his bookshelf alongside *Kiss of the Whip*,* *High Heels and Stockings* and *Mein Kampf* (not easily available in English, but the awful man hopefully acquired himself a *Teach Yourself German*). Brady and his accomplice, Myra Hindley, went on their sadistic child-murdering spree between July 1963 and October 1965. They were arrested shortly after the last killing.*

At the trial, in April 1966, Brady's reading matter was key evidence against him. The court was told that Brady had meditated deeply on the specific de Sadeian instruction: 'Is Murder a crime in the eyes of Nature? ... Destruction is Nature's method of progress ... Murder is often necessary, never criminal and essential to tolerate in a republic.'

Had the Moors Murders and all the publicity about de Sade not intervened, the British book trade would surely have followed the example of its American counterpart and published *The 120 Days*. But there was a backlash against de Sade in the wake of the most horrific and morally perturbing murder trial in post-war Britain. The Marquis was an accomplice, up there in the dock with Brady and Hindley. He, if not she, had evidently found *Justine* inspirational and would doubtless have found *The 120 Days* even more so. Both of them had toyed with the prospect of filming themselves in acts of extreme sex.

Thanks to Ian Brady, *The 120 Days* was a long time becoming generally available in the UK. Grove Press had editions available in the US (some of which dribbled across the Atlantic), and it was available, with full scholarly apparatus and at vast cost, in an *Oeuvres complètes*, published in France, in the early 1970s.

For a decade, de Sade was an exciting cultural topic. Around the 1980s, people ceased to care. So did I. When I finally got around to looking at *The 120 Days* I found it as anaphrodisiac as Euclid, in its geometric permutations on the postures, orifices and varieties of sex.

For example, this, from the 22nd day. Was this idiocy what one had been so long denied?

As a result of these all-night bacchanals, exceedingly little was accomplished on the twenty-second day of November; half the customary exercises were forgot, at dinner Messieurs appeared to be in a daze, and it was not until coffee they began to come somewhat to their senses. The coffee was served them by Rosette and Sophie, Zélamir and Giton. In an effort to return to his usual old self, Curval had Giton shit, and the Duc swallowed Rosette's turd; the Bishop had himself sucked by Sophie, Durcet by Zélamir, but no one discharged. They moved dutifully into the auditorium; the matchless Duclos, weak and queasy after the preceding day's excesses, took her place with drooping eyelids, and her tales were so brief, they contained so few episodes, were recounted so listlessly, that we have taken it upon ourselves to supply them, and in the reader's behalf to clarify the somewhat confused speech she made to our friends.

In keeping with prescription, she recounted five passions: the first was that of a man who used to have his ass frigged with a tin dildo earlier charged with warm water, the which liquid was pumped into his fundament at the same instant he ejaculated; nothing else was required to obtain that effect, he needed no one else's ministry.

The second man had the same mania, but was wont to use a far greater number of instruments; initially, he called for a very minute one, then gradually increased the calibre, ascending the scale by small fractions of an inch until he reached a weapon with the dimensions of a veritable fieldpiece, and only discharged upon receiving a torrent from its muzzle.

Far more of the mysterious was required to please the third one's palate: at the outset of the game, he had an enormous instrument introduced into his ass, then it was withdrawn, he would shit, would eat what he had just rendered, and next he had to be flogged. The flogging administered, it was time to reinsert the formidable device in his rectum, then once again it was removed, and it was the whore's turn to shit, and after that she picked up the whip again and lashed him while he munched what she had done; a third time, yes, a third time the instrument was driven home, and that, plus the girl's turd he finished eating, was sufficient to complete his happiness.

It is amazingly tedious. Nor was I much impressed with Pasolini's 1975 fantasia *Salò o le 120 giornate di Sodoma*, which uses de Sade to allegorise Mussolini's Italy.* Nothing decays faster than once-forbidden fruit.

At a certain point in my development, however, the important thing was that one *couldn't* read de Sade. It confirmed an important fact of cultural life. There would always be something beyond to push against – always something one would never be allowed to have; at least, not allowed to have when it might have its effect. And when one did, belatedly get it, something else, unallowed, would have taken its place. One has, case by case, to make a decision as to whether it's worth pushing.

Anyone found handling *The 120 Days*, in 1956, would have found themselves in extremely hot water. Certainly any business publishing or retailing it. Now it's not worth the labour of reading, even as cultural freeware. For those who want to sample, there's a website, with the witty nom-de-web supervert.com, which offers freely downloadable e-texts of all the major works, including *The 120 Days*.* Super-perversion doesn't come into it. It's less arousing, in the twenty-first century, than *Thomas the Tank Engine*. There's even a 'manga' version,* for those disinclined to undertake the labour of reading, or too young to have wholly mastered the skill.

Of course, the category of 'forbidden' is still there. In that dark socket where de Sade used to be, in the 1950s, there's now an inaccessible (to most of us, thank God) tier of web pornography that the police, apparently, label 'Category Five'. In time, doubtless, as it becomes domesticated, as has every generation of ne plus ultra offensiveness before it, a Category six will have to be discovered.

The 120 Days served a valuable function for me. It marked a boundary. As it happened, I would be entirely fulfilled on the safe side rather than the far side. But the boundaries, shifting as they may be, are always there.

Oblomov

(aetat. 17)

IN THE LATE 1940s the critic V. S. Pritchett* wrote a witty review in the *New Statesman* (a magazine which I liked, in my later adolescence, to be seen carrying) revolving around the paradox of what he called the 'Russian day'.

It must have been longer than our quotidian twenty-four GMT hours, Pritchett slyly suggested. Russian upper classes seemed, if Tolstoy, Dostoevsky, Chekhov and Turgenev were to be believed, to have so much burdensome *time* on their hands.

Clocks moved slower; weeks dragged; months crawled under the vast Russian skies. Life, for the Sashas, Pierres and Myshkins, seemed permanently on hold. It is true, of course, that during St Petersburg's summertime 'white nights', the hours of the day really do last longer, given the city's northern latitude. Even under the Great Bolshevik's ('Electrify! Electrify!') tyranny, there was presumably more leisure in Leningrad* than in – say – Chicago.

In Britain the 1957 day was longer than in crazy-hurry

2007. No mystery why. There were fewer TVs and cars, less disposable cash (films and theatre constituted a special 'outing' or 'weekly treat'), foreign holidays were only for the rich, famous or those (like Sir Bernard and Lady Docker, with their gold-plated Daimler*) who could fiddle the tiny foreign currency allowance, pubs closed at 10 p.m. (10.30 p.m. in summer). There was, particularly in your late teens, frequently 'nothing to do'.

Books could fill some of those yawning chasms between the young person's daily reveille and lights out. The fact that Trollope, for example, enjoyed a huge vogue in the wartime and early post-war years was no accident. And there were even bigger novels than his with which to kill one's time. Under the enlightened editorship of E. V. Rieu,* Penguin issued a series of vastly long classics in translation in the 1950s (many of them done by the indefatigable polyglot J. M. Cohen* – one of the unsung heroes of British popular education). I, like others, ploughed through the Penguin *Don Quixote*, *Crime and Punishment*, *The Brothers Karamazov*. Long books for long days.

I had the feeling that these books, in their handsome but sternly typographic livery (Allen Lane despised pictorial covers), were doing me good: a phrase much bandied about at the time – usually for things one didn't at all like. There was, however, one novel in this set which I liked an awful lot: Goncharov's *Oblomov*.* It is eerily *about* Pritchett's peculiarly Russian day: or, put another way, the strange imbalance between time and action which Russian fiction (and Chekhov's drama) records.

Goncharov's novel (which came out in Russia in 1859, and under Penguin colours in 1954) is set in the period shortly before the emancipation of the serfs. A period in which, like the antebellum American South (as all 'Peel me a

grape, Beulah' caricatures would have one believe), serfdom
has rotted all willpower in the serf-owning class. Goncharov
calls the Russian disease, eponymously, 'Oblomovitis'. As the
French poet put it, 'Living? Our servants will do that for us.'*

Oblomov is 'a gentleman by birth and a collegiate secretary
by rank' who could more accurately be called an upper-class
layabout. Lying about is his main occupation in life. He can
barely be bothered to get out of bed (where he's discovered
as the story opens), unless it's to lumber across to his sofa
and pass the day there, recumbent, dressing-gowned, doing
nothing other than wait for bedtime to roll round. He lives
on the revenue of an estate, a thousand miles (what was a
'verst',* one vaguely wondered?) away from the city. The
estate is wormholed by parasites nearer and more energetic
than he. Oblomov doesn't care.

The novel describes, at extraordinary length, the Oblo-
movian day. He eats voraciously, and unmercifully nags his
luckless serf, Zakhar – who has 'boundless loyalty' to the
master whom nonetheless (like everyone else) he cheats
whenever he can. Friends call. Oblomov never goes out to
meet or call on them. This 'sublime sluggard', as Pritchett
called him, is contemptible, but lovable and even admirable.
He embodies 'the poetry of procrastination'.

And, the novel tells us, truths are to be found in that state
of forever suspended animation in which Oblomov lives, if
it can be called living. And what is the greatest truth to be
found? That truth, paradoxically, will finally, probably, elude
us. To quote Pritchett again:

> In 19th Century Russia, under the simpler feudal division
> of society, there is more room to breathe, to let the will
> drift, and the disparate impulses have their ancient

> solitary reign. In all those Russian novels we seem to hear
> a voice saying: 'The meaning of life? One day all that will
> be revealed to us – probably on a Thursday.'

I don't honestly know if that elegant riff really catches the
spirit of Russia. But it surely reflects the ennui of adolescence.
Particularly in the 1950s. Plenty of room in those desolate
years to let the will drift. Life was not, as the proverb put it,
your oyster: more like the oyster bed. And always Thursday –
that most useless day of the week.

Oblomov is a grossly obese version of Beckett's anorexic,
similarly bed-bound, even more *ennuyé* hero in *Malone Dies*.★
That slim work was on sale, a few years later, as a red-backed
Penguin. I recall carrying it (as I did not *Oblomov*, which
was very much a book for the easy chair and required too
much explanation), cover visible, into the coffee bar I then
frequented: The Bamboo.★ One felt 'existential'; not quite *rive
gauche*, but not *gauche* either with it lodged, artfully visible, in
the crook of one's arm ('Incredibly *good*', one would confide
to some kindred cappuccino bibber – 'Much better on the
textures of existential weltschmerz than Camus.')

Looking at the pages of the Penguin Classic *Oblomov* (as
translated by David Magarshack) and the too-small type
crammed on to the slightly too-small page, I wonder at how
slowly my own clock must have moved in those interminable
Essex days. There are some 485 pages in the 1954 edition –
close on 300,000 words. A hundred hours of reading: not for
an exam, not for thrills, just to pass 1950s time. The time was
there, the book was there, I was there. As the witty George
Bernard Shaw said about cricket, it gave one an intimation
of eternity.★

In the climax (so to miscall it) of Goncharov's narrative,

after nothing happening, apart from gorging, loafing, bickering, not working and not marrying (his friend gets the girl, Olga, whom he might have had), Oblomov is found, years on, in reduced circumstances, living in the country, still loafing, still scoffing, still serenely at peace with his world. He is stuffed, nowadays on homelier fare than in St Petersburg, by his housekeeper, Agafya, who treats him rather as French peasants might do a particularly valued Strasbourg goose:

> His coffee was as carefully and nicely served and as well made as at the beginning, when he had moved into the house several years before. Giblet soup, macaroni and Parmesan cheese, meat or fish pie, cold fish and vegetable soup, home-grown chicken – all this followed each other in strict rotation and introduced pleasant variety into the monotonous life of the little house ... The canaries trilled gaily; the geraniums and the hyacinths the children occasionally brought from the count's garden exuded a strong scent in the small room, blending pleasantly with the smoke of a pure Havana cigar and the cinnamon or vanilla which the landlady pounded, energetically moving her elbows. Oblomov lived, as it were, within a golden framework of life, in which, as in a diorama, the only things that changed were the usual phases of day and night and the seasons.

And, of course, they change more slowly than anywhere else on the face of the turning planet.

Oblomov has a stroke – is paralysed (when has he been anything else?) – and five slow years later dies, well short of the statutory three score and ten; although doubtless his lifespan felt positively Methuselean to him (time, psychological time as it's called, goes slower in bed; in Heller's *Catch-22* there's a character, Dunbar, who is extending his life by never getting out of his bunk*). Oblomov's departure from life happens off stage. One cannot call it an 'event'. In a sense, it can barely be said to happen. So torpid is his life, in his final years, that it is indistinguishable from rigor mortis; or is like twilight merging into night. He drifts out of life, as he drifted into it, and through it, leaving nothing behind him but a word: Oblomovitis. His monument.

The novel can be seen as a parable of Russia, in terminal, pre-Revolutionary decay. Or it can be read as high comedy (which is how Spike Milligan travestied it, in his long-running 1960s stage version*). Or one can read *Oblomov* as a one-off literary curiosity. Goncharov was deranged while writing the novel and in later years was wholly paranoid – cultivating a mad jealousy of Turgenev.* But I doubt whether schoolboys, normal schoolboys, that is, nowadays have time to read Russian novels of Goncharovian, Dostoevskian or Tolstoyan length. Chekhov's short stories are probably as much as the current schedule allows. Even MTV clips go on too long.

Their day, in short, is too short. Why? Their life is too full. Lucky them.

'Red Wind'

(aetat. 17)

I BECAME A CALIFORNIAN in 1983, late in life. But I *knew* Southern California, and it had a formative influence on me, long before I got my green card and my place in the sun.

I was, in fact, one of the few. There was a whole generation alongside me, and at least a couple before me, who resided, spiritually, in Hollywoodland (particularly on Friday nights) – thanks to the movies. They knew Grauman's Chinese Theatre (with all the cement footprints*) as well as they knew Piccadilly Circus. But whereas (if only as the English provincial equivalent of the Hajj) they might expect to see Eros in their lifetime, they would die never having seen how incredibly tiny Fred Astaire's tootsies were (he could have come in as the eighth dwarf). There were even writers (see, for example, Dennis Wheatley) who set stories in California, never having set foot there.

Aldous Huxley *had* seen the place. He went to live in Southern California, as did a rootlessly cosmopolitan diaspora of other intellectuals, writers and artists, as trouble brewed up disturbingly in Europe in the late 1930s. Like others at the time, Huxley thought Europe was finished: a toothless bitch. And, of course, the studios were suckers, ripe for a clever person's picking. As the writer Herman Mankiewicz telegrammed his New York buddy Ben Hecht on arrival in Los Angeles: 'Millions are to be grabbed out here and your only competition is idiots.'* (Coincidentally, both Mankiewicz and Huxley would make money lampooning William Randolph Hearst – as 'Citizen Kane' and 'Jo Stoyte'.)

Huxley was all for grabbing, if not millions, then a good handful of the dollars lying around. He would go on to enrol his talent in the cause of such travesty film adaptations as Disney's *Alice in Wonderland* and a scarcely more palatable *Pride and Prejudice*.*

Southern California, comfortable bomb shelter as it may have been in the late 1930s, was not to Huxley's refined taste. He reproduces his first brush with the place in the opening paragraphs of *After Many a Summer* (a novel which I knew, at this stage of my life, rather better than I knew my A-level texts). Jeremy Pordage, effete Oxford bibliophile, arrives, carrying, preposterously, a calf-bound volume of Wordsworth for identification purposes, at Union Station. There he is met by a 'blackamoor' chauffeur (Huxley was oddly fond of that word). They drive in their limousine through downtown LA, a mongrel slum:

> Southern California rolled past the windows; all Jeremy had to do was to keep his eyes open.
>
> The first thing to present itself was a slum of Africans and Filipinos, Japanese and Mexicans. And what permutations and combinations of black, yellow, and brown! What complex bastardies!

At the end of the trip, deep in the San Fernando valley, lies the ultimate Southern Californian bastardy, 'Xanadu' (as Mankiewicz labelled it in *Citizen Kane*), Jo Stoyte's pleasure dome:

> But what a castle! The donjon was like a skyscraper, the bastions plunged with the effortless swoop of concrete dams. The thing was Gothic, mediaeval, baronial – doubly baronial, Gothic with a Gothicity raised, so to speak, to a higher power, more mediaeval than any building of the thirteenth century.

'What on earth is that?' Pordage is reduced to asking. 'Southern California', would be the answer.*

As with the Oxford scholar, the multifarious images of Southern California which bombarded me, from my first movie experiences onwards, never cohered into any single image. It was the Land of Oz. I lived for many childhood years under the delusion that apples in California were black (as they were in pre-Technicolor movies), that there was a lot of darkness (noir strongly suggested the nights were interminable) and every Californian carried a handgun (I was partly right about that).

A green-backed Penguin Crime volume which my mother left around gave me my first thoughtful impression of the place. She'd liked the book a lot and since she was the most worldly thing in my world at the time, I read it. It was dated 1950. I came across it, somewhat battered, a few years later. It had probably passed through a few hands by then.

The title was *Trouble is My Business*, a scooping up of early Raymond Chandler pulp stories, from a period when he was honing his style on genre, as a barber might sharpen his cut-throat on a strop. The series hero, later to mutate into Philip Marlowe, was a 'shamus', or 'Private Eye', John Dalmas.*

Penguin livery was highly respectable: it graced none but authors who had passed Allen Lane's stringent entry standards. Chandler was (thanks, mainly, to the publisher Hamish Hamilton) a much more highly thought-of author in the UK than in his own country. It was something that pleased him inordinately, out there in Long Beach, Anglophile to the core that he was. It even flattered his delusion that he might, one day, get the Nobel Prize for Literature (if Pearl S. Buck, why not Ray Chandler?).

Penguin Books were at the other end of cultural life from *Dime Magazine*, *Black Mask* and *Detective Fiction Weekly*, where the stories in *Trouble is My Business* had originated. They brought with them a grittiness which leapt off the page. What gripped me tightest, as I read the stories, was the opening to the story 'Red Wind':

> There was a desert wind blowing that night. It was one of those hot dry Santa Anas that come down through the mountain passes and curl your hair and make your nerves jump and your skin itch. On nights like that every booze party ends in a fight. Meek little wives feel the edge of the carving knife and study their husbands' necks. Anything can happen. You can even get a full glass of beer at a cocktail lounge.

This overture leads in to a 'Night Hawks' scene in an LA bar (a favourite opening set of moves in Chandler's fiction). Dalmas, who has an apartment nearby, has drifted in for a nightcap. What follows, I would later realise, owes much to the classic 'hard-boiled' crime story, Hemingway's 'The Killers', which opens in exactly the same way. In that story, two customers – in fact assassins – turn up in a bar, looking for the 'Swede', their prey.* They make over-the-counter tough small talk. Violence hovers in the air, like a black cloud. It's an opening scenario which has become archetypal (at random, think *Pulp Fiction* or *A History of Violence*).*

In 'Red Wind', the bar is empty apart from a drunk who is sitting soddenly in the corner, a pile of dimes in front of him (a shot only cost a quarter in those days). There is some bar badinage, of a high-Chandlerian nature, between Dalmas and the young, smart-as-paint barkeep:

> The kid came back and put more beer in my glass. Outside the wind howled. Every once in a while it blew the stained-glass swing-door open a few inches. It was a heavy door.
>
> The kid said: 'I don't like drunks in the first place and in the second place I don't like them getting drunk in here, and in the third place I don't like them in the first place.'
>
> 'Warner Brothers could use that,' I said.
>
> 'They did.'
>
> Just then we had another customer.

Chandler does this kind of thing even better than Hemingway. Or Warner Bros, come to that.

It emerges that the drunk is no drunk, but a contract killer, waiting patiently for his luckless prey. That would be the customer who has just walked through the door, inevitably. He gets two 22s in the chest and falls to the floor: 'he might have been poured concrete for all the fuss he made,'

Dalmas comments, laconically. Trouble is his business – but he's off duty at the moment.

As is usual with Chandler, the plot thereafter goes entirely haywire. No one ever read this author for the story. Famously he himself never quite knew what was happening in his narratives. 'Who knows?' was his usual riddling response when asked about some peculiarly baffling twist.* His long and short fictions were merely occasions for the kind of writing he did better than anyone else, even Dashiell Hammett, his closest rival in the hard-boiled crime genre.*

What most enthralled me was the idea of that red wind.* You get a lot of weather in England, but most of it is grey and damp. What was a hot dry wind – a *red* wind – like? Like a gust from the oven doors of a rather interesting hell, Chandler suggests. The wind blows, redly, throughout the story (the Santa Anas normally last one or two days). They come in from the Mojave and are further heated by compression as they swirl, angrily, over the San Gabriel mountain ridge, howling through the Jeffrey pines.* By the time they arrive at the coast – and LA – the humidity is down to single figures, practically. However hot it is indoors (only Casablanca fans, then, no a/c), you keep the windows closed when the red wind blows. But you can't keep the devilry out.

When I lived in Southern California, years later, the Santa Anas (which, oddly, always seemed to blow at weekends) were to me the essence of the West Coast. They were dangerous. It was a Santa Ana fire, barrelling up the residential canyons like a flamethrower, which destroyed Aldous Huxley's house, and all his books and papers, in 1961. They often were literally red; literally, as embers are red. After the catastrophic October 1993 mountain fires – driven across the chaparral at speeds of up to sixty mph by the Santa Anas – the hillsides glowed, sparked and sporadically flamed, for nights, from Laguna Beach to Sierra Madre, like something out of Dante. I would go out and look at them, hours-long.*

That, for me, was when the place was most itself. The apples weren't black, but the wind, the real Californian wind, was hot, dry, red and tinged with danger.

Waiting for Godot

(aetat. 17)

'THE REVOLUTION,' we are authoritatively informed, 'will not be televised'.* It can, in my experience, be dramatised. In August 1955, the English translation of an Irishman's French play, *En attendant Godot*, was performed in London.* The theatre of the absurd had arrived in a country which had traditionally prided itself on being immune from Higher Froggy Nonsense.

A month or two later, *Waiting for Godot* was performed at my local 'rep', in Colchester's High Street (the theatre, a converted insurance office, vacated in the Depression-hit 1930s, was called – absurdly – the Albert Hall). Disturbing metropolitan – cosmopolitan even – ripples slapped into the provincial backwaters with Beckett's play.*

I had never enjoyed live theatre as much as film. But, for a year or two, in the mid-1950s, I was a regular theatregoer. One of the English teachers at my school – 'George' Young – a man of extraordinary energy and wit – had started something he called the Junior Rep. Boys and girls would hold play-readings in the Albert Hall on late afternoons and put on occasional productions. They were also given concessionary admission to the mid-week live performances. Since the grammar schools in Colchester were sex-segregated, it was lipstick, as much as greasepaint, which recruited me into the Junior Rep. But I faithfully, once a week, attended the theatre.

I remember the evening of *Godot* vividly. One of my other schoolteachers (maths – he had no time for me, unlike George) exited the theatre – mid-play – in a rage, waving his fist and shouting, 'This is balls!' No waiting around for him.

George Young (still, thank God, alive) vouches for the fact that one of the rep cast, David Baron, had grabbed him by the lapels during rehearsals and said, excitedly, 'I've just experienced the most important thing in my life. It will change everything.' Baron was then a supporting actor in the rep. He was in the troupe from February 1955 until early 1956. He had, as I recall, an unusually still way with his parts – avoiding any theatricality.*

Like those of the other actors, a studio photograph of Baron was visible from the pavement outside in the High Street. One could sit in the bus stop six feet from the Albert Hall and admire it. The bus service was infrequent in those days. Baron subsequently reverted to his birth name, Harold Pinter. And he took to writing plays rather than performing in them. In 1957, a couple of months after it was performed in London, *The Caretaker* came to Colchester. More balls.

In the interval between Beckett and Pinter, during the build-up to Suez, came Osborne's *Look Back in Anger*. The Angry Young Man had exploded on the English scene. Less balls than cannonballs. Kenneth Tynan recalls the impact:

The salient thing about Jimmy Porter was that we – the

underthirties [Tynan was just twenty-nine in 1956, Osborne two years his junior] generation in Britain – recognized him on sight. We had met him; we had pub-crawled with him; we had shared bed-sitting-rooms with him [in point of fact, Ken 'Peacock' Tynan, would as like be found in a pigsty as a bedsit]. For the first time the theatre was speaking to us in our own language, on our own terms.

Those three plays did to the English Establishment what Samson did to the temple of the Philistines. Anger and absurdity dismantled the ideological pillars on which my parents' England had complacently rested since time immemorial. *Godot* mocked the God-waiters, Jimmy Porter defecated all over the Empire and the household of Mick, Aston and Davies subverted whatever sense of 'care in the community' had hung over from the Second World War. 'Scum', Somerset Maugham had called them – unaware that scum is often carried on a flood tide.*

What these plays represented wasn't iconoclasm, but vandalism in a good cause. It was a three-voiced 'everlasting Nay', and immensely hygienic, culturally and spiritually. And for me it started in a dusty repertory theatre in Colchester, Essex.

I was present at a lunch with Pinter half a century later. 'Yes,' he said (without much evident pleasure), he remem-bered Colchester. When he was there, the matinee idol in the cast was Bryan Drew. I, certainly, had idolised the other actor and had modelled my laconic off-hand remarks, for a month or two, on Drew's performance in Ustinov's *The Love of Four Colonels* (which, as I recall, came to Colchester in 1954). Drew, Pinter informed me, had gone into theatrical agency. The first step on the road to international stardom did not begin in Colchester's Albert Hall for him.*

Less fondly, Pinter remembered Robert 'Bob' Digby, the dictatorial founder-manager of the rep in 1937.* The corpulent Digby had a disconcerting resemblance to Robert Morley – but was less jolly. Digby would take to the boards (*his* boards) once a year, for a ritual appearance as the moronic giant, Lennie, in the dramatised version of Steinbeck's *Of Mice and Men*. The theatre was always loyally packed that week. I found it incredibly ham, and the American accents appalling compared to the real thing which one could hear, two hundred yards away, in the Hippodrome.

Digby was a ruthless manager. He exploited stage-struck youngsters as ASMs. They were expected to slave, painting sets and scavenging props and wardrobe ('Stockings by Kayser Bond, Cigarettes by Abdullah, Standard Lights by the Cooperative Society', etc.). Digby saw the Junior Rep as nothing more than slow-evening fodder. He paid his cast nothing – fired matinee idols when their looks faded, or their hair receded (one, I recall, sitting in tears, in the Waggon and Horses, across they way, where in happier days he'd learned his lines, and happily gossiped about what was happening in the West End. What remained for him? That pit at the end of Clacton Pier?)

But Digby kept the doors open during grim days for the 'live' theatre and had a keen eye for good plays. It was at the rep I saw Anouilh's *Antigone*, Donald Wolfit's histrionic *The Master Builder* and a lot of Shakespeare.

Some future biographer, doubtless, will succeed in discovering the effect of that dash of Colcestrianism in the complex mixtures that resulted in our greatest modern playwright. They were, I suspect, more inspirational than the town was on me.

W. R. Rodgers

(aetat. 18)

POETRY MEANT LESS to me growing up than fiction, film and even – for a couple of years – drama. There was, however, one living poet whom I read, whose verse I listened to and thought about.

W[illiam] R[obert] ('Bertie') Rodgers does not live in the annals of literature. He was never, except possibly for a couple of years in the early 1940s, a player in the first division: up there with Eliot or Auden. Not even, like the poet whose biography I would later write, Stephen Spender, was Bertie at the top of any discriminating critic's second division. Which, of course, means posthumous oblivion – other than the occasional footnote in some dry-as-dust thesis. More true of W. R. Rodgers than of any other gifted poet I've read is it that his achievement was written in water. Flushed away in a couple years after his largely un-noticed death, in 1969.*

From the scant biographical evidence I have since seen (principally a sympathetic essay by Dan Davin – connoisseur of the wine-soaked muse*), Rodgers's background was, even for a poet of the 1930s, unusual. He was Ulster born (1911). His father, an 'iron-buttocked' Protestant, would not permit any son of his to go to university unless he took orders afterwards. Learning was for the service of God, not the pleasure of man. At Queen's University Belfast, Bertie duly did theology after a first degree in English – already his principal interest. From 1934 to 1946 he was a minister in County Armagh – on the uneasy border between the two Irelands, or, as Rodgers put it, a place marked by 'through otherness'. Like Seamus Heaney, also North-born, the literary side of Rodgers was attracted, magnetically, southwards. Conor Cruise O'Brien described him as 'an Ulster Presbyterian who sought and enjoyed the company of Southern Catholics ... He was ... a good Dubliner and Dublin loved him.'

In his Ulster church Rodgers was also a famed preacher in a denomination which valued the sermon and rhetoric (one of his poems is an anthem of praise for 'that brave man [Ian] Paisley', then a brave young Ulsterman*). The clerical profession was 'reserved': the Reverend Rodgers was not obliged to serve in the Second World War. Family circumstances may also have prevented him volunteering. He had married, and his wife – tragically – was diagnosed as schizophrenic in the late 1930s. And the Dublin-loving element may have disinclined him to serve the English king, although many Southern Irish did.

At the same period, Rodgers launched into an explosive outburst of poetry. His poems found favour with the editors of the few places where verse had worthwhile circulation: in London weeklies, that is, such as the *Listener*, the *New Statesman* and, most influentially, *Horizon*, where Cyril Connolly and Spender sifted out the very best that was currently being done. Yeats's death in 1939 had created a vogue for eloquent Irish

Protestant grandiloquence. It was, as Auden famously put it, the 'climate' at the time.*

Secker and Warburg (not Faber – Eliot, the grand patron, did not, apparently, approve) brought out a collection of Rodgers's work entitled, rousingly, *Awake! And Other Poems*. It carries on its title-verso page the bleak information:

> These poems were written between 1938 and 1940. They were originally sent to press in 1940, and the first printing was entirely destroyed by enemy action. Reset and first published July 1941.

At the height of the Blitz, that is. A Wagnerian overture for any slim volume.

In 1946, Rodgers resigned his ministry and drifted over into the post-war London literary world. He found a spiritual home in that brilliant coterie of poetic drunkards in the Stag's Head and the George ('the gluepot' – once there, you were stuck all day) by Broadcasting House.* There, thanks to their leader (and Rodgers's principal patron, Louis MacNeice), they could pick up whatever work was going at the BBC. The bibulous Langham Place pantheon included MacNeice, Dylan Thomas and Roy Campbell (the most violent of the crew, Campbell once gave Stephen Spender a bloody nose, with the screamed exclamation 'You bloody lesbian!'*). Their genius dissolved into conversation of which only fragments remain, transmitted as oral anecdotes. Rodgers, by all accounts, was among the best of the talkers. And drinkers.

Rodgers's debut volume, *Awake!*, was extremely well received and the BBC (particularly the Third Programme*) supplied him gainful employment. He did little to advance his career at Broadcasting House, however, when (his first wife having died in 1953) he fell in love with the ex-wife of his boss and married her. Thereafter, W. R. Rodgers was freelance and his income always more precarious.

The Rodgerses managed to get by and moved to a farmhouse on the outskirts of Colchester, the poetically named Rookery. This was the mid-1950s. Colchester was a 'dormitory town' (and, of course, my town) just an hour from Liverpool Street. I would sometimes see Bertie, a full-faced, rubicund, tweed-coated, white-haired (not, alas, smiling) public man walking stiffly off the train at North Station. He was, one gathered, drunk as a lord – as the simile was. In the 1950s, drunk as a BBC poet would have been as appropriate.

As a poet, he was, after his wake-up call to England's poetry readers, strangely silent. A second slim volume, *Europa and the Bull* (1952) had fallen flat. Exciting things were happening in English poetry (Dylan Thomas, for example). Rodgers was no longer one of those exciting things. He had waited too long since the éclat of *Awake!* and the iron was no longer hot. He was bogged down in large collaborative projects (an ambitious anatomy of Ireland with MacNeice, for example) that never went anywhere, stuck as they were in the friendly gluepot in Mortimer Street (I dropped by the pub the other night and it no longer has the faintest poetic aura, alas; the only imagery is on the fruit machine).

I had my own inklings of what had happened to Bertie: Colchester had got him, as I swore it would never get me. And, of course, the drink (or, as his DNB entry delicately puts it, 'pub talk'). That, as it happened, I was (then) quite happy to be got by. His last serious volume (locally published, at his own expense) was entitled *The Essex Roundabout*. I knew exactly what roundabout Rodgers had in mind – a bewildering double set, laid down in the late 1950s just off Station Road, as you hit the town bypass. Once on them, you just can't get off the damn things. They lock you in, like a hamster on a treadmill. An image of Colchester.

I came to know Rodgers in the dead, 1950s, ground of his career. 'Stickit' as he was as a poet and broadcaster, he was always good for local 'readings'. And, preacher that he had once been, he managed such events flamboyantly, even to a meagre audience of hearing-aided ladies and fidgety school-boys which, often enough, was his 1950s congregation. I must have heard Rodgers half a dozen times over a period of three years. I could even have been said to be a fan. I was not alone in my admiration (although it often felt like that). On receiving an honorary doctorate, late in life, the East Anglian laureate Ronald Blythe (author of the magnificent *Akenfield*), a near contemporary of mine, recalled in his acceptance speech that Rodgers, on such occasions, had opened his eyes to what poetry was and what it could do.* Who knows, I may have sat alongside Blythe. I don't recall.

At these readings, Rodgers would trot out the same stories. It was in the air, apparently, that he might at one time have been an authorised biographer of W. B. Yeats. He had done a profile on the Nobelist for a well-received radio series on Irish writers. He had, Bertie recalled, communicated with the great man, by telephone, to congratulate him on something or other. Yeats replied, 'Rodgers, I am cooking some sausages [the word was dragged out in the telling, 'sorsaaages']. You are welcome to come round and have one.' Rodgers evidently dined in, as well as dining out, on the Yeatsian banger.

At the readings Rodgers would, of course, read his own work. Usually the same poems – evidently his personal favourites. I particularly liked the poem which featured as the highpoint: 'Stormy Day'. It opens, windily:

O Look how the loops and balloons of bloom
Bobbing on long strings from the finger-ends
And knuckles of the lurching cherry-tree
Heap and hug, elbow and part, this wild day,
Like a careless carillon cavorting;*

The euphonic alliteration and assonance go on for another ten lines before reaching the delayed relief of the poem's first full stop. 'Stormy Day' was evidently composed in late 1939 and the final image is of newspapers, headlines screaming war, blown about to be 'crucified on palings'. There is, the poet warns, more than one storm warning to be issued.

Rodgers does not merely load the rift with Keatsian ore. He overloads it until the syntax dissolves into a kind of adjectival hemiplegia. He had (like Yeats) another, more declarative, voice. But it was this full-blown, all-stops-out Rodgersism which captivated me. Or, perhaps, the rich Ulster delivery.

In 1962 I found myself at a dinner party, at a fine farmhouse in the Essex countryside, with Rodgers. I was dating a girl who lived there. It was a congenial setting. There was a cask of bitter to the side of the table for soft drinkers, a bottle of whisky for the guest of honour, a fire and hours of after-dinner conversation. Rodgers claimed to remember me. Perhaps he did. His audiences were few enough and I had bought signed copies of his two volumes. Drinking steadily, he dominated the conversation. I'd just read Richard Ellmann's *Yeats: The Man and the Masks*. Injudiciously, and hoping to impress, I dropped the fact into the conversation. Bertie exploded: he was full-faced, swollen with thyroid, whisky and frustrated biographer's ire. 'What?' he asked glaringly. 'What does a Romanian *Jew* know about Yeats?'* Or an Essex twenty-three-year-old, I thought ruefully. I'd never been too sure about whether there really was a Lake Isle of Innisfree, or whether it was as imaginary as Brigadoon. I knew no more of Dublin than of Bucharest.

Was Rodgers right? Could one ever know anything about poetry, that strange inward-turned language, unless one belonged to the Masonic communities and inbred coteries which created the stuff? More importantly, people who were *there* when it was created and saw it taken, still glowing from the forge (talking about poetry, it's impossible not to catch the metaphorical contagion, I find).

By this stage of his career, Rodgers's own output had completely frozen over. That forge was very unglowing in his later years. As regards what was the most important thing in a poet's life, he was extinct; although, as his literary remains (currently resting, undisturbed by the scholar's hand, in the Northern Irish PRO) testify, he was still packing notebooks with fragments and ideas for poems. They somehow never made it to print.

In 1966 W. R. Rodgers was invited to go to Pitzer College, in Claremont, Southern California, as their writer in residence. He resided in that place but did not, apparently, write (there is one light poem about potholes in freeways – nothing else as far as I can see from this phase of his career). At least it got him off the Essex roundabouts. Freeways, in my experience, are far preferable. Nor are they notably potholed.

Claremont, this nomadic poet's last port of call, is a college town, deep down the San Gabriel valley, along what is now called 'Historic Route 66'. The Joad family had rolled along it, thirty years before. There is not, to be honest, much in Claremont that one could term historic. Cynics, in allusion to nearby Disneyland, call the town 'Collegeland'.* The main streets are all named after Ivy League institutions (Yale,

Harvard, Dartmouth, etc.). It's unthreatening (unlike nearby Pomona or Riverside, which have large immigrant communities). Claremont nestles under the vastness of Mount Baldy, whose 10,000-foot peak, the poet Leonard Cohen claims, gives him early-morning hard-ons.* What its effect on Bertie was is not recorded. Less than aphrodisiac, I suspect.

The Claremont colleges are strong on three things: science (Harvey Mudd is one of the best science schools in the country), English and divinity. It was, presumably, Rodgers's unusual background as a Presbyterian poet which suggested the appointment to Pitzer's board of trustees, on which church-people are represented. That and the fact that he was such a powerful talker, reader and – as I can testify – lecturer.

He did not last long in the sunshine, dying in 1969. His body was transported from Los Angeles to be buried at Loughgall, where he had been a preacher thirty years before, and where there were lots of stormy days to blow over his tomb.

It's not just the great poets, it's the poets who speak (or read) to you who matter.

Room at the Top

(aetat. 18)

JOHN BRAINE'S *Room at the Top* was published in March 1957. The author had had a hard time getting his novel written and as much trouble getting a publisher to accept it. Eventually, after doing the usual dispiriting rounds, it was taken on by Eyre & Spottiswoode. They expected little other than a catalogue filler and a break-even 'safe library sale'. The author had no track record and had laboriously hacked out the text over many years at the Bradford Writers' Circle – not renowned in the London publishing world as a nursery of literary genius.

To their surprise, the publishers discovered they had a runaway best-seller on their hands. The novel sold 5,000 copies in its first week and earned Braine, a thirty-five-year-old, £15-a-week librarian, £10,000 in two months.*

The provenance of my copy of *Room at the Top* is not something I should be proud of. A faint purple stamp on the inside cover declares it to be the property of 'Fincham's Lending Library: 33 North Hill, Colchester'. Fincham's was, in 1957, the last surviving 'tuppenny' library in town. It went under in the early 1960s, as its humble patrons turned, en masse, to TV and bingo.

My *Room at the Top* was stolen property – something which can, perversely, make reading matter sweeter and more positively one's own (Abbie Hoffman, author of the hippie classic *Steal this Book*, was right about that). But I was not, in this instance, the book thief. My grandmother was the guilty party. Fincham's was, in addition to being a lending library, a spiritualist coven. My grandmother was among Colchester's most renowned tassologists (tea-leaf readers). She would drop in at Fincham's, as a privileged patron, and pop any book which appealed into her basket, under the morning's shopping, and the latest copy of *The Veil*. There might be a couple of paid-for loans as cover. These would be innocuous romances: having read them, she would insert in the flyleaf her 'mark', like an illiterate Victorian 'domestic', which she was, in fact, one generation away from being, poor woman.

Some 300 of Fincham's stolen books were found scattered around her artisan's cottage at the time of her death. She'd purloined, rather than borrowed, *Room at the Top*, with the vague feeling there might be something interestingly hot between its covers. People, she sensed, were talking about the book. Perhaps she overheard something in Fincham's on the subject. Having lifted it, however, she found Braine not at all to her taste. It might be hot (in 1957 the standards were something less than scorching) but it was kitchen-sink realism. She read books to put some distance between herself and the sink.

I scooped the unwanted volume up. Waiting for it at the public library would have been interminable, and buying it beyond my means. *Room at the Top* had a profound effect on eighteen-year-old me. This is strange, on the face of it, because it is not a good novel. One could go so far as to say it is a very bad one. *Room at the Top* is clumsily plotted, ill-written and melodramatic. Educationally, I should have been above such things in 1957. I have a fragmentary diary – steam-full of adolescent angst – which records that I was stoking that angst with *Aaron's Rod* and *Eyeless in Gaza*, two of the most pointless books, it now seems to me, ever published. But undeniably Lawrence and Huxley were of a higher literary character than the Angry Young Man from Bradford.*

Why did Braine's crudity have the impact it did? The automatic answer would be 'anger', an emotion which rarely depends on refined literary expression for its maximum effect. Braine, along with Amis, Osborne and the other AYMs, condensed Britain's post-Suez moment (spring 1957)* into articulate or, at least, semi-articulate rage. They gave rabid political protest a literary voice and packaged it as a threatening message to the 'Establishment'.* Typically with the bluntest of weapons: tirades in Osborne's case, unwarranted sarcasm in Amis's and head-butting frontal assault on the 'zombies' (as he scornfully called them) in Braine's.

Eyre & Spottiswoode were well aware of the potential offensiveness of what lay between the hard covers of their unexpectedly lucrative property. They prefaced Braine's novel with a statement of comical pusillanimity: 'This book,' they informed any prospective purchaser, 'is about the violence which a young man does to himself in his struggle to rise above the world of his childhood.'

Was it hell. The power of *Room at the Top* – what propelled it into best-sellerdom – was Braine's hobnailed, fist-flailing assault. A more honest blurb would have described it as 'about how a northern oick, with nothing but energy, good looks, native intelligence, abundant testosterone and vengeful ruthlessness, could, at this point in history, do a lot of violence to his class's traditional masters'. Screwing, that is, their wives (Alice) and daughters (Susan) and dipping his hands, up to the armpits, into their gold-plated trough. Oh, and getting a Mark II Jaguar and some silk shirts into the bargain. Payback for a thousand years of servitude was what the novel angrily celebrated.

There was a lot of rebellion about in 1957, and much of it was, like Braine's, crudely expressed. At exactly the same period that *Room at the Top* was published the court martial of pilot officer D. R. Kenyon* was going forward. Rather than bomb the Egyptians, during the Suez Crisis, Kenyon had retracted the undercarriage of his Canberra bomber on the tarmac. With National Service for me just ten months away, such 'direct action' (as it was called) had a painful urgency. Would I dare to do a Kenyon and wipe my backside with the warrant summoning me to the Queen's service? Or would I enlist, dutifully, as required?

I fell into line and took the Queen's shilling, of course. And, looking back, I can see now that the power Braine's bad book had on me was more complex than a simple 'Up-yours, England!' Nor, carefully read, was it exactly 'anger' which the novel finally communicated; or 'protest' which, in the final analysis, it advocated. *Room at the Top*, as Braine's literary remains record, was at least ten years in the writing. There is a reflective passage in the novel which marks this long gestation. Joe, as we are informed, is writing retrospectively in 1957 about formative events in his life in 1947–8. One of those events was shortage. Shortage of everything. As Lampton recalls (but has half forgotten, what with the silk sheets and good whisky of his years at the top):

It's already [i.e. 1957] difficult to remember the days of rationing [i.e. 1947] but I am sure of one thing: one was always hungry ... hungry for profusion, hungry for more than enough, hungry for cream and pineapples and roast pork and chocolate.

Forget AYM. It was HYM. 'H' for 'Hungry'.*

Things had changed, amazingly, over the years Braine was writing *Room at the Top*, as is mirrored in the novel by the 'unfallen' Lampton AD 1947 and the 'fallen' Lampton AD 1957. English society had moved from Austerity to Affluence.* It too might have been said to have fallen, over that decade, from innocence, what with chocolate and roast pork every day.

Affluence was official. On 20 July 1957, as *Room at the Top* was still flying off W. H. Smith's shelves, Harold Macmillan delivered his 'You've never had it so good' speech, at a Tory rally in Bedford. 'Go around the country,' the amiable old Whig instructed, with that famous finger-pointing: 'go to the industrial towns, go to the farms and you will see a state of prosperity such as we have never had in my lifetime – nor indeed in the history of this country.'*

And who did we have to thank for these good times – charcoal-grey suits (smartly drainpiped), floral ties, yellow socks, chukka boots, good liquor, rock and roll, thirty-six-inch waistlines and the prospect, not too far off, of a TR2 sports car, or even a TR3?* Not the unions, not the Labour Party, not even the 'wealth creators'.

The good times, as Supermac complacently reminded the suddenly affluent nation, were the gift of the Establishment. People like him. Tweedy, blue-blooded upper-class fellows, who belonged to the best London clubs, shot pheasants and had a palate for the finer wines.

How could the lower classes snap 'angrily' at the hand that fed one these 'sweeteners of our existence' (as Dr Johnson called them)? Macmillan's favourite author, as he often proclaimed, was Anthony Trollope. And Macmillan's favourite character was Plantagenet Palliser – MP, Cabinet minister, prime minister and, finally, Duke of Omnium: ruler of every-thing.* Palliser is a Whig. A well-meaning, One-Nation Tory (as Trollope himself was 'an advanced conservative liberal'). 'Planty Pall', one understood, was the literary equivalent of Harold Macmillan. An upper-class do-gooder, determined that his people should 'have it good'. An unrocked boat and a Tory government were what would get one there. Socialism led back to the ration book and Muscovite austerity.

So what, in the event, actually happened in the face of all that raging Jimmy Porterism and Joe Lamptonism? Rebellion remained a gesture: satisfying, but as historically inconse-quential as a furtive V-sign outside No. 10 Downing Street. No barricades, no stones, no bombs. Not even a protest vote for Labour. Buoyed up by the country's feel-good factor, Macmillan stayed in power for five more years, until the Profumo scandal brought him down in 1963. Not Anger, not Austerity, but *Affluence* was the trump card in 1957. Macmillan played it.

At the end of *Room at the Top*, Joe is in a taxi, whisking him off to the Bradford equivalent of *La Dolce Vita*,* while he blubs, his head on a friendly woman's bosom, about how terribly awful he feels. But is Joe going to return to his roots? Is he hell. He's on his way to the top.

What *Room at the Top* articulated, very effectively, for all its narrative crudity, was the terms of a sellout. A sellout which all my generation bought into. We had been, we knew, more authentic, more *real* in 1947. But did we want authenticity if it meant 'utility' clothes, fuel cuts, and bread and dripping? Drive on, taxi. Affluence next stop.

Braine's novel had a secondary effect on me which seems superficial now, but was very important to me then. By reference to *Room at the Top*, I can date, precisely, the moment at which I stopped using hair cream (which, up to that point, I had slathered on by the pot-full in homage to the 'Brylcreem Boy', Dennis Compton – I despised Silvikrin and that dourly Yorkshire run-machine Len Hutton*).

What rendered my post-March 1957 cranium forever unpomaded was the scene in the novel where the upper-class Alice Aisgill runs her fingers through working-class Joe's locks with the instruction to lose the hair oil. 'Too Palais de Danse, darling,' she drawls.

Remember that, Sutherland, I thought. You'll never get a sophisticated lady with gunk dripping like axle grease from your bonce. And better give up the Palais, as well (not that there was one in Colchester, but the Corn Exchange, a roller-skating rink during the week, doubled as a dance hall at weekends).

An element in the best-sellingness of *Room at the Top* was its usefulness as a manual for all those twenty-something grammar-school boys, emancipated by the 1944 Butler Education Act, who were angry as hell and weren't going to take it any more. And really confused by what not taking it any more meant. And what hairstyle was in order to make the point about anger.

If Elvis turned Revolt into Style, *Room at the Top* (for me, at least) turned Anger into Lifestyle. *Aaron's Rod* could never have done that.

XXVI

The Uses of Literacy

(aetat. 18)

THE GRAMMAR SCHOOL in which I was impounded for seven ungrateful years had a well-stocked library. I first read Thackeray's *Book of Snobs*★ there, over a succession of 'reading periods': blissful hours in which the pupil could select any book from the shelves. I was interested in snobbery, having been at the cutting edge of it – although the great snobographer's 1840s satire was well above my head in the 1950s. But I liked the turns of phrase describing, for example, Marrowfat's quixotic (and ineffably vulgar) attempts to eat garden peas with his table knife. I myself was constantly bullied, in the name of 'good manners', to waste time crunching them on to the tines of my fork.

A succession of English teachers deposited in the library works which had influenced them as undergraduates: names such as C. S. Lewis, Lord David Cecil, 'Q', A. C. Bradley, Dover Wilson were prominent, breathing an Oxbridge aroma of connoisseurship over the adjoining rows of high literature. The headmaster had purchased a fine fireplace from a local mansion which was being destroyed.* The Old Colcestrians had kicked in for a stained-glass window. There was a feel of Rugby Chapel, as immortalised by Matthew Arnold, about the place.* I saw the same library, a few months ago. It was a shell of its old self. Like the Colchester town public library, the range of literature on its shelves in 2007 would have been outmatched by any Oxfam shop. All the energy of the clever young minds once concentrated there had been diverted to the adjoining computer cluster. It thrummed away like a beehive in autumn. The library was a mortuary by comparison.

The school library was not the only book-supply system. The sixth-form common room in the late 1950s ran a Free-masonic circulating library of more or less under-the-shelf or edgy items. It was there, over the Nescafé, that a friend, about to go up to the LSE and more on the ball than most, passed on to eighteen-year-old me a hardback copy of Richard Hoggart's *The Uses of Literacy*.* The book had been published, and multiply reprinted, in 1957. Hoggart, as the flyleaf testified, had produced that rarest of things: a work of literary criticism which was a best-seller. Assuming, that is, *The Uses of Literacy* was literary criticism. Definition of that book has always been slippery. My two most used facilities, the London Library and UCL, categorise it as, respectively, 'Social Science' and 'History'. It could as well be shelved as autobiography, since main parts of the book are quarried, unprocessed, from Hoggart's own life experience.

Wherever it belonged according to Mr Dewey's decimal system, I couldn't tune in, at this latent stage of my intellec-tual life, to Hoggart's rabid mix of methodee-working-class-ILP-sub-Leavisite-WEA entirely *bloody* high-mindedness. Nor would I be able to do so until taught by the man himself, a few years later, at university. Then I could tune in, but not sing along. Even if he wanted me in his choir; which he didn't.

But I could take on board Hoggart's main point: that reading by itself wasn't enough. In fact, the printed word, taken in the wrong concoctions, could make populations more docile and more readily tyrannised. 'The one thing necessary' (there was a strong vein of Matthew Arnold in Hoggart's book) was *critical* reading. Reading which carved off the unworthy stuff, to be thrown away like so much cheese rind. That was the route to the only intellectual liberty worth having. One could, easily enough, trace Hoggartism back to Puritans like John Bunyan, who spent most of his life in Bedford Jail rather than modify his idiosyncratic reading of his one book, the Geneva Bible.* With Hoggart, it was D. H. Lawrence.*

The Uses of Literacy left me profoundly confused and, in ways I couldn't quite articulate, furious. It was hard to put one's finger on it, but Hoggart, I apprehended, wasn't writing *for* me, he was writing *against* me and what I represented (not that I'd consciously chosen to represent anything). For him, I was on the other side of a fence I would never be able to cross.

Hoggart is strikingly good at pen-portraiture. Two images in *The Uses of Literacy* – the 'Juke Box Boy' and the 'Scholarship Boy' – stared back at me like reflections in an unflattering mirror. Both boys are losers. The first, JBB, is anatomised in the section Hoggart labels 'The Newer Mass Art: Sex in Shiny Packets'. Juke-box boys, Hoggart explained:

> spend their evening listening in harshly-lighted milk-bars to the 'nickelodeons' ... I have in mind the kind of milk-bar – there is one in almost every northern

town with more than, say, fifteen thousand inhabitants – which has become the regular evening rendezvous for some of the young men. Girls go to some, but most of the customers are boys aged between fifteen and twenty, with drape suits, picture ties, and an American slouch. Most of them cannot afford a succession of milk shakes, and make cups of tea serve for an hour or two whilst – and this is their main reason for coming – they put copper after copper into the mechanical record player ... some of the tunes are catchy; all have been doctored for presentation so that they have the kind of beat which is currently popular; much use is made of the 'hollow cosmos' effect which echo-chamber recording gives ... The young men waggle one shoulder or stare, as desperately as Humphrey Bogart, across the tubular chairs.

The milk bars which so offended Hoggart were pallid, cis-Atlantic versions of the American drugstore soda-fountain (lovely name). 'Chemist's Pop-Shop' would not have worked, even in Wigan. Milk bars were a less permanent, and certainly a less significant, phenomenon than Hoggart and other cultural alarmists of the late 1950s imagined them to be; of no more danger to the soul than the wholly British 'transport caff' (where the despised juke box, with its hollow cosmos, continued to find a home). Milk bars were, very quickly, replaced by coffee bars, with their wheezy Gaggias, and an entirely different – pseudo-cosmopolitan rather than wannabe American – atmosphere. It wasn't drape jackets, but chukka boots, Viyella shirts, cavalry twill trousers, houndstooth jackets. They too had their falsities, but of a different kind. Lite muzak, not juke boxes, soothed the ears as one sipped exotic Italian brews.

Coming up, some years over the horizon, were the

ice-cream parlours (which would make the 'shake' fashionable again). The milky sinks of iniquity which so offended Hoggart, in which depraved 'boys' fermented their low, Americanised, cultural tastes, only flourished for a year or two, before passing into commercial oblivion. Many readers of Anthony Burgess's A Clockwork Orange, composed in 1959, may have wondered why Alex and his teenaged druggie droogs hang out in the Korova Milkbar.*

Burgess's novel remains the institution's lasting monument. I, personally, am rather nostalgic for them. I used, aged fourteen, to hang out in a milk bar alongside Colchester's bus station. I wasn't, in most ways, the juke-box boy that Hoggart describes. But the 'American slouch' hit home, painfully. I would indeed, at the time, hood my eyes, hunch my shoulders and try to look like something very much not myself. And I certainly favoured shoulder pads on the single 'sports jacket' in my wardrobe. But the desired image was not Bogart. He died of lung cancer in the same year The Uses of Literacy was published, 1957. Humpty's last, rather gallant performance was in the boxing melodrama (scripted by Budd Schulberg) The Harder They Fall (1956).* Bogart, who plays a corrupt but finally crusading journalist, had scarcely enough puff left in his ravaged lungs to get through more than a grunt and a monosyllable: deathbed grey showed through his make-up. No teenager, even in the most godforsaken northern town of 15,000 inhabitants, would have taken that sixty-year-old wheezing wreck as his role model. And certainly not with Jimmy Dean in glorious Technicolor there for the aping.

Did Hoggart go to the movies? And if he didn't, should one not shun those places of moral corruption oneself? It was perplexing. And was Hoggart right – was America the siren against whom one should stop one's ears? I was more of Norman Mailer's grandiloquent view: 'America is a hurricane, and the only people who do not hear the sound are incredibly stupid and smug.' I heard the mighty wind and loved its roar. But did destruction lie that way?

There was another, quite opposite portrait in *The Uses of Literacy*, which – painfully – I could have put in my attic of shame alongside JBB. This second portrait appears in the final, and most argumentative, pages of Hoggart's book, entitled 'Scholarship Boy'. These are lads plucked from their rich, organic, working-class soil, by having passed the 11+ (the 'scholarship', as the equivalent exam was called before the 1944 Butler Act),* only to find themselves at grammar school, in a machine which comprehensively uproots them from their background as it educates them. The Scholarship Boy has no more chance of 'growing' intellectually thereafter than a cut daffodil. His life, becomes a sham. He

> discovers a technique of apparent learning, of the acquiring of facts rather than the handling and use of facts. He learns how to receive a purely literate education, one using only a small part of the personality and challenging only a limited area of his being. He begins to see life as a ladder, as a permanent examination with some praise and some further exhortation at each stage. He becomes an expert imbiber and doler out; his competence will vary, but will rarely be accompanied by genuine enthusiasms. He rarely feels the reality of knowledge, of other men's thoughts and imaginings, on his own pulses; he rarely discovers an author for himself, and on his own.

I suppose like many grammar-school boys in the late 1950s reading that passage I wondered, 'How does he know?' How

does he know *me*, John Sutherland, personally, that is, so intimately? Nor is there any redeeming sense of confession here.
Hoggart was, palpably, *not* talking about Richard Hoggart.
He was authentic; one of the culturally saved. He was talking
about me. The imbiber and doler out; as inauthentic as a
plug nickel (whatever that might be); rejected by the great
nickelodeon of life. The Great Pretender. 'Oh yes!' – as the
Platters' 1957 hit put it:* a recording that made full use of
what Hoggart, laughably, calls 'the hollow cosmos effect'. No
cosmos hollower than mine, apparently.

I had the odd experience of being taught by Hoggart, a few
years later, when he was briefly a senior lecturer at Leicester
University. I couldn't help but feel, desperately eager as I
was to impress him, that he was less than impressed by me,
professionally courteous as his demeanour always was. He
had my number. I had the satisfaction, though, of being told
by the head of sociology there that they had opposed his
promotion to professor – on the grounds that he overpopu-
larised their subject. Or perhaps they, too, like the librarians
and the Dewey Decimal System, simply couldn't classify him.
It wasn't until he defined a wholly new discipline, 'Cultural
Studies', at Birmingham, that Hoggart's career took off,
meteorically.

My third book, *Fiction and the Fiction Industry* (an oblique
homage to *The Uses of Literacy*, in one of its aspects) was read
by him for publication. He condemned it, with the remark (as
reported to me by my editor) that 'UCL smart-aleckiness had
never been to his taste'. The University of London Press had
to find other, friendlier, readers before it could get my type-
script into print. A later effort, *Bestsellers* (again something of
an offshoot from *The Uses of Literacy*), was reviewed, harshly,
by Hoggart in the *Listener*, with the dismissive remark that

the book was like a glossy plastic pack of disposable razors. Sharp, perhaps; but worth spending time on? No. Read, toss, forget and move on to something more worthwhile.

Half smart-aleck, half disposable Bic. It was a cruel verdict. I was in the odd situation of having idolised (the word is not excessive) a critic for whom I was, in a sense, the enemy; and always would be. It had an odd effect on me. It did not lead me to mend my ways. That milk was hopelessly spilt. It made me, if anything, more wayward. Damn it, I'll slouch, modo Americano, if I feel like it. And I did.

The Tenement Kid

(aetat. 19)

ONE OF THE CULTURAL THREATS Hoggart anathe-matises in his 'Sex in Shiny Packets' section is what he calls 'Sex and Violence Novels'. This pulpy poison comes in for his unforgiving lash:

> The authors are usually American, or pseudo-American, after the manner of the American shirt-shops in the Charing Cross Road [I confess, this simile flummoxed me in 1957, and still does]. Most of them have 'tough names' with forenames in the style of Hank, Al, Brad and Butch ... these are novels of violent sex, in which sex seems to be regarded as thrilling only when it is sadistic. There must be violence all the time: between the men, prolonged arm-twistings, razor-slashings, long-drawn-out beatings with rubber tubes ... When man meets woman the air is heavy with violence, with drug-inspired moans, with embraces ending in bloody bites on both sides.

When Hoggart submitted his manuscript to Chatto it was,

apparently, lavishly illustrated with the kind of material he anatomises above. The publishers' lawyer pointed out that even writing as loathsome as this is protected by the law. The legal expert went so far as to venture the opinion that *The Uses of Literacy* 'was the most dangerous book he'd ever read for libel purposes'. Hoggart was instructed that he would have either to drop the extensive quotations, or, if he was up to it, to invent the 'Sex and Violence' stuff himself. He would need, that is, for the purpose of his attack, to transform himself into 'Butch' Hoggart – pulp hack. It was like Lord Longford doing a pole dance, full-on naked, to alert the nation to the dangers of pornography.

The following is one of the 'Hank Hoggart' pastiches, demonstrating the rhetoric of violence:

> Suddenly Fatsy brought his knee hard up into Herb's groin. Herb's face came down sharp and Fatsy met it with his ham-like fist. The knucks splintered the bone and made blood and flesh squelch like a burst pomegranate. Herb fell back to the tiled floor, retching teeth. He was bubbling gently as he lay there, so Fatsy gave him one in the belly with his steel-shod shoe. Then – just for luck – Fatsy ground his foot straight on to the squelchy mess that useter be Herb's face.

It's not at all bad. One can't help feeling Hoggart might have had a future in the pulpy literary underworld, had he been so inclined. How close it is to the real thing can be judged by comparing the above to a passage in a genuine sex and violence novel, *The Tenement Kid*, by Karl Edd (a mugging has just taken place in the narrative, and the utterly amoral hero is coolly bragging about his expertise in such things):

After blowing coolly on my knuckles I knocked the bridge right out of his mouth, splattering his lips to mush. They looked like frozen strawberries when they're starting to thaw out. I frisked the guy. His wallet had some bills and change, and a card that said he was an automobile salesman. I kicked him in the stomach hard. Some sort of greenish stuff started to come out of the corner of his mouth. Dirt from the garage floor started to float in it ...

Strawberries, pomegranates – what's the difference?

When asked why he sold so many copies of his ultra-hard-boiled Mike Hammer books (he was the best-selling novelist in the world in the late 1940s), Mickey Spillane blandly replied, 'People like them.'* My problem was not that I liked them, exactly, but that I found them extremely interesting. And, for what they were, extremely readable.

Hoggart's blast against the sex and violence novel was clearly inspired by George Orwell's 'Raffles and Miss Blandish' essay, published in 1944.* In it, Orwell diagnosed the disease which had infected the British reading public's taste over the last twenty years like some surgically masked medical examiner looking at a decomposed cadaver.

Once, Orwell nostalgically sighed, in the not so distant past, the British reading public had relished the exploits of the 'amateur cracksman' – invented by E. W. Hornung. Raffles and his sidekick, Bunny, were, like their author (Uppingham School), 'gentlemen'. Raffles was public-school-educated, handsome (with a 'strong, unscrupulous mouth') and a superb athlete who plays cricket for the Gentlemen of England against the 'Players' as 'the very finest slow bowler of the decade' (that decade being the 1890s). Off the pitch, he and Bunny pull off daring cat burglaries – typically snatching the tiaras and necklaces of rich women of the hero's own class. In the last episode, in 1901, the genteel crook is seen giving his life for queen and country in the war against the Boers.

In the *Strand Magazine*,* where he shared top billing with Sherlock Holmes, Raffles was vastly popular. Switch to the end of the 1930s. Or, as Orwell graphically puts it, 'take a header into the cesspool'. Propelled by the corrosive influence of American gangster movies (such power was certainly dangerous), another kind of crime novel had risen into best-selling popularity, displacing Raffles entirely.

The epitome of this vile new genre was, for Orwell, *No Orchids for Miss Blandish*, by James Hadley Chase.* English by upbringing and residence, Chase was a 'pseudo-American' (his taste in shirts is not recorded; doubtless he acquired them in Charing Cross Road). The story in *No Orchids* is one of kidnapping, sadistic rape and even more sadistic violence – the rape and violence coming along, with increments and ingenious variations, every few pages. Chase was, Orwell stresses, with some chauvinistic indignation, fully as English as Hornung, and a cultural traitor to his nationality. Chase was also highly educated, as Orwell clearly did not know, and was currently (1944) serving as a pilot in the RAF. He would leave the service a squadron leader. Like Raffles, he put his life on the line for king and country. Orwell, as I say, did not know this. Or care to know it.

True, Chase had never even been to the country where his best-sellers were set, and for *No Orchids* he had worked from slang dictionaries and dialogue picked up (not very perfectly) in the cinema. He had taken to writing gangster novels in the depressed 1930s, to keep the wolf from the door. The alternative was encyclopedias or panhandling. Like Graham Greene (a friend in later life), he found he rather enjoyed writing 'entertainments' for the masses. He would go on to turn out over eighty of the things and retire, rich, to Switzerland.

Had he known something of Chase's background, it might have mitigated Orwell's disgust and encouraged a more subtle analysis. As it was, so tightly does he hold his nose that the contempt he feels for the author of No Orchids can hardly get through. 'It should be noticed,' Orwell writes:

> That No Orchids for Miss Blandish is not in the ordinary sense pornography ... The real highspots of the book are cruelties committed by men upon other men: above all, the third-degreeing of the gangster, Eddie Schultz, who is lashed into a chair and flogged on the windpipe with truncheons ... In another of Mr Chase's books, He Won't Need it Now, the hero, who is intended to be sympathetic and perhaps even a noble character, is described as stamping on somebody's face, and then having crushed the man's mouth in, grinding his heel round and round in it.

No one reading this and knowing Orwell's work will miss the echo in Nineteen Eighty-Four, where O'Brien is torturing Winston, and instructing him in the realities of world history:

> 'If you want a picture of the future, imagine a boot stamping on a human face – for ever. ... And remember that it is for ever. The face will always be there to be stamped upon. The heretic, the enemy of society, will always be there, so that he can be defeated and humiliated over again.'

Orwell records two things as significant. The first is that

A bad book

there is a congruence of the taste for 'Mr' Chase's kind of fiction and the rise of fascism in the 1930s. No Orchids is a plague spot, or bubo: it is the outer symptom of the lethal totalitarian disorder afflicting the European body politic. Secondly, No Orchids is, genetically, a slavishly pseudo- (we would say 'wannabe-') American novel. Another bubo. 'The career of Mr Chase shows,' Orwell gravely tells us, 'how deep the American influence has already gone.' And, he implies, how dangerously deep. To the vital organs, perhaps. Will the patient recover? Can England be England again? The prognosis is not good.

For Hoggart, the indiscriminate popularity of Yank fiction such as Don't Tempt Me, Hotsy (he was obliged to invent his titles as well – this is one of the less convincing) pointed inexorably in the direction of what he called 'shiny barbarism': cultural fascism. For Orwell, No Orchids pointed to political fascism. And the way stage, in both dire signpostings, was America.

I could never bring myself to feel that harshly about America, even though (like Orwell, as it happened, and I suspect Hoggart in the early 1950s) I had never (yet) crossed the Atlantic. I was like the sisters at the end of Chekhov's play – looking forlornly towards Moscow.

Even if one was resolutely English, why couldn't one read both Raffles and James Hadley Chase? Orwell and Hoggart clearly read them both. And both of them emerged from the 'cesspool' with interesting (if to my mind entirely wrong-headed) things to say. They seemed, unfairly, to place themselves in the same position as those 'authorities' who had themselves read (for inspection purposes, of course) Lady Chatterley's Lover, then denied my right to read it on the grounds that it would 'deprave and corrupt me'. But not, apparently, them.

The issue was crystallised for me by a novel of an ephemerality so complete that, in terms of literature, it might just as well never have happened. Namely *The Tenement Kid*. It was, as the earlier quotation from it confirms, a 'Yank' novel of the kind Orwell and Hoggart saw as so much cultural pus.

Karl Edd's novel tells the story of a young thug, brought up in the high-rise slumland of Cleveland. The book was merchandised in 1959 as a fifty-cent, drugstore paperback 'original', published by the Newsstand Library. As the endpages record, other titles under the imprint available to the newsstand browser in 1959 included:

Fear of Incest: by March Hastings; 'She was afraid of her brother's love. A tense and dramatic novel – inflamed, passionate!'

She had to be Loved: by Edward Culver; 'Imagine your mistress a nymphomaniac who blackmails her way into your bed! A fast-paced and intriguing novel.'

The Tenement Kid, in addition to regular doses of splattering violence, contains sex scenes, and tough sex talk – such as the following, reproduced as cheese-on-the-trap on the back cover (the young hero is anticipating his first sex, on release from the state reformatory):

... When I thought of Gertie's big, plump breasts – even though they did get more business than a corner drug store – I got real shook up. I figured she'd be the only broad around that ever got it with a doorknob in her hand...

It's important to register (as neither Orwell nor Hoggart

care to) the different commercial origin of the mass-market paperback in the UK and the US – those machineries which produced on one side of the Atlantic that elegant, green-backed Penguin Crime edition of Chandler's *Trouble is My Business* and on the other the radioactively garish *Fear of Incest*.

Allen Lane launched his Penguin imprint in 1935.* After the briefest of flirtations with Woolworths, Lane's stylish reprints established themselves in conventional bookshop outlets, as paperbacks that sold like hardbacks. For an author like Raymond Chandler to be 'Penguined' was a mark of high merit. Lane eschewed pictorial covers for much of his long career as Britain's leading paperback publisher. He thought them vulgar. And American – which was the same thing.

In America, the mass-market paperback pioneer was Robert de Graff.* His strategy was less to embed his product in the traditional bookstore than to circumvent that outlet entirely. De Graff's twenty-five-cent 'Pocket Books' (launched the same year as Lane's Penguins) were, essentially, 'drugstore' paperbacks. They had eye-grabbing illustrated covers, news-print-quality paper (barely one notch up from the Bronco toilet roll*) and, typically, slapdash typography. They were designed to sell less like books than short life magazines. 'Spicy' magazines (as Hoggart labelled them) principally.

The 'spiciness' of Edd's narrative is prominent on the front-cover blurb: 'Unwatched and unwanted, kids spawned from drunken orgies throng the streets. They live by their own code, respect only the law of the knife and the knuckle, and the whore is their emblem of womanhood ...'

I came across *The Tenement Kid* accidentally, in early 1960. It, in a sense, came across me, as has been the case with many of the books which have meant something in my ramshackle reading career.

the

the **tenement kid**

50¢

N
A
L

**by
karl edd**

Unwatched and unwanted, kids
spawned from drunken orgies throng
the streets. They live by their own code,
respect only the law of the knife and the
knuckle, and the whore is their emblem
of womanhood. . . .

Another bad book

I had, at the time, a room over a busy garage. All day long there would be the sounds of metal upon metal, engines revving, men bawling out whatever was the latest hit song. A copy of Karl Edd's paperback (an American original, brought in by who knows whom, but most likely from the nearby American airbase) had passed from hand to hand among the fitters as an agreeably dirty book for men whose work was dirty and whose literary sensibilities scarcely cleaner. Having served its multiple purposes, it was left around in the shop. I picked it up, wiped the grease off it, and – as Orwell would say – took a header into Karl Edd's cesspool.

In fact, the book is considerably more interesting than its tawdry cover illustration conveys. The narrative is halfway between Holden Caulfield (Edd had obviously read *Catcher in the Rye* and plays with the hero's litmus-paper term, 'phony', throughout*) and Hubert Selby Jr's *Last Exit to Brooklyn* (a shocker still to come).

The Tenement Kid is narrated autobiographically, like Salinger's book. It covers the childhood and adolescent years of Ronnie – a clever and wholly feral young hood. At the end of the novel, he is leaving the reformatory – about to join Big Nick's gang, and embark on a professional life of crime. As the quotations above confirm, *Tenement Kid* fits the template which Orwell and Hoggart lay down, in their anatomy of the sex 'n' violence novel. But, as is often the case with such works, read carefully and there is something interesting beneath.

Take, for example, a late scene in which the hero has some conversation with Fred, a 'flower' (i.e. pansy) in Juvenile Hall. How's it going? Ronnie asks.

> Fred, like a lot of those flowers, recited some fancy poetry by a guy by the name of Oscar Wilde or something like

that, and it went on about how it was to be lonesome in prison or something. Anyhow, Fred told me then how this Wilde was a hero or something because he'd served time for bein' a homo, and I suppose that's why a lot of these literary characters go fruity over his poems. I don't know.

This guy Fred, he was a character, for sure. Besides this character Wilde, he said something about Thomas Mann and something he wrote, and a guy called something like Plato, and anyhow it was all about how it's OK to be a homo, and maybe grand. I had Fred figured now. His trouble was he read too much. Maybe it wasn't the reading, I figured, but it was *what* he read. Any guy reads trash like that'll be affected, I figure.

'Trash', that is, like *The Ballad of Reading Gaol*, *Death in Venice* and *The Symposium* (all of which, like Fred, I'd read by 1959; in somewhat more comfortable conditions). The author, we apprehend, is laughing at any highbrow taking a prurient tourist's look at his depraved novel. Lurking round every corner of *The Tenement Kid* is a literary in-joke, an allusion, a sly echo, or putdown to the moralistic reader. Edd clearly anticipated readers, like himself (or myself), who – whatever they were doing with his book – prided themselves, in a pharisaical way, as being 'better read' than its other readers.

The Tenement Kid, like 'Red Wind', belongs to the category of tough crime writing originated by Hemingway's 'The Killers', the short story, first published in 1928, which gave birth to 'hard-boiled' crime fiction. Arguably, the genre trickled down from high literature. It did not bubble up, like some mephitic underground sewage from a broken pipe. The genre was brought to its highest pitch in *Black Mask*⋆ magazine in the late 1930s and its essence refined into 'noir' by French theorists of the 1940s and 1950s (commentators much more tolerant of things American – whether jazz, Negroes or pulp fiction – than their British counterparts).

One of the reasons for paying sex and violence novels more attention than Hoggart would allow one was the fact that (as with Hadley Chase) there were often interesting backgrounds to them. The 'March Hastings' novel *Fear of Incest* (see above), which nestled alongside *The Tenement Kid*, was (it was revealed, years later) actually written by Sally M. Singer* – now a highly respected figure in the history of lesbian fiction. Ms Singer – university-educated (she at one point hoped to be a neurosurgeon) – could only smuggle in the gay themes that interested her via the sewers of literature. And often, by transgendering her characters. S&M books such as those she wrote for Newsstand were, she claimed in June 2007, 'yellow bricks in Stonewall'.

Who, then, was Karl Edd – this hacker out of pulp, who was also, clearly, not entirely what his trashy covers implied? He was known to the authorities as a dubious practitioner. A 1960 US Mails memorandum lists 'Edd, K.' as a purveyor of pornography. *The Tenement Kid* obviously did well, commercially. Edd followed it up with *Tenement Tramp* – the female of the species – in 1961. This is a very rare volume in present-day used-book markets. It did not, apparently, sell well enough to encourage him to continue along this track. Or perhaps he just got tired of the game.

Pulp was not, as far as one can make out, Edd's main career. Library and second-hand catalogues identify him as the editor and founder in the mid-1960s of the *Mustang Review* (horses, not Ford motor cars were alluded to in the title), which ran for a few years. His first published book under the name Karl Edd would seem to have been *A Printer's Prayer*, in

1965. He and his wife, Joy Edd, may have been in the trade. There are references to fine editions produced by them. There is a clutch of books – of a wildly various kind – identified as being by Karl Edd in the early 1970s: *The Ballad of Helen Smythe Jones* (1970), *Billy the Kid* (1970) and *Love is a Moment of Grace* (1971). He did a biographical study of the African-American Booker T. Washington – offprinted, apparently, from the *Mustang Review*, as were others of his titles.

The Tenement Kid suggests Edd (his own name, it would seem – much as it fits Hoggart's 'Hank, Butch, Al' sneer) was brought up in Cleveland, Ohio. There are a couple of precise topographical references and some of his literary remains are currently deposited at the University of Ohio. Edd seems to have been resident, for many years, in Denver. Here it was that he published his *Mustang Review*, whose contents are described as having a 'Western and Northwestern emphasis', featuring 'Poems, folklore (with resident folklorist, Fred Red Cloud), and ruminations'. A long way from Gertie getting it with her hand on the doorknob. He co-edited the magazine with Irene Wilkins, about whom nothing is known. Copies are very rare and go for a lot of money in the collectors' market.

The author of *The Tenement Kid*, it would seem, wrote his sex and violence product on a casual basis, whether to raise some cash, to subsidise more important things or, possibly, out of sheer mischief.

The next time I'm in Ohio, I'll investigate further.

Absolute Beginners

(aetat. 20)

BY 1959 I had crossed a barrier. I was no longer a teenager. But that barrier was a mile high and a mile broad at the time. There was always acute adult nervousness as to what was happening on the teenage side. See, for example, the warning message, masquerading as blurb, to MacGibbon & Kee's 1959 first edition of Colin MacInnes's *Absolute Beginners:**

A spectre has arisen in our cities – the spectre of lawless, carefree youth. Bemused parents, restless citizens, outraged authority – all show distress at the sight of young people (unnaturally clean and appearance-aware) visibly enjoying their own company.

In *Absolute Beginners* Colin MacInnes has gone right inside the 'teenage' world – of coffee bars, motor-scooters, casual and alarming elegance – and race riots. Yet his hero is neither crazy nor mixed up; a saner, brighter and more resourceful youth it would be hard to find, but he's way out from being hobbled by fossilized good form. Though the language is jazz and the mood very hip, this

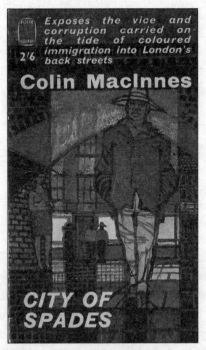

The image of black England, 1961

is the truest, shrewdest and kindest eye that has looked over the new world made by the 'kids' themselves – right slap in the middle of the enemy.

What idiot wrote this is not recorded. But it is clear he was no teenaged idiot. Nor, as it happened, was the kind-eyed MacInnes in the first flush of youth. He was forty-five years old in 1959; no absolute beginner.

I read *Absolute Beginners*, in a couple of sittings, in the year of its publication, riding up and back, second class, between Colchester and London on the train. A day return was dirt cheap and allowed one an hours-long cruise up and down the record and book shops around Shaftesbury Avenue. It was highly appropriate, since *Absolute Beginners* is the second in MacInnes's 'London trilogy'. I've always enjoyed reading cabined in trains or (later on in life) planes. I'll take books with me into my coffin. Contemporary teenagers, I have read, sometimes ask for their mobile phones to accompany them into eternity. I may take a book.

The opening scene in *Absolute Beginners* introduces MacInnes's hero-narrator. He is unnamed (i.e. 'everyteen-ager'), a freelance photographer, with remunerative lines in fashion and pornography. Converging styles, we understand. He is on the age cusp, between nineteen and twenty. He converses, chippily, on the subject with 'the Wiz', over a smoked-salmon sandwich and ice coffee (it is June) in the roof café whose 'glass garden' they favour (I think it must be Simpson's, in Piccadilly). So much for Richard Hoggart's seedy milk bars. They are meditating, portentously, on the record of the day, thirteen-year-old Laurie London's April 1958 no. 1 hit, 'He's Got the Whole Wide World in His Hands'.*

'Laurie L.,' I said, ' 's a sign of decadence. This teenage thing is getting out of hand.'

The Wiz looked wise, like the middle feller of the three old monkeys.

'It's not the tax-payers,' he said, 'who are responsible. It's the kids themselves, for buying the EPs these elderly sordids bribe the teenage nightingales to wax.'

'No doubt,' I said, for I know better than ever to argue with the Wizard, or with anyone else who gets his kicks from an idea.

Mr Wiz continued, masticating his salmon sandwich for anyone to see. 'It's been a two-way twist, this teenage party. Exploitation of the kiddos by the conscripts, and exploitation of themselves by the crafty little absolute beginners. The net result? Teenager's become dirty word or, at any rate, a square one.'

I smiled at Mr W. 'Well, take it easy, son,' I said, 'because a sixteen year old sperm like you has got a lot of teenage living still to do. As for me, eighteen summers, rising nineteen, I'll very soon be out there among the oldies.'

I had been eighteen summers, rising nineteen not that long ago. And to my ear, this dialect was double-distilled tosh. Bill and Ben, the flowerpot men, were closer to the actual speech of teenagers than what MacInnes hopefully invents here, and throughout his novel.

The fabricated teenage idiom of *Absolute Beginners* made no impression on me at all other than haughty disdain for the middle-aged man who created it. And wonder that anyone could seriously publish such outlandish gibberish. There was, however, another aspect of the book which did make a powerful impression: namely its treatment of race.

In 1963 the American Jewish critic Norman Podhoretz, following a stand-up row with James Baldwin,* wrote a hugely influential essay for *Commentary* entitled 'My Negro Problem – and Ours'.* Podhoretz recalls that as a child ('my head was full of movies and English novels') growing up in New York, he had been afraid of Negroes, and 'hated them'. Correcting that hatred was a long process. But it was necessary to start, honestly, from the ground up: not from skin-deep liberal attitudes, but from the fear and prejudice of an ethnic 'enemy', deep-rooted in childhood.

I too had a Negro problem, as did everyone in my age group and social background. Unlike Podhoretz, whose Jewish tenement life was cheek by jowl, often violently so, with Negro areas of the city, I was not familiar with them – or not until late teenage life. I was, in that sense, a first genera- tion. I remember my stepfather, a man of brutal simple- mindedness, reminiscing about the first 'darky' he'd ever seen. It was at a travelling summer fair. Among the various raree shows (bearded woman, mermaid, midgets, etc.) there was 'the world's strongest man' – an African. 'We all paid our penny and went in,' my stepfather recalled, 'not because we wanted to see him lift those fake wooden barbells, but because we'd never seen a real Nigger before.' This must have been the early 1920s. But that generation was still there, wholly unregenerate in its views on race, in the 1950s. And the prejudice was passed on – or, at least, freely ventilated. It was then inflamed with the state-encouraged immigration from the West Indies in that decade.

I had two solutions to my own Negro problem. One, and the easiest, was unthinking prejudice of my stepfather's kind. The other was jazz. I loved the music and collected it. But the standoff between the British and American musicians' unions meant that, until 1956, no American jazz artist could perform in the UK. In that year a 'band for band' agreement was signed (what American aficionado, I forlornly wondered, would want Ted Heath in return for Lionel Hampton*?). I knew the sounds of black jazz, intimately. I had listened to thousands of hours of it. I had seen photographs, films even. But I knew no black jazz in the flesh. I was, in a sense, like my stepfather in the fairground. (The first black performer I saw was Louis Armstrong: he did his vaudeville act, rather than his hot-five stuff. It was deeply depressing.)

Absolute Beginners, hopelessly lame as its depiction of teenage culture might be, was helpful in solving my problem. MacInnes's narrative climaxes with the late September 1958 race riots in Notting Hill (stamping ground of MacInnes's hero and MacInnes himself).* At the height of the disorder, 2,000 white youths went on the rampage in the streets of west London – seeking out, beating up and verbally abusing any blacks they could find. There was retaliation by young blacks. MacInnes's narrative makes clear that although the National Front (British Nazis) were in there, stirring things up, the riot was teenage-fuelled. The main culprits were lumpen 'Teds' (working-class kids whose uniform was faux-Edwardian – they would later mutate into 'rockers'). The more enlightened, Vespa-riding, coffee-sipping jazz-loving youth ('mods', as they would later be called) were ineffectual. But even 'The Wiz' ends up shrieking 'Keep Britain White'. It was not merely ethnic, but a generational internecine war between two kinds of teenager that was developing. MacInnes depicts all this subtly and dramatically.

The hero despairs and resolves to emigrate to the place that he has been told has no race problem: Brazil. But, at the airport, he meets 'a score or so of Spades from Africa'. They all look 'so dam pleased to be in England', even though it's pelting rain. The hero relents, and hope is reborn:

> I ran up to them through the water, and shouted out above the engines, 'Welcome to London! Greetings from England! Meet your first teenager!' ... And I flung my arms round the first of them, who was a stout old number with a beard and a brief-case and a little bonnet, and they all paused and stared at me in amazement, until the old boy looked me in the face and said to me, 'Greetings!' and he took me by the shoulder, and suddenly they all burst out laughing in the storm.

The authorities' response to the riots (encouraged by the

politicians) was a mixture of Knacker of the Yard and Judge Jeffreys. They handed down 'exemplary' sentences – to deter any other teenagers with a taste for race-rioting. On the public level it worked. Changing minds – that intractable problem where race in post-colonial England was concerned – would prove harder.

In my case, MacInnes was instrumental in making the twenty-year-old me think about the subject, and think differently. Novels can, sometimes, do that. And not always the novels that think they are doing it. Colin MacInnes was an inveterate Negrophile – the roots of that were sexual and, if one dug down deep enough, not entirely to his credit. But, for public consumption, MacInnes spoke eminently good sense on the subject of black–white relations. No one, in 1959, more so. Certainly no politician. 'I don't understand my country anymore', he wrote: 'the English race has spread itself all over the world ... No one invites us, and we didn't ask anyone's permission ... Yet when a few hundred thousand come and settle among our fifty millions, we just can't take it..' He was right.

Absolute Beginners is a preposterously condescending and tin-eared book. But, for me, in the year of its publication (and the year of my passing out, as it were, from teendom) it was extraordinarily tonic. It didn't deracialise me. But it loaned me a set of ideas by which I could begin liberalising, and dismantling, a set of inherited (wholly malign) attitudes. If only it were a better novel.

The Claverings

(aetat. 20)

I READ A LOT of Victorian fiction in my last, lazy hours at school (to the detriment of my A-level performance, which was D-level dismal). And I read even more in the army, recumbent on my 'charpoy' (the lovely barrack-room name for one's bed; a word imported back from the regiment's service, long ago, in India – quite possibly the beds were as well). There being no war at the time, those khaki hours were even lazier than in the blazered sixth form.

Reading was one way of getting through the two years National Service.* It beat bayonet polishing. Nor, as one waited in Germany for the Russian hordes to attack, was there any shortage of reading matter to fill the vacant hours. British Council libraries were treasure houses of the stuff. Brothels for the mind. As Simon Raven* – an author I was reading at the time – never stopped complaining, the British Army, nervous Nellie that it was, shied away from providing the real thing. In Raven's view, some well-regulated red-lamp houses (blue lamps for officers, as in the First World War) would have done wonders for military morale and for the local overseas economy. As it was, curling up with a good novel had to suffice (not, however, for Raven, who was dismissed from the service for conduct flagrantly unbecoming an officer – he got some lively fiction out of the experience, notably his soldier's novel, The Feathers of Death, 1959).

Trollops were not on the menu. But it was at this period I became a Trollopian (as, indeed, was Raven – who later adapted Trollope's The Way We Live Now for TV). Having since edited some seventeen of the Chronicler of Barsetshire's works, I would nowadays rate myself as the league's seventeenth most eminent Trollopian (there are, alas, about eighteen of us in all). As is usual with private reading in one's formative years, my preferences among his impressively many chronicles (Anthony had, one publisher sourly noted, the fecundity of 'the herring') were a mirror image of myself, in my early twenties. Or, more precisely, I sought to catch reflections of myself in Trollope's pages. And, gratifyingly, the reflections I sought were indeed there – framed, as in a fine Victorian pier glass.*

My favourite novel in the late 1950s was, ironically, one of the author's less-favoured among his forty-seven full-length works: The Claverings.* My copy of the novel, which I still possess, was bought in Doncaster's Bookshop. Of seventeenth-century construction, without a straight wall or floor in the place, every nook and cranny was packed and stacked to overflowing with books, some of them almost as old as the walls around them. The shop had the exhilarating aroma that old books exude, kippered as they have been in wood-fired libraries. Bookworms and woodworms did their slow work in unison, in that wonky building. I romanticise, of course. But what I loved, still love, about bookshops was that one could go into them, spend hours there, read whole books and leave without spending a penny, and without so much as a black look from the proprietor.

The flyleaf informs me that my copy of The Claverings cost 2/6 – half a crown (a beautiful coin, abolished with the florin and threepenny bit in an act of numismatic vandalism in the early 1970s*). It was a World's Classics 'double' volume.* Almost all Trollope was available in the series. It was initiated at OUP by Michael Sadleir.* A scholar who revived interest in Trollope, Sadleir was himself a neo-Victorian novelist (author of the classic of the genre, Fanny by Gaslight) and a bibliophile. Unfashionable as it was between the wars, Sadleir believed that Trollope deserved noble treatment. OUP duly supplied it with hard, impressed covers, fine India-quality paper, richly swashed typography and Lynton Lamb illustrations on the dust jacket – if your second-hand copy was lucky enough to have retained them.*

Trollope, as I say, affected rather to dislike The Claverings, even though it was the best-paid work he ever did in fiction. It attracts that self-flagellation which runs, angrily, through An Autobiography. Rarely has an author bared his buttocks more willingly to any and all critics of Trollope than Trollope himself. The main fault in The Claverings, he complains, is the 'weakness' of the hero, who 'vacillates' – unheroically. 'I doubt now,' he bleakly concludes, 'whether any one reads The Claverings.' If by 'now' he meant 1960, he was wrong.

The plot of The Claverings is easily summarised (there are rarely complexities in that department with Trollope). A young man, aged twenty-four, has done brilliantly at Cambridge. It being the 1860s, a college fellowship entails clerical orders, lifelong allegiance to the thirty-nine articles and formal celibacy. Harry Clavering, however, wants a fuller life than high table, good claret and discreet sex with one of the numerous Cambridge prostitutes who served the needs beneath the gown. Often, apparently, these comfort women were allowed to stay overnight; Cambridge fellows, like all fellows, had their needs. 'Do you have doubts?'* Harry's clergyman father delicately asks, rather hoping, as fathers do, that his wonderful son will follow in his footsteps. No, Harry replies, he merely wants a life.

The narrative opens with Harry rashly proposing marriage to the beautiful Julia. Nonsense, the sensible girl says. He, as a schoolteacher (albeit with good prospects in that line of work), has £200 p.a., while Julia has £600 in debts. She will sell her beautiful self to the vicious, but rich, Lord Ongar. She too has her needs.

Rebuffed, Harry decides he must put money in his purse. Julia used the dreadful word 'usher' in turning him down. To stay a schoolteacher, though respectable enough in the world's eyes, is now, for Harry, an impossible thing. In his mind's eye he would not be Dr Arnold of Rugby, but Nicholas Nickleby of Dotheboys' Hall. Unthinkable. He goes on to do something scarcely less thinkable in the 1860s. He joins a builder's firm, as a trainee. Harry has made that most daring of leaps in Victorian middle-class life: he has gone into 'trade'.

He promptly falls in love with a tradesman's daughter, Florence, and proposes marriage to her, very urgently, overriding her comely maidenly modesty (Trollope hints, insistently, at the sexual needs driving his hero, who, we apprehend, is probably a twenty-four-year-old virgin). Julia meanwhile becomes widowed. Now rich, titled, sexually experienced and, if anything, more beautiful than ever, she cunningly lures Harry back into her web. He, foolishly, weakly or immorally, neglects to inform her that he has engaged himself to Florence (who is no great beauty; but a very good woman and just the wife for a rising businessman).

Harry Clavering, as the novel hits its middle sections, finds himself in the position of loving two women simultaneously: one worldly, one pure. He has neither the life skills, nor the experience, nor (like most of us) the backbone to do the right thing. If, that is, he actually knew what the right thing to do was. The novel itself seems to have an open mind on the subject.

Trollope is supremely good at this kind of moral quandary. For him, life is a series of situational crises in which honest action is confused by frustratingly unique situations – a priori rules ('Stick to your word', 'Do no harm') do not help in these situations. And the crises are most critical, with most at stake, in early manhood. Trollope's tone, as he turns from his narrative to the reader, is wise, tolerant and wholly commonsensical. And characteristically rueful. As, for example, an interim judgement on his 'hero', and his wholly unheroic conduct towards the two women he loves:

> Harry Clavering, who is the hero of our story, will not, I fear have hitherto presented himself to the reader as having much of the heroic nature in his character. It will, perhaps, be complained of him that he is fickle, vain, easily led, and almost as easily led to evil as to good. But it should be remembered that hitherto he has been rather hardly dealt with in these pages, and that his faults and weaknesses have been exposed almost unfairly. That he had such faults, and was subject to such weaknesses, may be believed of him; but there may be a question whether as much evil would not be known of most men, let them be heroes or not be heroes, if their characters were, so to say, turned inside out before our eyes.

In the absence of psychoanalysis – a technique still to come –
we must rely on novelists, Trollope suggests, to see what lies
within when we turn men inside out.

What worked most powerfully for me in The Claverings, in
1960, was that aspect which the author principally deprecates:
the 'weakness' of the hero. Trollope had created a bewildered
young man, like myself, in my early twenties, unable to handle
'manhood'. Trollope had a name for the genus. Harry is what
Trollope called a 'hobbledehoy'. It was a type which he introduced, with wonderful effect, into a number of his best novels
(e.g. Johnny Eames in The Last Chronicle of Barsetshire, Charley
Tudor in The Three Clerks, Phineas Finn, et al.). Young Anthony
had himself been a hobbledehoy in his early twenties, as An
Autobiography records. I too was one.

The term 'hobbledehoy' (which, as far as I know, no
other novelist of the time used) describes a young person,
out of youth and in the adult world of men, but incapable of
holding his own in that world. Typically, the hobbledehoy
gets himself (as did young Anthony) into a financial mess
and what the novelist obscurely calls 'dirt'. Typically (as did
young Anthony) the hobbledehoy pledges himself to two or
more women; inviting disaster. Trollope saw the condition as
something essentially English, and no great disgrace to the
nation. He defines it thus:

> Englishmen of this class in question are boys for a more
> protracted period of their life and remain longer in a state
> of hobbledehoyhood, than the youths probably of any
> other nation. They are nurtured on the cold side of the
> wall, and come slowly to maturity; but the fruit, which
> is only half-ripe at the end of summer, is the fruit that
> we keep for our winter use. I do not know that much has
> been lost in life by him who, having been a boy at twenty,

is still a young man at forty. But even in England we are changing all this now-a-days. Let us hope that what we gain in time may not be lost in flavour.

I loved the congenial texture of Trollope's narrative, the easygoing tolerance of what he calls 'weakness', and his inspiriting belief that weakness, and the experience moral weakness brings (painfully but usefully) in its wake, was – or could be, if you were lucky – the royal road to maturity ('manhood', as Trollope would have put it). At this stage in my life, I was forever falling in love, or making rash assurances to women. I was overspending. I was drinking too much. Trollope did not condone any of that, but in his worldly way, he held out the possibility that one could come through. And come through stronger. I read Trollope for the story, for the characters, for the high literary comedy. But also for the moral education.

When asked in later life what *good* all his novels did, Trollope replied, mischievously, that they instructed young women how they should receive proposals from young men who wished to marry them. Perhaps his novels did that. But they also helped young men. Or at least me as a young man.

Mein Kampf

(aetat. 21)

ONE OF MY EARLY MEMORIES is cowering, under German bombs, in the dank vaults of Colchester Castle.* In 1944 a municipal shelter, they had been, a few centuries earlier, the town dungeon. The castle withstood the bombardment. Large sections of the town were knocked about.*

In the last year of my National Service I was moved with my regiment into the Montgomery Barracks, at Kladow, on the 'wire' (literally a symbolic few strands of barbed wire) between the Russian and British sectors in Berlin.* This was where the Third World War, we were solemnly informed, would start. With a single Soviet boot crossing that line. On wire patrol, one would encounter partnering Russian patrols, walking towards one a couple of feet away, with fur hats (much more sensible than our ear-chilling berets) and Kalashnikovs. I doubt they worried about us crossing the wire.

The barracks was, by comparison with the British Army counterpart, palatial. It had been planned and built during Hitler's crazed military expansion in the mid-1930s, along with the neighbouring airfield at Gatow. Kladow's barrack rooms, messes, canteens, gleaming shower rooms, firing ranges, parade grounds and a thousand thoughtful details expressed the Prussian reverence for the jackboot. Gibraltar Barracks in Bury St Edmunds (my regiment's depot), by contrast, expressed the ineradicable British contempt for Tommy Atkins.* Kladow, being in the woods some miles from the city, had been spared the destruction visited on the capital itself. A spectral regiment of the Wehrmacht could have walked in and found it unchanged from the glory days of 1940.

This seemed to me the place to read a book which had been known to me by title for almost as long as I could remember: *Mein Kampf*. The first, and surprisingly vexing, problem was finding a copy to read. There must have been as many of them in the years of the Third Reich as there are Gideon Bibles in motel America.* Every married couple was obliged to buy a copy, every soldier was issued one, as were schoolchildren. Where, one could not but wonder, had all those millions of books gone, in summer 1945? Burning books, whatever Goebbels decreed, is not easily accomplished. Was there a gigantic, foul-smelling landfill somewhere, like the pits where they throw and burn carcasses during a foot and mouth epidemic?

From being part of the furniture of every home, *Mein Kampf* had suddenly become a 'rare book' – a collector's item, even.* (There is a persistent rumour that Prince Philip has one of the world's best collections of author-associated copies of *Mein Kampf*; I once had a conversation with a drunken friend-for-the-night in a pub who claimed he had been a Buckingham Palace servant and that he could swear to the fact – if he hadn't already sworn by the Official Secrets Act to keep it to himself.) Hitler's own copy, bound in white calf, ended up as part of General George Patton's conqueror's booty, in the Huntington Library (Patton's family lived along the road in San Marino, CA). The library, to forestall annual pilgrimages on 20 April by squads of bikers with Stalhelms and dubious tattoos, does not publicly exhibit the object.*

There were, with the fall of the Third Reich, fierce prohi-bitions against circulating, selling, publishing or owning this most German of books. Particularly in Germany (*Mein Kampf* is still banned in Austria, the author's birthplace). Resident as one was in Berlin, one could visit the Olympic Stadium (I played rugby for my regiment on the turf where Jessie Owens had sprinted), stroll down Unter den Linden and over where the bunker had been, before taking a *Weiss-bier* in sight of the Brandenburg Gate. One could tread where Nazidom had goose-stepped. But one could not, for the life of one, get hold of a copy of *Mein Kampf* – legally or illegally. Or, at least, I couldn't.

The overnight disappearance of this book was a fasci-nating fact, as is its post-war publication history, and its nervous resurfacing into availability. In the 1960s, the copyright holder of the English version of *Mein Kampf* was Hutchinson (via its Hurst and Blackett division). They judged the work too offensive to reissue in England, after the death camps became widely known about. The stench of Auschwitz was too strong on the thing. The firm ran into stiff opposition with a later translation which they had intended to bring out in autumn 1965. Principally (and understandably) outraged were the German government and British Jewish organisa-tions. Publication was postponed. Had it not been, Ian Brady, the Moors Murderer (see above) could have had his copy of *Mein Kampf* in a language he understood, and spared himself

He struggled

the expense and vexation of a *Teach Yourself German*. In 1969 an expensive hardcover version was, finally, put on sale. But as the publishers piously declared: 'the selling price has been set intentionally high so as to avoid any imputation of catering to a mass audience'. In 1972 a paperback version was at last issued, again to widespread indignation. The publishers claimed, rather feebly, that at £1.75 it could not be thought a 'mass-market' commodity. Which, of course, it was. Nonetheless, it sold feebly.*

This was all too late for me. I finally got hold of a copy of *Mein Kampf* – not in Germany, but while on leave in England. It was the James Murphy translation. Hutchinson had been producing it until 1942, when, fortuitously, the stereotype plates were destroyed by German bombing. I found my copy in a seedy second-hand shop. The provenance was interesting. Public libraries in Britain in the late 1930s and early 1940s had prominently acquired and openly shelved the book as a practical demonstration of the democracy we (the country) were fighting for. Our values did not require censorship (nor, for example, the jamming of Lord Haw-Haw's broadcasts). In the late 1940s, however, the book had become an embarrassment. My copy of *Mein Kampf* was deaccessioned from, of all places, Ipswich library.

After my struggle, I found Hitler's book impossible to read. Even in Berlin, even to dance on the grave of the creed which had so comprehensively messed up my life (robbing me of a father, a family, a stable education). It wasn't the disgustingness of chapters such as that on the 'Race' (i.e. Jewish) problem. It was the awfulness of the writing, even in Murphy's admirably straightforward English. Every part of the book worked up to some mad rant.

It was clear, too, that the book was in sad need of a

sub-editor. Anyone daring enough to criticise the text after 1934 would, of course, have found themselves on a one-way railway journey to the only place in the Reich where *Mein Kampf* was not required reading.

One passage in the chapter on propaganda (by far the most interesting in the book) did, however, catch my attention. Hitler was reminiscing about his first experiences at the front, in July 1917, at the battle known on the Allies' side as Passchendaele. (Oddly Erich Maria Remarque, author of *All Quiet on the Western Front*, was in the same sector, fighting in the same battles: a few miles of trench, and the same few months, produced the two most influential German books about the First World War.*) Corporal Hitler was, he recalls, ill prepared for the foe – not as regards training, or equipment, or battle-readiness, but as to *imagery*:

> In Germany, through the medium of the schools, the Press and the comic papers, an idea of the Englishman was gradually formed which was bound eventually to lead to the worst kind of self-deception. I can vividly recall to mind the astonished looks of my comrades when they found themselves personally face to face for the first time with the Tommies in Flanders. After a few days of fighting the consciousness slowly dawned on our soldiers that those Scotsmen were not like the ones we had seen described and caricatured in the comic papers and mentioned in the communiqués. It was then that I formed my first ideas of the efficiency of various forms of propaganda.

If they were 'Scotsmen', they weren't 'Tommies' (the English word is used in the German original) but 'Jocks', those kilted soldiers of whom Robert Graves (alias Robert von Ranke), who was also around that blood-soaked stretch of mud, fighting in a Welsh ('Taff') regiment, said tartly, 'They charge like hell (in both directions).' But it's hard to wield the editorial blue pencil when the right arm is raised in a Heil Hitler salute.

Mein Kampf turned out to be an utter dud. I left the copy by my bedside, with the faint expectation of perhaps amazing my comrades. But I couldn't, in the event, bring myself to do more than skim through its pages with any attention. A struggle too far.

There was, however, another book I read at exactly the same period which did work for me. Paradoxically this book gave me a much more entertaining and comprehensible understanding of the excesses of xenophobia and the madness of dictatorship than ever Adolf Hitler could.

It was a Victorian novel (just), published in 1901, by M. P. Shiel, called The Lord of the Sea.* I found the book, of all places, on a 'help yourself' table in the Officers' Club in Charlottenburg. Judging by the inscriptions, this literary waif had been first bought by a well-educated German in the 1930s and prudently dumped (along with all that Mein Kampf tonnage) in 1945. It had escaped the flames, or entombment, visited, as I surmised, on Hitler's book. It must have been picked up by some bored British soldier to while away the tedium of post-war occupation. It was, as I further surmised, dumped again, when this unknown second owner was posted away, or demobilised. Then it waited patiently on its table for me, its next owner.

The reason for this minor work of English fiction, by the century's zaniest novelist, finding itself in pre-war Germany is evident from the opening pages. The Lord of the Sea starts, at a rattling pace, with a pogrom, in the present day (i.e. 1900) in middle Europe:

One midnight the people of Prague rose and massacred most of the Jewish residents; the next day the flame broke out in Buda-Pesth; and within a week had become a revolution.

On the twelfth morning one of two men in a City bank said to the other: 'Come, Frankl, you cannot fail a man in this crisis – I only want 80,000 on all Westring.'

One of the men in the bank is an English aristocrat, Lord Westring, who is attempting to raise a loan on his country estate in East Anglia, from a Jewish moneylender, Baruch Frankl. Frankl is a modern day Shylock (Rothschilds are hinted at). He is 'of the Cohanim, the priestly class – a Jew of Jews'.

Westring is having no luck at all, until a news bulletin changes everything:

'No good to me, my lord,' answered Frankl, who, though a man of only forty – short, with broad shoulders – already had his skin divided up like a dry leaf; in spite of which, he was handsome, with a nose ruled straight and long, a black beard on his breast.

But the telephone rattled and Frankl heard these words at the receiver: 'Wire to hand from Wertheimer: Austrian Abgeordneten-haus passed a Resolution at noon virtually expelling Jewish Race....'

When Frankl turned again he had already resolved to possess Westring Vale, and was saying to himself: 'Within six months the value of English land should be – doubled.'

The bargain was soon made now: and within one week the foresight of Frankl began to be justified.

Austria, during those days, was a nation of vengeful hearts: for the Jews had acquired half its land, and had mortgages on the other half: peasant, therefore, and nobleman flamed alike. And this fury was contagious: now Germany – now France had it – Anti-Semite laws – like the old May-Laws – but harsher still; and streaming they came, from the Leopoldstadt, from Bukowina, from the Sixteen Provinces, from all Galicia, from the Nicolas Colonies, from Lisbon, with wandering foot and weary breast – the Heines, Cohens, Oppenheimers – Sephardim, Aschkenasim. And Dover was the new Elim.

With alarm Britain saw them come! but before she could do anything, the wave had overflowed it.

'Swamped', as a later British prime minister would put it.*

This tidal wave of Jewry are not (as they historically were at the turn of the century) poor huddled masses, destined for ghetto existence in the East End of London and three generations of social struggle to make it into the middle classes. They are rich, idle parasites, battening like so many Judaic vampires on England and its traditional ruling classes. 'Hofjuden' take over the government, through the 'Jew-Liberal Party' (these paranoid delusions were not unique to Shiel; an influential tract, Joseph Banister's *England Under the Jews*, came out in the same year as *The Lord of the Sea*).

The results for England are dire: 'In Westring Vale, as everywhere, times were hard. It was now the property of Baruch Frankl: for at the first failure of Lord Westring to meet terms, Frankl had struck.' As the new owner of the old English estate, the Jewish moneylender decrees that all his serfs (as the local populace now find themselves) must wear a 'fez', with ornate tassels, and bow low when the new, Jewish, lord of the manor passes. This is the livery of servitude to the Jewish master. Lord Westring dies of shame. His son, Richard, is too much of a man (and too much of an

Englishman) to crook the knee and bow the head to any Jew. He horsewhips Frankl, breaking into the synagogue, during a religious service, to do so.

Frankl's revenge is terrible. He has Richard framed for murder. There is the added convenience that the villain lusts after Richard's beautiful sister, Margaret: removing her guardian will make the accomplishment of that vile plan easier.

Richard is reprieved from the gallows and consigned to life imprisonment, on an impregnable island jail, Colmoor. The novel at this point mutates into *The Count of Monte Cristo*. Richard (Prisoner 76) escapes by feigning death (with the cunning use of chloroform), smuggles himself out, disguises himself as a Bedouin (so orientalised has Britain become, this guarantees inconspicuousness) and, free at last, becomes, overnight, fabulously rich. How? Not by the pirates' treasure that transforms Edmond Dantès into the Count of Monte Cristo. Too easy. Shiel has a more ingenious plot twist – and with one leap, he takes his novel from the swashbuckling world of Dumas père to that of the young scientific romancer, Mr H. G. Wells.

A meteorite has crashed into Earth's atmosphere. Richard has learned some interesting facts about it in prison (an obvious parallel with Dantès and the Abbé Faria). He locates the main fragment of the meteorite which (1) has landed in Westring and (2) is encrusted with diamonds (never let it be said that M. P. Shiel was frightened of plot improbability).

What will Richard do with his wealth? Personal revenge, of course; but much else besides. His name resounds meaningfully at this point of the narrative – Richard will *launch a crusade*. And what else did the Lionheart do? His coronation in 1189 was the occasion for the ugliest anti-Semitic violence in all British history and led the way to the 'Edict of Expulsion' – the world's first state sanctioned ethnic cleansing (or final solution, to give it another name) – in 1290.* Richard, as his namesake failed to do, will solve the 'Jewish question', once and for all.

Richard sets out on his crusade by taking charge of the oceans: he builds huge steel forts, commanded by blue-blooded British admirals, and called 'Boodahs'. Shiel, whose writing is ever teetering on mania, goes into blueprint specificity:

> There were no keel-blocks, for there was no keel – or rather, the keel was a circular plate a yard in diameter, resting on a single block, the shape of the structure to be a perfect square, along the sides of which four battleships might lie like toy-boats: the bottom, from circular keel to upward bend, having the same shape as a battleship's seen in midship section, only with four faces instead of two. From the knee-bend the sides ran up perpendicular; but at the level evidently intended to be the water-line they struck inward, so that the flat roof was smaller than the area below; the position of this water-line giving a definite clue to the intended displacement; and this again showing that the whole – roof, sides, bottom, and all – would be one wall of Simmons armour – steeling and backing – layer on layer – no less than 4ft. $9^{1}/_{4}$ ins. thick.
>
> Yet this stupendous ark, or citadel – so simple was its plan – would be turned out in less time than a second-class cruiser; and its cost, apart from yard-modifications and groundways, small in proportion.

The great European navies' fifteen-inch guns might as well

be peashooters, for all the damage they can wreak on the Boodah. Impregnable on his worldwide constellation of marine pillboxes, the Lord of the Sea (as he now is) sinks the odd liner or two, as an exemplary demonstration of his sovereign power (a little light-fingered lifting, at this point, from Jules Verne's Captain Nemo★). Dissatisfied with mere lordship he appoints himself regent of Britain ('King Richard IV', that is). He taxes anything ('four shillings a ton') that moves across his watery domain. 'The world is at his feet': he issues a 'manifesto', abolishing any ownership of land (a crotchet of Shiel's derived from the utopian socialist Henry George★).

And now, his final solution. Each and every Jew in the length and breadth of England – the Regent decrees – shall be 'returned' (i.e. deported) to Palestine. Within three months of the edict, no Jew may be employed or own property. Synagogues and Jewish schools will be illegal and pulled down. No Jewish signature will have legal force (thus making inter-marriage illegal). 'Throughout Britain,'

> this piece of Russian despotism sent a wave of quiet gladness, and an epidemic of jest broke out, in club, factory, 'Lane', and drawing-room: 'You hurry up – to Jericho!' became the workman's answer to a Jew; it was remarked that the chimney of train and steamship would furnish a new pillar of cloud by day, and pillar of fire by night, to go before the modern Exodus.

The narrative, in its last sections, cartwheels into the surreal. Richard discovers what he has long suspected, that he himself is in fact a Jew: Raphael Spinoza. He elects to abdicate from his virtual monarchy over England (and his lordship over the oceans) to lead 'his' people to the promised land. In an epilogue, we learn that 'he took the title of Shophet, or Judge, and for sixty years ruled over Israel'. Now the Messiah, he is united with his lifelong love, Frankl's sister, Rebecca. It is the last of this novel's strange mutations – into a parody version of *Daniel Deronda*.

Shiel dreams on, madly, unstoppably. Under Richard/ Raphael's guidance, Israel becomes the most advanced, progressive and prosperous country in the world. There is more than one solution to the Jewish problem, we are to understand. And kindness to the chosen people requires, we apprehend, considerable cruelty.

The Lord of the Sea was written in the run up to the 'Aliens Act' of 1905, an unpleasant piece of legislation specifically designed to block off the immigration of persecuted Jews from Europe into an England which conceived itself as being 'swamped'.* Shiel, of mixed race (born in Montserrat, his mother was a mulatto), was a connoisseur of xenophobia. His novels must have been flagons of gasoline poured on the never-extinguished flames of race hatred.

Shiel was catholic in his racism. Even more influential than *The Lord of the Sea* was his 1898 novel *The Yellow Danger* (i.e. 'peril'), which fantasises a 'tide' of Chinese sweeping over Europe.* It all starts when the Oriental potentate Yen How becomes infatuated with a Fulham nursemaid and starts a world war – with his countless armies – to possess her (yellow swine). England is saved by another hero – 'John Hardy' (think Nelson). The novel climaxes with a sea battle which claims twenty million lives. Some 150 million of the world's population die in a subsequent cholera epidemic.

Shiel was never a novelist to blink in the face of casualties.

In *The Purple Cloud*, published the same year as *The Lord of the Sea*, the hero, Adam Jeffson ('the second parent of the world') is at the North Pole and so misses the poisoning of the rest of humanity by a cloud of 'cyanogen gas'.* He spends seventeen years in solitary, pyromaniac splendour, before finding a mate, sheltering in a cellar in Constantinople. They set out to restock the human race from scratch.

It is easy to see why *The Lord of the Sea* would have found a place on the shelf for a certain kind of German reader in the early twentieth century. Any novel which opens with a pogrom and ends with a final solution was grist to the Nazi mill. Had it come his way, Shiel's disgusting novel would have found favour with the Austrian arch-anti-Semite himself. The wild fantasies of omnipotence, the militarism, the fascination with the 'overman', the careless extinction of millions of human beings, the apocalypticism: all find echoes in *Mein Kampf*. Above all, Shiel's obsession, and mad fantasies, about the Jews (whom he has taken the trouble to study obsessively: his is no vulgar anti-Semitism) would chime with Hitler's *Weltanschauung* (the word that Murphy found hardest to translate, there being no exact English equivalent, and 'worldview' being too tame).

Whatever else, Hitler was no tinpot dictator. Shiel was; or, to be more precise, a tin-box dictator. At the end of his life, the novelist came into the ownership of a barren island in the Caribbean. When he died he left the domain to his disciple, the writer John Gawsworth, who promptly crowned himself 'King Juan of Redonda'. It was his habit, in the Fitzrovia pubs he frequented, to issue honours and posture royally. Gawsworth was also left the ashes of Shiel, which, it is said, he kept 'in a biscuit tin on the mantelpiece, putting a pinch in the stew for special guests'.*

If there was a supremely right place to read *The Lord of the Sea*, it was Berlin in 1936. If there was a supremely satisfying place to read *The Lord of the Sea*, it was Berlin in 1960.

The Resistible Rise of Arturo Ui

(aetat. 21)

WHILE IN GERMANY, having at last reached majority, I had a crowning experience. It was not a book but the theatre which delivered it. I had Berliner friends who took me, a number of times, across the line into the Soviet sector, to the Theater am Schiffbauerdamm: the House of Brecht and his Berliner Ensemble.* The visits were entirely legal, even though the theatre was in the Soviet sector. Berlin was technically, in 1960 (until the Wall went up a year later), an open city under four-power administration.

Oddly (although I did not know it until much later), Kenneth Tynan was having his first, epochal, experience of Brecht and epic theatre at exactly the same period.* Who knows, we may have been in the auditorium at the same time. Tynan describes the physical layout of the place as reverently as John Ruskin might have described an admired Italian cathedral. One went through the 'grandiose, bullet-chipped pillars of the Brandenburg Gate', then:

the short sally past the skinny trees and bland neo-classical facades of Unter den Linden (surely the emptiest of the world's greatest streets), and the left turn that leads you across the meagre, oily stream of the Spree and into the square-cum-parking-lot where the theatre stands, with a circular neon sign – 'BERLINER ENSEMBLE' – revolving on its roof like a sluggish weather vane. You enter an unimposing foyer, present your ticket, buy a superbly designed programme, and take your seat in an auditorium which is encrusted with gilt cupids and cushioned in plush. When the curtain, adorned with its Picasso dove, goes up, one is usually shocked, so abrupt is the contrast between the baroque prettiness of the house and the chaste, stripped beauty of what one sees on the expanses, relatively enormous, of the stage.

Tynan neglects to mention the huge slogans in the auditorium – the last of which declares that the theatre is always the servant of the state.

The play which had huge impact on me (and on Tynan – for different reasons) was *The Resistible Rise of Arturo Ui*. It had an unusual history. A 'parable play' (*Lehrstück*), it was conceived and first drafted in 1941. The playwright, whose life had been rendered chaotic by events in Germany, had been strongly influenced by Warner Brothers crime movies, and the work was labelled 'ein Gangster Spektakel'. Particularly influential had been the Bogart/Cagney movies *Public Enemy* and *The Roaring Twenties*.

Brecht allegorised the Nazi Putsch and takeover of Germany in terms of Al Capone's first taking over Cicero, then Chicago. The play – written as Brecht awaited refugee entry into US – was shelved, and not produced until two years after his death, at the Schiffbauerdamm.

The production was breathtaking. Tynan describes the production we both saw, at the same period, with his customary brilliance:

> The whole play is performed in a style that is somewhere between Erich von Stroheim and the Keystone Cops. The Roehm murders are staged like the St Valentine's day massacre: a truck drives into a garage, its headlights blazing straight at the audience, and silhouetted gunmen mow down the victims. The entire cast wears the sort of distorted make-up that one associates with puppets; the revolving stage whizzes around; and squalling Dixieland jazz interlards the scenes. Macabre farce on this level of inventiveness was something I had never struck before in any theatre. Its quality was condensed in the performance of Ekkehard Schall* as Ui – one of the most transfixing human experiments I have ever seen on a stage, and a perfect image of Brechtian acting. Schall, who is under thirty, plays Ui with a ginger moustache, a ginger forelock, a trench coat, and a hat with the brim completely turned down. He invests the part with all the gymnastic agility of the young Chaplin.

What, wonderfully, the production did was to fuse almost all the elements which had been uneasily floating in my sensibility for fifteen years. Brecht made no division between German history, American popular culture, Marx, Groucho Marx, Chaplin, Warner Brothers gangster movies, jazz, high theatre. There were no divisions, no hierarchies, no disdainful aversion of the eyes from 'sex and violence' unter-literatur. Brecht wasted nothing, however low. Everything was grist. I began with Coleridge, and there is a Coleridgean neologism for this: 'esemplastic'.*

For Tynan, Brecht was a salutary bomb under the London West End theatre. For me, Brecht and this play in particular pulled into focus everything from *Tarzan's Desert Mystery* to *Mein Kampf*. Nothing, if one put one's mind to it, need ever be discarded. I was part of everything I'd read, seen and listened to.

Epilogue

IN 2004 I sold a house. It was a second home in the country, in whose large, rambling structure (it was 400 years old, with a 200-year-old sycamore in the garden) I stored, miscellaneously, what I grandly called my library. Many of the books, particularly the Victorian fiction, were a century old. And I was sixty-five.

I have never been a methodical – or shrewd – collector; any more than my reading has ever been organised (anyone who has looked into the previous pages will be well aware of that). But there were thousands of books which had passed my way and somehow stuck: they were, I liked to think, my personal archaeology.

As the young realtor looked round the house – 'sussing' it out, as he would have said – he turned to me. 'The place looks tired,' he said. 'Lose the books.' Sensible advice: Wordsworth once said something similar. But I don't think I could lose them, even if I parted with them physically.

Portal Notes

www.magicmomentbook.com

IN THE PORTAL OR 'GATEWAY' notes to websites which follow I have, in the main, avoided reference to the obvious Wikipedia, IMDb, ODNB and Britannica sites – although in many cases they will be a reader's first port of call. The principal aim of this e-annotation is to thicken the cultural texture of the book, in a number of places by offering audio-visual as well as conventional annotation.

Conventional annotation aims to encase knowledge, as *apparatus criticus*. What I have attempted here is something different. William Gibson, the pioneer of 'cyberpunk', who has popularised this kind of web reference, likens the reader to a worm crawling through cheese. The cheese doesn't change, but every worm creates a different passage through it. The following are my suggested wormholings through, and out of, what I have written.

Chapter I: Tarzan's Desert Mystery

p. 1 For a clip of Hal9000 and Dave in 2001: *A Space Odyssey*, see http://www.youtube.com/watch?v=klw8MVkSBwk &feature=related. On Hal9000, see http://pages.prodigy. com/kubrick/kub2001.htm.

p. 1 The 'Daisy, Daisy' song may be heard at http://kids.
niehs.nih.gov/lyrics/daisy.htm/.

p. 1 For a pictorial synopsis of *Tarzan's Desert Mystery*, with
all the scenes referred to in this chapter ('Boy' reading
to Tarzan, for example), see http://www.erbzine.com/
mag6/0624.html.

p. 2 For the pulsing RKO logo, see http://en.wikipedia.org/
wiki/RKO_Pictures.

p. 3 For the Fieseler 'Storch' and its amazing landing
capacity, see http://www.warbirdalley.com/storch.htm.

p. 3 On Tarzana, Burroughs's second most valuable
invention, see http://www.snopes.com/lost/tarzan.htm.

p. 4 On the Los Angeles Arboretum and Tarzan's 'jungle',
see http://faculty.oxy.edu/jerry/arbor.htm.

p. 5 On *One Million Years BC*, see http://www.imdb.com/title/
tt0032871/.

p. 5 To hear the inimitable Tarzan yell, go to http://www.
youtube.com/watch?v=WylcBisy39Q.

p. 7 On the complex issue of black soldiers and their white
'comrades' in the US Armed Forces in the Second World
War, see http://www.history.army.mil/documents/
cold-war/EI-Ch1.htm.

p. 7 On doomed John Garfield and his career in films, see
http://themave.com/Garfield/menu.htm.

p. 8 On Johnny Weissmuller's bare-chested careers in sport
and film, see http://www.geostan.ca/.

p. 8 On Triffids and the cult Wyndham's homicidal
vegetables have generated, see http://www.bbc.co.uk/
cult/classic/triffids/.

p. 8 On Frank Matcham's work and his design for the
hippodromes across England (particularly in Colchester

High Street), see http://www.frankmatchamsociety.org.
uk/.

p. 10 For a history and illustration of the Colchester
Hippodrome and the erotic 1905 cartouche, see http://
www.theatrestrust.org.uk/search?type=image&q=colche
ster+hippodrome.

Chapter II: Henry V

p. 12 For the film's cast see http://www.imdb.com/title/
tt0036910/.

p. 13 For a Technicolor clip of Laurence Olivier and his
rousing St Crispin's Day speech to the troops, see http://
www.youtube.com/watch?v=3jXFnQUU7yg. On À rebours,
see http://www.ibiblio.org/eldritch/jkh/rebours.html.

p. 14 On archery, Agincourt and the victorious English
tactics, see http://www.stortford-archers.org.uk/
medieval.htm.

p. 14 On Operation Market Garden and its failure to deliver,
see http://www.rememberseptember44.com/.

p. 14 For a video clip of the dreaded Waffen SS at Arnhem,
see http://www.youtube.com/watch?v=6-30w-dPGe0.

p. 15 To hear Adrian Mitchell reading his rousing anti-war
poem 'Tell Me Lies about Vietnam', go to http://
www.democraticunderground.com/discuss/duboard.
php?az=view_all&address=104x1486318 and http://www.
inminds.co.uk/stopbush-1-20nov03.html#mitchell.

p. 15 On the fabled Angel of Mons, see http://www.
westernfrontassociation.com/thegreatwar/articles/
research/angelofmons.htm.

Chapter III: The Wind in the Willows and Great Expectations

p. 16 For *The Wind in the Willows*, text and audio versions, see http://www.gutenberg.org/etext/7308.

p. 17 On Larkin's poem alluded to here, see http://plagiarist.com/poetry/4855/. For a selection of cocoa tins alluded to in the poem, see http://www.tias.com/140/InventoryPage/4698/1.html. On the 'shut shops' (i.e. as a result of the 1908 half-day-closing act), see http://books.google.co.uk/books?id=qeAHc4FQKakC&pg=PA16&lpg=PA16&dq=%22half-day+closing+act%22&source=web&ots=gwExq9JGPm&sig=6047boNGkSnXFXNOYz_zELakD_M&hl=en#PPA16,M1.

p. 17 For *The History of Mr Polly*, see http://www.gutenberg.org/etext/7308.

p. 18 For the charming poster of the movie, showing Mr Polly, jubilant, on his bike, see http://www.eyeforfilm.co.uk/reviews.php?film_id=12109.

p. 18 On the practice of 'urchins blowing up toads', see George Barker's poem, at http://www.artofeurope.com/barker/bar5.htm.

p. 18 On the gay Holmes and Watson liaison, see http://www.trashfiction.co.uk/sherlock_dearest.html and for 'slash' fantasy on the subject, see http://liquidfic.net/Holmes_Watson.html.

p. 20 For the current National Curriculum in English, see http://www.ncaction.org.uk/subjects/english/index.htm.

p. 21 The IMDb entry has full filmography and clips of *Great Expectations*: http://www.imdb.com/title/tt0038574/.

p. 22 For *Great Expectations*, text and audio versions, see
http://www.ncaction.org.uk/subjects/english/index.htm
and www.gutenberg.org/etext/8608.

p. 23 For details on the Norton–Rosenberg *Great
Expectations*, see http://www.amazon.com/Great-
Expectations-Charles-Dickens/dp/0393960692.

p. 25 On Woodfall Films' kitchen-sink realism, see http://
www.imdb.com/company/c00103083/.

p. 25 The wartime blackout is graphically described on the
BBC website: http://www.bbc.co.uk/ww2peopleswar/
stories/39/a4035539.shtml. See also the fictional
depiction of blackout England in the Powell and
Pressburger film *A Canterbury Tale*: http://www.
criterion.com/asp/release.asp?id=341&eid=483&sec
tion=essay and http://www.powell-pressburger.org/
Reviews/44_ACT/.

p. 26 On the history of Zoe Gail's anthem to the blackout
and the long-awaited reillumination of London,
see http://findarticles.com/p/articles/mi_qn4158/
is_20040331/ai_n12776671.

p. 26 On the BBC's 'Big Read' 2007 and 2008, see http://
www.thebigread.org/.

Chapter IV: The Amazing Wilson

p. 27 For an account of the uplifting *Boy's Own Paper*, see
http://www.collectingbooksandmagazines.com/bop.
html.

p. 28 The most informative site with details on the boys'
comics discussed here is Vic Whittle's: http://www.
britishcomics.20m.com/.

p. 28 On Godfrey's Cordial, see http://answers.google.com/ answers/threadview?id=527947.

p. 28 For *Guy Livingstone*, see www.gutenberg.org/ etext/17084.

p. 29 On Paavo Nurmi, the 'Flying Finn', see http:// virtual.finland.fi/netcomm/news/showarticle. asp?intNWSAID=26157.

p. 32 On Gilbert Dalton, the creator of 'Wilson', see http:// www.amazon.co.uk/Sporting-Supermen-Stories-Childhood-Heroes/dp/1845131657/ref=sr_1_2?ie=UTF8& s=books&qid=1207071757&sr=1–2.

p. 32 On Dalton's Alf Tupper, 'tough of the track', see http://www.toughofthetrack.net/.

p. 32 On Britain's dismal Olympic 1948 performance, see http://www.bbc.co.uk/history/british/modern/ olympics_1948_gallery.shtml.

p. 32 On Colonel Harry Llewellyn and Foxhunter's sole 1952 gold, see http://www.oundlesociety.org/ SirHarryLlewellyn.asp.

p. 33 On the all-conquering 1945 Moscow Dynamo tour of Britain, see http://www.bramalearangersclub.com/ dynamo_1945.html.

p. 33 On Bruce Woodcock's career in the ring and British disappointments, see http://www.britishboxing.net/ boxers_17581-Bruce-Woodcock.html and http://prints. paphotos.com/pictures_682985/Boxing-Heavyweight-Bruce-Woodcock-v-Joe-Baksi-Harringay-Arena-London. html.

Chapter V: Lorna Doone

p. 34 The Lorna Doone cover is the work of the talented African-American artist Matt Baker. See his subtly erotic work (for young readers) at http://www.americanartarchives.com/baker,matt.htm.

p. 34 On the frigid hardships of the 1947 winter, see http://www.winter1947.co.uk/.

p. 36 On the complex background to Plievier's novel Stalingrad, see http://en.wikipedia.org/wiki/Theodor_Plievier.

p. 36 On the Hungerwinter and its long-term effect in Holland, see http://www.dutchfamine.nl/index_files/study.htm.

p. 37 For the full text of Lorna Doone, see www.gutenberg.org/etext/17460. For film versions of Blackmore's Exmoor romance, see http://www.youtube.com/watch?v=90FAMCLpZJg&feature=related.

p. 37 For the coldest winters in the seventeenth century, including Lorna Doone's of 1683–4, see http://www.wirksworth.org.uk/A14WEATH.htm.

p. 38 For Jack London's 'To Build a Fire', see http://www.jacklondons.net/buildafire.html.

p. 38 For audio-visual clips of the film of Scott of the Antarctic, see http://www.screenonline.org.uk/film/id/457209/.

p. 38 On the popular balladeer Robert W. Service, see http://www.robertwservice.com/.

p. 39 For the most thorough account of 'The Ballad of Eskimo Nell', see http://en.wikipedia.org/wiki/Eskimo_Nell.

p. 40 On Derek Humphry and death assistance, see http://assistedsuicide.org/blog/.

p. 40 For Arnold's 'Empedocles on Etna', see http://
whitewolf.newcastle.edu.au/words/authors/A/
ArnoldMatthew/verse/EmpedoclesonEtna/index.html.
A commentary on the poem will be found at http://
victorian.lang.nagoya-u.ac.jp/victorianweb/authors/
arnold/works.html.

Chapter VI: Noyes + Noyes

p. 41 On Alfred Noyes, his career (successful) and his
reputation (low), see http://litterature.historique.
net/noyes.html. For the text of 'The Highwayman',
see http://www.potw.org/archive/potw85.html. The
poem has inspired illustrators of a higher calibre
than the poet. See Charles Keeping's depiction of the
ghostly highwayman, for which he won the 1981 Kate
Greenaway Prize, at http://www.amazon.com/gp/
reader/0192723707/ref=sib_dp_pt#reader-link and
Murray Kimber's superb modern comic-strip version of
'The Highwayman' at http://www.theartark.com/kimber.
html.

p. 41 On Palgrave's many 'golden treasuries', see http://
en.wikipedia.org/wiki/Palgrave's_Golden_Treasury.

p. 43 On Hale's 100-inch telescope on Mount Wilson, see
http://www.mtwilson.edu/.

p. 44 On Saul Bellow and Caltech, see http://www.eands.
caltech.edu/articles/LXVIII_3/Random-Walk.pdf.

p. 44 For Robert Millikan and 'Millikan's School' (e.g.
Caltech), see http://nobelprize.org/nobel_prizes/
physics/laureates/1923/millikan-bio.html and http://
www.aip.org/history/gap/Millikan/Millikan.html. For

Arthur A. Noyes at Caltech, see http://en.wikipedia.org/
wiki/Arthur_Amos_Noyes.

p. 45 On the three founding spirits ('stooges') at Caltech,
and their presiding portrait, see http://athenaeum.
caltech.edu/dining.html.

p. 47 On the Mount Wilson toll road, see http://
en.wikipedia.org/wiki/Mount_Wilson_Toll_Road.

p. 47 For the whole text of *Watchers of the Sky* (be warned),
see http://www.gutenberg.org/etext/6574.

Chapter VII: Horizontal Heavyweights

p. 49 On the witty boxing commentator Stewart
Macpherson, see http://www.broadcasting-history.ca/
personalities/personalities.php?id=140.

p. 49 For clips of the epic Tommy Farr vs. Joe Louis fight
in 1939, see http://www.broadcasting-history.ca/
personalities/personalities.php?id=140. On Tommy Farr,
the famed 'Welsh Battler', see http://www.johnnyowen.
com/tommy_farr.html.

p. 49 On Freddie Mills, the 'fairground battler'
see http://www.findagrave.com/cgi-bin/
fg.cgi?page=gr&GRid=6792216.

p. 49 On Joe Baksi, conquering American, see http://www.
findagrave.com/cgi-bin/fg.cgi?page=gr&GRid=6792216.

p. 49 On Eamonn Andrews, amateur boxer and
professional commentator, see http://www.screenonline.
org.uk/people/id/569940/.

p. 49 On Jack Gardner, British champion and international
flop, see http://www.britishboxing.net/boxers_12585-
Jack-Gardner.html.

p. 50 On the Turpin vs. Robinson fights, see http://
randyturpin.com/. For a clip of the great fight itself, see
http://www.youtube.com/watch?v=cWo2wUJ2d6U.

p. 51 On Odets's boxing melodrama, *Golden Boy*, see http://
en.wikipedia.org/wiki/Golden_Boy_%28play%29.

p. 51 For a clip from *When We Were Kings*, Ali vs. Foreman,
see http://www.youtube.com/watch?v=N44vdCqI7LI.

p. 52 On Clark Gable's 'Dumbo' ears and the remedies
surgery now offers, see http://www.plasticsurgery4u.
com/procedure_folder/ears/big/hiding_big_ears_gable.
html.

Chapter VIII: This Gun for Hire

p. 53 On buying guns in the US (very easy), see http://
books.google.co.uk/books?id=SDG_By1cAkMC&pg=PA1
23&lpg=PA123&dq=%22a+gun+for+sale%22+greene&s
ource=web&ots=PDrpgTzzkx&sig=pk6HqQVQW7U586
hIOstuOECuPzQ&hl=en#PPA124,M1.

p. 54 For details on the film *This Gun for Hire*, and the
pictures alluded to in this chapter, see http://www.
eskimo.com/ffinoir/ftitles/thisgun/index.shtml.

p. 54 On Chandler's 'Moronica Lake' crack, see http://
en.wikipedia.org/wiki/Veronica_Lake.

p. 54 On Alan Ladd and Robert De Niro ('You talkin' to
me?'), see http://www.bighousefilm.com/reviews/this_
gun_for_hire.htm.

p. 55 To hear Karas and watch his zithering fingers, see
http://www.youtube.com/watch?v=gFz79SBnuk8.

p. 55 On Harry Lime and the cuckoo clock, see http://www.
screenonline.org.uk/film/id/592079/. To hear Welles's

speech itself, in clip form, go to http://mraybould.
wordpress.com/2007/12/20/the-third-man/.

p. 56 On Himmler and the display massacre at Minsk, see
http://www.deathcamps.org/occupation/minsk%20
ghetto.html.

p. 57 On the huge RAF Bomber Command casualties in
the Second World War, see http://www.raf.mod.uk/
bombercommand/dresden.html.

p. 57 On the peacenik blitz on London's 'Bomber' Harris
statue, see http://www.ukattraction.com/london/
sir-arthur-bomber-harris-statue.htm.

Chapter IX: Peter Ibbetson

p. 58 For Old St Paul's, see http://www.gutenberg.org/
etext/11082. On Harrison Ainsworth, see http://www.
litencyc.com/php/speople.php?rec=true&UID=54/

p. 59 For Colchester's impressive war(s) memorial, see
http://www.camulos.com/war/memorial.htm.

p. 60 Carlyle expands on the subject, in ultra-conservative
fashion, in his essay on the second reform bill, *Shooting
Niagara – And After?*: http://www.efm.bris.ac.uk/het/
carlyle/shooting.htm.

p. 61 For *Masterman Ready*, see http://www.gutenberg.org/
etext/21552.

p. 61 On *The Swiss Family Robinson* and its
absurdities, see http://en.wikipedia.org/wiki/
The_Swiss_Family_Robinson.

p. 61 For Percy F. Westerman and his 170-or-so rattling
tales, see http://www.collectingbooksandmagazines.
com/wester.html.

p. 61 For *Peter Ibbetson*, see http://www.gutenberg.org/etext/9817.

p. 62 Henry James's declining the idea of *Trilby*, when offered it by du Maurier, is the subject of David Lodge's novel *Author, Author* (2005): http://www.reviewsofbooks.com/author_author/.

p. 62 On 'scientific romance', as opposed to 'science fiction', see http://www.foolquest.com/Scientific%20Romance.htm.

p. 64 On Sigmund Freud and dreams, see http://www.wsu.edu:8080/ffiwldciv/world_civ_reader/world_civ_reader_2/freud.html.

p. 68 On the film of *Peter Ibbetson*, see http://en.wikipedia.org/wiki/Peter_Ibbetson.

p. 68 On Éluard, *Peter Ibbetson* and the novel's elevation to a surrealist manifesto, see http://www.alsolikelife.com/shooting/?p=110.

p. 68 For a clip of the slashed eyeball in Buñuel's *Un chien andalou*, see http://movies.nytimes.com/movie/51646/Un-Chien-Andalou/overview. For Salvador Dalí's famously floppy watches, see http://www.moma.org/collection/browse_results.php?object_id=79018.

Chapter X: Svengali

p. 69 On making up Alec Guinness for the Fagin caricature, see http://lean.bfi.org.uk/material.php?theme=1&type=Photograph&title=oliver.

p. 69 On the horrors of Belsen, see http://www.scrapbookpages.com/BergenBelsen/Introduction.html.

p. 70 On *Spark of Life*, see http://www.fantasticfiction.co.uk/r/erich-maria-remarque/spark-of-life.htm.

p. 70 On the novelist and refugee Erich Maria Remarque, see http://www.kirjasto.sci.fi/remarque.htm.

Chapter XI: Such Power is Dangerous

p. 71 On *Rasselas*, see http://www.st-andrews.ac.uk/ffiwww_se/personal/cjmm/Rasselas.html and www.gutenberg.org/etext/652.

p. 72 For a view of North Hill, Colchester, in the 1950s, see http://www.francisfrith.com/search/england/essex/colchester/photos/colchester_photos.htm.

p. 72 Dennis Wheatley still has his enthusiastic admirers. See http://www.denniswheatley.info/. Rider Haggard has his admirers too. See http://www.riderhaggardsociety.org.uk/.

p. 72 Likewise, the 'King of the Thrillers', Edgar Wallace. See http://www.edgarwallace.org/.

p. 73 For Wheatley's innovative 'crime dossiers', see http://www.fantasticfiction.co.uk/w/dennis-wheatley/malinsay-massacre.htm.

p. 73 A good starting point on Burroughs, Johnson and their 'cut-up' (non-)narrative technique can be found at http://www.eyemagazine.com/feature.php?id=151&fid=644.

p. 73 On Dumas's *The Three Musketeers*, see http://www.hoboes.com/html/FireBlade/Dumas/Musketeers/.

p. 73 On the Hammer horror industry and its highpoints, see http://www.hammerfilms.com/, and http://www.unofficialhammerfilms.com/ and http://www.fortunecity.com/lavendar/judidench/339/hammer.html.

p. 73 On the *The Lost Continent*, a distinct Hammer low point, see http://www.hammerfilms.com/arts/themes/dennis_wheatley/lost_continent.htm.

p. 75 On Aldous Huxley, *Brave New World* and his highbrow social engineering schemes, see http://www.huxley.net/.

p. 77 On Budd Schulberg's Hollywood novel *The Disenchanted*, see http://books.google.co.uk/books?id=pS KLfQYNYDAC&pg=PA1126&lpg=PA1126&dq=schulberg +disenchanted&source=web&ots=rpAqLWDoiK&sig=uU B38-ICRxKeH5pwsikgwX3CsTM&hl=en.

p. 77 On Clifford Odets's Hollywood melodrama *The Big Knife*, see http://en.wikipedia.org/wiki/The_Big_Knife.

Chapter XII: The Cruel Sea

p. 79 On novelist Nicholas Monsarrat, see http://en.wikipedia.org/wiki/Nicholas_Monsarrat. On the film of *The Cruel Sea* starring Jack Hawkins, see http://www.britmovie.co.uk/studios/ealing/filmography/72.html.

p. 79 On novelist James Jones and the film of his novel *From Here to Eternity*, see http://www.filmsite.org/from.html.

p. 83 For a clip of this cruellest scene in the film of *The Cruel Sea*, see http://kllrchrd.livejournal.com/tag/jack+hawkins.

p. 85 For *Lord of the Flies* and its long road to publication, see http://education.yahoo.com/homework_help/cliffsnotes/lord_of_the_flies/2.htm.

Chapter XIII: The Puppet Masters

p. 86 On 'tuppenny libraries' in twentieth-century Britain, see http://books.google.co.uk/books?id=ZaW75ok9N

HIC&pg=PA185&lpg=PA185&dq=%22twopenny+librar
ies%22&source=web&ots=e8_eesR2_R&sig=wB181RJ-
EMoXvtHB34bvPUKzuXs&hl=en

p. 86 On the history of commercial circulating libraries
in Britain, see http://www.sensationpress.com/
victoriancirculatinglibraries.htm.

p. 87 On lofty John Reith and the BBC he created, see http://
www.spartacus.schoolnet.co.uk/Jreith.htm.

p. 87 For a recollection of the impact of Kathleen Winsor's
steamy *Forever Amber* on the young female reader in the
early 1950s, see http://books.guardian.co.uk/reviews/
classics/0,6121,771986,00.html.

p. 87 For a lurid display of Hank Janson covers (always
promising, alas, much more than the books deliver), see
http://www.fantasticfiction.co.uk/j/hank-janson/.

p. 87 On Victor Gollancz and his firm's pioneering science-
fiction list, see http://johnfair.brinkster.net/Booksite/
Books/Gollancz/index.htm.

p. 87 On *The Puppet Masters*, see http://en.wikipedia.org/
wiki/The_Puppet_Masters.

p. 89 On the United States Air Force, protecting the
homeland from their outpost base at Wethersfield,
Essex, see http://en.wikipedia.org/wiki/
RAF_Wethersfield.

p. 89 On the nuclear-capable Thunderjet, see http://www.
globalaircraft.org/planes/f-84_thunderjet.pl.

p. 90 On alleged germ warfare by the US in Korea, see
http://www.kimsoft.com/1997/us-germx.htm.

p. 91 On the Heinlein-inspired film *Destination Moon*, see
http://www.imdb.com/title/tt0042393/.

p. 92 On TANSTAAFL and Robert Heinlein's titanium-
nosed philosophy based on the absence of free lunches,

see http://en.wikipedia.org/wiki/TANSTAAFL and http://www.heinleinsociety.org/.

p. 92 On brainwashing by the Chinese on American prisoners in the Korean War, see http://changingminds.org/techniques/conversion/brainwashing.htm.

p. 92 On Skinner's unattractive 'behavioural psychology' utopia, *Walden Two*, see http://www.sparknotes.com/lit/walden2/.

p. 92 On the 'Glorious Gloucesters' and their bloody battle at the Imjin river, see http://en.wikipedia.org/wiki/Battle_of_the_Imjin_River.

p. 92 On 1950s 'peaceful coexistence' and the Khrushchev 'thaw', see http://en.wikipedia.org/wiki/Khrushchev_Thaw.

p. 93 On Joseph McCarthy and the Communist 'enemy within', see http://www.spartacus.schoolnet.co.uk/USAmccarthy.htm.

p. 93 For *Invasion of the Body Snatchers*, and a clip of the film, see http://www.imdb.com/title/tt0049366/trailers-screenplay-E14099–310.

p. 93 For the car and flick-knife scene, at Griffith Park, Los Angeles (a long way from Colchester), in *Rebel without a Cause*, see http://www.youtube.com/watch?v=uaIq234nLo4.

p. 94 For the final scene on the Sierra Madre highway in *Invasion of the Body Snatchers*, see http://www.youtube.com/watch?v=SR32SqbdQtg.

Chapter XIV: The Feather Merchants

p. 95 On the carnage at Omaha Beach, see http://www. thehistorychannel.co.uk/site/tv_guide/full_details/ Conflict/programme_2054.php.

p. 96 On *A Tree Grows in Brooklyn* and the ASE edition thereof, see http://web.njit.edu/fficjohnson/tree/pub/ pub3.htm.

p. 96 For the picture of an American soldier reading the ASE edition of *A Tree Grows in Brooklyn*, see http:// en.wikipedia.org/wiki/Armed_Services_Editions. For a history of ASE in the Second World War, see http://catdir. loc.gov/catdir/toc/becites/cfb/84600198.html.

p. 96 On Hubert Selby Jr's *Last Exit to Brooklyn* and its prosecution, for obscenity, in England, see http:// en.wikipedia.org/wiki/Last_Exit_to_Brooklyn and http:// www.marionboyars.co.uk/Amy%20individual%20 book%20info/LastExit.html.

p. 98 On *The Feather Merchants* and its author, see http:// en.wikipedia.org/wiki/Max_Shulman and http://query. nytimes.com/gst/fullpage.html?res=940DEFDD113EF93 AA1575BC0A96E948260.

p. 99 For information on the film of *For Whom the Bell Tolls* starring Gary Cooper, and a clip (note the Spanglish), see http://www.imdb.com/title/tt0035896/.

p. 101 On the super-patriotic film *Across the Pacific*, see http:// www.imdb.com/title/tt0034428/. For a clip featuring Sydney Green(Fat)street, see http://video.aol.com/video-detail/across-the-pacific-trailer/2226908184.

p. 102 On pre-Nazi Berlin cabaret, see http://www.youtube. com/watch?v=Eyxa1Sfq6Q8.

p. 102 On James Thurber's life and hard times, see http://
en.wikipedia.org/wiki/James_Thurber

p. 103 For a clip from The Dam Busters, happily celebrating
civilian carnage, see: http://simscience.org/cracks/
advanced/dams1.html.

Chapter XV: Lady Chatterley's Lover

p. 104 For Jammin' the Blues, see http://www.dailymotion.
com/video/xrxyq_jammin-the-blues-1944.

p. 104 On Dien Bien Phu and its disastrous consequence
for colonial France, see http://www.dienbienphu.org/
english/.

p. 105 On Pierre Mendès-France, see http://en.wikipedia.
org/wiki/Pierre_Mend%C3%A8s-France.

p. 105 This vast quantity of wine may seem incredible, but
see Miles Kington at http://findarticles.com/p/articles/
mi_qn4158/is_20020905/ai_n12632666.

p. 105 For a brief history of the Kahane–Girodias, Obelisk–
Olympia publication of Lady Chatterley's Lover, see http://
www.bbc.co.uk/dna/collective/A12737829.

p. 106 On John Sparrow and heterosexual buggery in Lady
Chatterley's Lover, see http://www.robertfulford.com/
Dons.html.

p. 106 On the spicy weekly Reveille, see http://www.
geocities.com/rosemarytimperley/articles.htm.

p. 107 For Catherine Tate, see http://www.youtube.com/
user/kenzoidthealien.

Chapter XVI: On the Waterfront

p. 108 On Martin Scorsese and the influence of *Waterfront* on him, see http://www.scorsesefilms.com/article2.htm.

p. 108 For a clip of the 'I coulda been a contendah' exchange, see http://www.youtube.com/watch?v=prXXOxCPNek.

p. 108 On the Regal picture house, Colchester, see http://cinematreasures.org/theater/17575/.

p. 111 On Budd Schulberg and *Waterfront*, see http://books.google.co.uk/books?id=ssvuDCFBhUEC&pg=PA174&lpg=PA174&dq=schulberg+waterfront&source=web&ots=IgElSoZiB5&sig=LOHaQImz27–oRAuzL5yoziGEkKU&hl=en#PPA177,M1.

p. 111 For the complex evolution of the movie *On the Waterfront* from its newspaper and novel sources, see http://66.102.9.104/search?q=cache:tZHSvMabsBYJ:www.wga.org/uploadedFiles/news_and_events/101_screenplay/Waterfront.pdf+%22schulberg%22%2B%22waterfront%22%2B%22novel%22&hl=en&ct=clnk&cd=4&gl=uk.

p. 111 For a clip of the ending of *On the Waterfront*, with Malloy brutally kicked, and Johnny Friendly kicked off the jetty, see http://www.youtube.com/watch?v=S1AopoF_iH8.

p. 112 On the 2007–8 Writers' Guild strike, see http://en.wikipedia.org/wiki/2007_Writers_Guild_of_America_strike.

p. 112 On John Wayne vs. Budd Schulberg, see http://query.nytimes.com/gst/fullpage.html?res=9E05E3DF163CF936A15750C0A9679C8B63.

p. 113 On Elia Kazan vs. the House UnAmerican Activities
Committee, see http://www.wsws.org/articles/2003/
sep2003/kaz-s30.shtml.

p. 113 On Churchill, troops and the Tonypandy strikers,
see http://libcom.org/history/1910-cambrian-combine-
miners-strike-and-tonypandy-riot.

Chapter XVII: Nineteen Eighty-Four

p. 116 On Piccadilly Circus's appearance in the early 1950s,
see http://www.guinntiques.com/piccadilly/index_pages/
Piccadilly1950.asp.

p. 116 For an encyclopedic account of science fiction in the
1950s, see http://www.magicdragon.com/UltimateSF/
timeline1960.html.

p. 117 On Nigel Kneale, TV adapter and SF maestro, see
http://www.nigelkneale.cwc.net/.

p. 117 On Peter Cushing, see http://home.earthlink.
net/ffimhoaglin/sfilm/artists/petercushing/.

p. 117 On Charles Wheeler and his impressive hair, see
http://www.bbc.co.uk/bbcfour/documentaries/timeshift/
charles-wheeler.shtml

p. 118 On Gilbert Harding, and his famed grumpiness, see
http://www.transdiffusion.org/emc/tvheroes/gilbert.
php.

p. 118 For the whole broadcast of the 1954 *Nineteen Eighty-
Four*, see http://www.youtube.com/watch?v=UmHVooJ
qSMo&feature=PlayList&p=AC65E19055A43295&inde
x=14.

p. 121 For a clip of the 1931 film *Dracula*, see http://www.
youtube.com/watch?v=wlsMWuaoukQ.

p. 121 On the 'Doomsday Bomb', see http://www.rense.
com/genera140/dooms.htm.

p. 121 On the horrified Dr Frederic Wertham and his
'seduction of the innocent' campaign, see http://
en.wikipedia.org/wiki/Seduction_of_the_Innocent.

p. 121 On *Vault of Horror*, E.C. comics and horror comics of
the 1950s, see the unhorrified connoisseur site http://
www.watt-evans.com/theotherguys.html.

p. 122 On Stephen King, George Romero and
inspirational E.C. comics, see http://www.avclub.com/
content/interview/george_romero and http://www.
sensesofcinema.com/contents/directors/07/romero.
html.

p. 122 On John Major's Cones Hotline (now inoperative – to
be honest, always inoperative) see http://en.wikipedia.
org/wiki/Cones_Hotline.

p. 123 On *The Scourge of the Swastika*, see http://
en.wikipedia.org/wiki/Edward_Russell,_2nd_
Baron_Russell_of_Liverpool.

p. 123 On the highly unfrightening Abbott and Costello
encounter with Dr Jekyll, see http://eu.movieposter.com/
poster/MPW-12355/Abbott_And_Costello_Meet_Dr_
Jekyll_And_Mr_Hyde.html. For a clip, see http://www.
youtube.com/watch?v=L2qOW3R3fus.

p. 123 On the extremely frightening 2007 film *Saw IV*, see
http://www.officialsaw.com/.

p. 123 On the 1958 Hammer film of *Dracula*, see http://
en.wikipedia.org/wiki/Dracula_%281958_film%29.
For the 'too horrific' (in 1958) ending, see http://www.
truveo.com/Dracula-1958-Trailer/id/674897023.

p. 124 On *Marjorie Morningstar*, see http://www.epinions.
com/book-review-118-ADFDF64–3A185B53-prod4.

Chapter XVIII: 'Shake Rattle and Roll'

p. 125 To watch and hear 'Rocket 88', see http://www. youtube.com/watch?v=Gbfnh1oVTko.

p. 125 On Keats's erroneous 'stout Cortes', see http://www. cs.rice.edu/ffissiyer/minstrels/poems/12.html.

p. 125 On philosopher Herbert Marcuse and his influence in the rebellious 1960s, see http://www.marcuse.org/ herbert/.

p. 126 On pioneering songwriter Jesse Stone, see http:// en.wikipedia.org/wiki/Jesse_Stone and, for a clip of music, http://www.soul-patrol.com/soul/jessiestone. htm.

p. 126 On Bill Haley, his Saddlemen and his Comets, see http://www.billhaley.com/.

p. 126 For Big Joe Turner's and Bill Haley's versions of 'Shake Rattle and Roll', see http://www.youtube.com/ watch?v=20Feq_Nt3nM and http://www.youtube.com/ watch?v=uo_vvA_lzEY.

p. 127 On New Orleans clarinettist Johnny Dodds, see http://www.redhotjazz.com/jdodds.html.

p. 127 On swing band clarinettist Artie Shaw, see http:// www.artieshaw.com/.

p. 127 To hear recordings of 'Begin the Beguine' and 'Potato Head Blues', see http://www.youtube.com/ watch?v=GhEnpEfT3j4 and http://www.youtube.com/ watch?v=NpVgSxsP5Vo.

p. 129 A starting point for Elvisology is the 'official' fansite: http://www.elvis.com/.

p. 130 On songwriters Leiber and Stoller, see http://www. geocities.com/spectropop/hleiberstoller.html.

p. 130   On R&B singer Jimmy Witherspoon, see http://www.jimmywitherspoon.com/.

p. 131   For Big Mama Thornton's rousing 'Hound Dog', see http://www.youtube.com/watch?v=5XUAg1_A7IE.

p. 132   On the British blues-shouter and much missed 'personality' George Melly, see http://music.guardian.co.uk/obituaries/story/0,,2119216,00.html.

Chapter XIX: Ulysses

p. 135   On Jeremy Bentham's 'Panopticon' and its ominous significance, see http://www.cartome.org/panopticon1.htm.

p. 135   On the troubled publication of Nabokov's novel *Lolita*, see http://en.wikipedia.org/wiki/Lolita (in general, avoid any website with 'Lolita' in its title).

p. 136   For a tense clip from *Le salaire de la peur*, see http://www.youtube.com/watch?v=MvtVozPqJVU.

p. 136   On the Blue Gillette razor blade, see http://www.historyworld.co.uk/admuseum.php?11=Shaving&sort=0.

p. 137   On James Joyce's 'dirty letters', see http://www.guardian.co.uk/uk/2004/jul/09/books.booksnews.

p. 137   On the Orton–Halliwell 'criminalised' Islington library books, see http://www.joeorton.org/Pages/Joe_Orton_Life11.html.

p. 138   On Larkin's sad 'annus mirabilis', see http://www.wussu.com/poems/plam.htm.

Chapter XX: The 120 Days of Sodom

p. 139   On Huxley's novel *After Many a Summer*, see http://en.wikipedia.org/wiki/After_Many_a_Summer.

p. 140 On Citizen Kane and citizen William Randolph
Hearst, see http://homepage.ntlworld.com/alm005/
citizen_kane.htm.

p. 140 On Hearst's long-time mistress, Marion Davies, see
http://www.imdb.com/name/nm0203836/.

p. 140 On Mario Praz, author of *The Romantic Agony* (and,
oddly, a Knight Commander of the British Empire),
see http://en.wikipedia.org/wiki/Mario_Praz. On
The Romantic Agony and romantic agony generally,
see http://66.102.9.104/search?q=cache:uqOeHgVa-
FEJ:www.h-net.org/reviews/showpdf.cgi%3Fpath%3D26
206966636723+%22the+romantic+agony%22&hl=en&c
t=clnk&cd=4&gl=uk.

p. 142 On Simone de Beauvoir's questioning (unanswered)
essay, 'Must We Burn de Sade?', see http://books.google.
co.uk/books?id=y9Zth6INdqQC&pg=PA182&lpg=PA182
&dq=%22burn+de+sade%22+beauvoir&source=web&ot
s=X2hToD3G0E&sig=cHDUcxWdJmpV7oo8NQC9C6gbI
vY&hl=en#PPA183,M1.

p. 142 On Ian Brady's sex-novel, *The Kiss of the Whip*, see
http://www.aks-books.co.uk/titles/kisswhip.htm.
High Heels and Stockings I have been unable to locate,
and I suspect it may have been a 'spicy' magazine, of
the *Razzle* kind see http://www.magforum.com/mens/
mensmagazinesatoz10.htm.

p. 143 On the Moors Murders and murderers (Ian Brady
and Myra Hindley), see http://www.crimelibrary.com/
serial_killers/predators/moors/index_1.html.

p. 145 For a clip from Pasolini's (retch-inducing) *Salò*, see
http://www.youtube.com/watch?v=002ul-UwOvU.

p. 145   For the full text of de Sade's (yawn-inducing) *The 120 Days of Sodom*, see http://supervert.com/elibrary/marquis_de_sade.

p. 145   For a manga (strip-cartoon) version of *The 120 Days of Sodom*, see http://www.englishmangas.com/e-mangas/120%20Days%20of%20Sodom/index.html.

Chapter XXI: Oblomov

p. 147   On the critic V. S. Pritchett, see http://en.wikipedia.org/wiki/V._S._Pritchett.

p. 147   On V. I. Lenin's 'Electrify!' slogan, see http://www.time.com/time/magazine/article/0,9171,757368–4,00.html.

p. 148   On Sir Bernard and Lady Docker's height-of-vulgarity gold-plated Daimler, see http://www.joesherlock.com/Docker.html.

p. 148   On Penguin Classics' founding editor, E. V. Rieu, see http://en.wikipedia.org/wiki/E.V._Rieu.

p. 148   On Penguin Classics' all-purpose translator J. M. Cohen, see http://en.wikipedia.org/wiki/J._M._Cohen.

p. 148   On novelist Ivan Goncharov, see http://www.kirjasto.sci.fi/ivangont.htm and http://en.wikipedia.org/wiki/Ivan_Goncharov.

p. 149   On the world-weary utterance, 'Living? Our servants will do that for us,' see http://en.wikipedia.org/wiki/Auguste_Villiers_de_l'Isle-Adam.

p. 149   On the Russian unit of distance, the 'verst', see http://mw1.m-w.com/dictionary/verst.

p. 150   On *Malone Dies*, see http://en.wikipedia.org/wiki/Malone_Dies.

p. 150 On coffee-bar culture (so to call it) in the 1950s, see
http://www.classiccafes.co.uk/Links.html.

p. 150 The Irish, because they do not much play the game,
love being rude about cricket. Note the ethnic origins
of the names at http://www.quotesea.com/Quotes.
aspx?about=Cricket.

p. 152 On *Catch-22* and the passing of time, see http://news.
bbc.co.uk/1/hi/magazine/6926500.stm.

p. 152 On Spike Milligan and his *Oblomov* stage fantasia, see
http://mikeagnew123.tripod.com/spikemilliganshop/
id20.html.

p. 152 On Goncharov, paranoia and Turgenev, see http://
www.answers.com/topic/ivan-goncharov.

Chapter XXII: 'Red Wind'

p. 153 On the much-footprinted Grauman's Chinese
Theatre, see http://www.manntheatres.com/chinese/.

p. 154 On the witty Herman J. Mankiewicz, see http://film.
guardian.co.uk/features/featurepages/0,,2224021,00.
html.

p. 154 On Aldous Huxley and Hollywood, see http://
somaweb.org/.

p. 155 On the 'original' of the Stoyte mansion and Kane's
Xanadu – Hearst Castle – see http://www.hearstcastle.
com/.

p. 156 On the genetic relationship of Chandler's private
eyes, Philip Marlowe and John Dalmas, see http://www.
thrillingdetective.com/dalmas.html.

p. 157 For the full text of Hemingway's (taut and short)
'The Killers', see http://www.geocities.com/cyber_
explorer99/hemingwaykillers.html.

p. 157 For the corresponding greasy-spoon scene in David
Cronenberg's film *History of Violence*, see http://www.
youtube.com/watch?v=gEUuZVN-Hwk&feature=related.

p. 158 On *The Big Sleep* and Raymond Chandler's riddling
'Who knows?' telegram to film director Howard Hawks,
who could not make sense of the plot, see http://www.
detnovel.com/BigSleep.html.

p. 158 On Dashiell Hammett, see http://www.pbs.org/wnet/
americanmasters/database/hammett_d.html.

p. 158 On the Santa Ana ('red') wind, and its meteorology,
see http://www.atmos.ucla.edu/ffifovell/ASother/mm5/
SantaAna/winds.html.

p. 158 On the hardy, high-altitude Jeffrey pine, see http://
www.na.fs.fed.us/pubs/silvics_manual/volume_1/pinus/
jeffreyi.htm.

p. 159 On the catastrophic 1993 fires in the Southern
California San Gabriel mountains, see http://www.
eqecat.com/documents/SouthernCAFire1993.html.

Chapter XXIII: Waiting for Godot

p. 160 On the origins of the assertion, 'The Revolution
will not be televised', see http://en.wikipedia.org/wiki/
The_Revolution_Will_Not_Be_Televised.

p. 160 On first productions of *Waiting for Godot* in London
and Britain, see http://books.guardian.co.uk/review/
story/0,12084,868126,00.html.

p. 160 On recollections of working in Colchester Repertory
theatre at this period, see http://www.bl.uk/projects/
theatrearchive/chater2.html.

p. 161 On 'David Baron' (i.e. Harold Pinter) and Colchester, see http://www.haroldpinter.org/acting/acting_otherrepwork.shtml.

p. 162 On Somerset Maugham's dismissal of the Angry Young Men as 'scum', see http://facstaff.unca.edu/moseley/maugham.html.

p. 163 On Bryan Drew's theatrical and film career, see http://www.imdb.com/name/nm1731383/.

p. 163 On Colchester rep impresario 'Bob' Digby, see http://www.theatrestrust.org.uk/resources/theatres/show/99-repertory-colchester.

Chapter XXIV: W. R. Rodgers

p. 164 On W. R. Rodgers's life, career and poetry, see http://en.wikipedia.org/wiki/W._R._Rodgers and http://www.ricorso.net/rx/az-data/authors/r/Rodgers_WR/life.htm and (most informatively) http://66.102.9.104/search?q=cache:s7W8ooy2s0sJ:www.proni.gov.uk/introduction__rodgers_papers_d2833.pdf+%22w.+r.+rodgers%22&hl=en&ct=clnk&cd=3&gl=uk.

p. 164 On critic and publisher Dan Davin, see http://en.wikipedia.org/wiki/Dan_Davin.

p. 165 For the full text of Rodgers on Paisley, approving, but not entirely flattering, see http://www.womenpriests.org/teaching/mcalees2.asp.

p. 166 On the making of cultural climates, see W. H. Auden, writing on the death of Freud, in 1939 http://www.poemhunter.com/poem/in-memory-of-sigmund-freud/.

p. 166 For the poets' drinking school in the environs of Broadcasting House, see the account of Paddy Fraser,

wife of G. S. Fraser http://jacketmagazine.com/20/fraser.
html.

p. 166 On Catholic, dangerously pugnacious poet Roy
Campbell, see http://www.catholicauthors.com/roy_
campbell.html.

p. 166 On the high-cultural BBC 'Third Programme', see
http://www.bbc.co.uk/radio3/classical/thirdprogramme/
introduction.shtml and http://en.wikipedia.org/wiki/
BBC_Third_Programme.

p. 168 On Ronald Blythe and Rodgers, see Blythe's
response, on receiving his honorary degree from Essex
University http://66.102.9.104/search?q=cache:SK88u-
h3s38J:www.essex.ac.uk/vc/orate2002/Blytheresponse.rt
f+%22Ronald+Blythe%22%2B%22w.+r.+rodgers%22&h
l=en&ct=clnk&cd=1&gl=uk.

p. 169 For a broad selection of Rodgers's poems, and
to hear the poet reading them, see http://www.
poetryarchive.org/poetryarchive/singlePoem.
do?poemId=3157.

p. 169 On Joycean and Yeatsian critic Richard Ellmann, see
http://en.wikipedia.org/wiki/Richard_Ellmann.

p. 170 For a 'virtual tour' of the town of Claremont and
its many colleges, see http://www.cusd.claremont.edu/
www/community/tour/index.html.

p. 171 For Leonard Cohen, his erections and Mount Baldy,
see http://www.leonardcohensite.com/baldy/index.htm
and http://www.leonardcohenforum.com/viewtopic.
php?f=19&p=114045.

Chapter XXV: Room at the Top

p. 172 On Angry Young Man and novelist John Braine, see
http://www.newi.ac.uk/rdover/popfic/room_at_.htm and
http://en.wikipedia.org/wiki/John_Braine.

p. 174 On the Angry Young Man school of writers
and satirists, see http://en.wikipedia.org/wiki/
Angry_Young_Men.

p. 174 On the 1956 Suez Crisis, and the British crisis it
provoked, see http://www.bodley.ox.ac.uk/dept/scwmss/
projects/suez/suez.html.

p. 174 On the 1950s anti-establishment sentiment,
among the AYM and the young generally, see http://
www.poetryarchive.org/poetryarchive/singlePoem.
do?poemId=3157. On the sarcastically named
Establishment Club in Soho, founded by Peter Cook,
see http://stabbers.truth.posiweb.net/stabbers/html/
biography/biography_01.htm.

p. 175 On Pilot Officer D. R. Kenyon's crime and
punishment, see http://www.time.com/time/magazine/
article/0,9171,809045,00.html?promoid=googlep.

p. 176 On 1940s rationing and its depressive effects, see
http://www.fashion-era.com/utility_clothing.htm.

p. 176 On 1950s affluence and its exhilarating effect, see
http://news.bbc.co.uk/onthisday/hi/dates/stories/july/20/
newsid_3728000/3728225.stm.

p. 176 On Prime Minister Harold Macmillan's 'You've
never had it so good' address to the nation, see http://
news.bbc.co.uk/onthisday/hi/dates/stories/july/20/
newsid_3728000/3728225.stm.

p. 176 On the lusted-after Triumph TR2 sports car, see
http://www.motorbase.com/vehicle/by-id/368/.

p. 177   On Harold Macmillan the inveterate Trollopian,
see http://64.233.183.104/search?q=cache:
YCvrEGIit6UJ:www.cercles.com/n11/catterall.pdf+%22h
arold+macmillan%22%2B%22trollope%22&hl=en&ct=c
lnk&cd=1&gl=uk.

p. 177   On the Fellini film *La Dolce Vita* (untranslatable in the
1950s), see http://www.imdb.com/title/tt0053779/.

p. 178   On 'Brylcreem Boy', Dennis Compton, see http://
www.ba-education.demon.co.uk/for/sport/cricket/
compton.html. On dour Yorkshireman (Sir) Len Hutton,
see http://en.wikipedia.org/wiki/Len_Hutton.

Chapter XXVI: The Uses of Literacy

p. 179   For *The Book of Snobs*, see http://www.gutenberg.org/
etext/2686.

p. 180   For Colchester Royal Grammar School's fine library
furnishing, see http://www.crgs.co.uk/inside/?page=1.

p. 180   On Matthew Arnold and 'Rugby Chapel' (even more
finely furnished), see http://www.bartleby.com/42/703.
html.

p. 180   On Professor Richard Hoggart and his pioneering
of 'cultural studies' in the UK, see http://www.
publications.bham.ac.uk/birmingham_magazine/b_
magazine1996–99/pg14_98.htm. On his influential
The Uses of Literarcy, see http://www.litencyc.com/php/
sworks.php?rec=true&UID=15068.

p. 181   On Puritan John Bunyan, see http://acacia.pair.com/
Acacia.John.Bunyan/.

p. 181   On latter-day Puritan D. H. Lawrence, see http://
www.online-literature.com/dh_lawrence/.

p. 183 For a clip of the Burgessian milk bar in *The Clockwork Orange* (film), see http://www.youtube.com/watch?v=vaNdncWHoio.

p. 183 For the Bogart-starring film *The Harder They Fall*, see http://www.imdb.com/title/tt0049291/.

p. 184 On the social revolution brought about by the 1944 Butler Education Act, see http://www.spartacus.schoolnet.co.uk/EDbutler.htm.

p. 185 For a clip of the Platters tunefully crooning 'The Great Pretender', see http://www.youtube.com/watch?v=PtXnUEW_OXw.

Chapter XXVII: The Tenement Kid

p. 189 On tough-guy author Mickey Spillane and his ultra-tough private eye, Mike Hammer, see http://pages.interlog.com/ffiroco/hammer.html.

p. 189 For George Orwell's essay on 'Raffles and Miss Blandish', see http://gaslight.mtroyal.ab.ca/Orwell-C.htm. On the creator of Raffles, E. W. Hornung, and the text of Raffles's exploits, see http://www.mysterynet.com/books/testimony/hardknox.shtml and http://www.gutenberg.org/etext/707.

p. 190 On the *Strand Magazine*, in which Sherlock Holmes and Raffles were introduced into mass readership, see http://www.strandmag.com/hist.htm.

p. 190 On *No Orchids for Miss Blandish* and its author, James Hadley Chase, see http://www.kirjasto.sci.fi/jhchase.htm and http://www.thrillingdetective.com/fenner.html.

p. 195 On the 1935 launch of Penguin paperback books, see http://www.penguin.co.uk/static/packages/uk/aboutus/history.html.

p. 195 On the launch of Robert de Graff's Pocket Book
series, in the US, see http://findarticles.com/p/articles/
mi_g1epc/is_tov/ai_2419100931.

p. 195 For the ubiquitous Bronco toilet paper, see http://
web.ukonline.co.uk/stephen.johnson/steve/bronco.jpg.

p. 197 For *Catcher in the Rye* and the hero, Holden's, scorned
'phoniness' of American society, see http://www.
bookrags.com/notes/citr/TOP4.htm.

p. 198 On *Black Mask* magazine and its 'hard-boiled'
detective stories, see http://www.blackmaskmagazine.
com/.

p. 199 On pioneer lesbian writer Sally M. Singer (alias
pulp novelist 'March Hastings'), see http://www.
expressgaynews.com/2007/6–22/locallife/feature/.

Chapter XXVIII: Absolute Beginners

p. 201 On novelist Colin MacInnes and his novel *Absolute
Beginners*, see http://arts.guardian.co.uk/theatre/
drama/story/0,,2057327,00.html. For photographs
of MacInnes around the period of writing *Absolute
Beginners*, see http://www.npg.org.uk/live/search/person.
asp?LinkID=mp05543.

p. 203 For the lyrics of Laurie London's 1958 hit, 'He's Got
the Whole World in His Hands', and the infant singer
of them, see http://www.lyrics007.com/Laurie%20
London%20Lyrics/Hes%20Got%20The%20Whole%20
World%20In%20His%20Hands%20Lyrics.html and
http://www.boysoloist.com/artist.asp?VID=1012.

p. 204 On black American novelist James Baldwin, see
http://www.kirjasto.sci.fi/jbaldwin.htm.

p. 204 For the text of Norman Podhoretz's angry essay,
'My Negro Problem – and Ours', see http://www.google.
co.uk/search?hl=en&q=%E2%80%9CMy+Negro+Proble
m%22%2B%22podhoretz%22&meta=.

p. 205 On British band leader Ted Heath ('and his music'),
see http://www.45-rpm.org.uk/dirt/tedh.htm and http://
nfo.net/brit/bh4.html. On American bandleader and
vibraphonist Lionel Hampton, and a clip of 'Hamp's'
tear-it-up performances in the 1950s, see http://www.
uidaho.edu/hampton/index.html and http://www.
youtube.com/watch?v=BnjKCVc781s.

p. 206 On the 1958 London race riots, around Notting
Hill, and the authorities punitive response, see http://
en.wikipedia.org/wiki/Notting_Hill_race_riots.

Chapter XXIX: The Claverings

p. 208 On post-Second World War National Service,
see http://www.bbc.co.uk/history/british/modern/
peacetime_conscripts_01.shtml.

p. 208 On the raffish novelist Simon Raven, see http://www.
guardian.co.uk/obituaries/story/0,3604,491484,00.html.

p. 209 For what a Victorian pier glass looked like,
see http://www.artfact.com/catalog/viewLot.
cfm?lotCode=19WPEV1F.

p. 209 The full text of The Claverings is available at http://
www.gutenberg.org/etext/15766. For contemporary
illustrations to the novel, see http://www.jimandellen.
org/trollope/pictures.Claverings.html.

p. 210 On the decimalisation of British coinage and
currency in 1971, see http://www.tclayton.demon.co.uk/
dec.html.

p. 210 On 'double' volumes in the Oxford World's Classics series, see http://www.edu.uwo.ca/worldsclassics/index.html.

p. 210 On bibliophile, publisher and passionate Trollopian Michael Sadleir, see http://en.wikipedia.org/wiki/Michael_Sadleir.

p. 210 On illustrator Lynton Lamb, see http://www.chrisbeetles.com/pictures/artists/Lamb_Lynton/Lamb_Lynton.htm.

p. 211 On Victorian religious 'doubt', see http://bookshop.blackwell.co.uk/jsp/id/Victorian_Doubt/9780389209386.

Chapter XXX: Mein Kampf

p. 215 For the 'dank vaults' of Colchester Castle – here more cheerfully portrayed – see http://www.colchestermuseums.org.uk/castle/castle_index.html.

p. 215 On bomb damage in Colchester in the Second World War, see www.colchestermuseums.org.uk/infodesk/downloads/WW2-supportingnotes.pdf.

p. 215 For a 'virtual tour' of Montgomery Barracks in Kladow (as they were), see http://baor-locations.com/montgomerybks.aspx. For a reminiscence of 'wire patrols' at Kladow, see http://www.bbc.co.uk/ww2peopleswar/stories/94/a4294794.shtml.

p. 216 On Gibraltar barracks, Bury St Edmunds, depot of the Suffolk Regiment (as it was), see http://www.stedmundsbury.gov.uk/sebc/visit/sufreg.cfm.

p. 216 On the Gideon Bible movement and its distribution of texts, see http://en.wikipedia.org/wiki/Gideons_International.

p. 216 For *Mein Kampf* as a rare, 'collectable' item, see
http://hitlernews.cloudworth.com/nazi-relics-rings-
leader.php.

p. 217 On *Mein Kampf*, the Huntington Library and General
Patton, and prudent reasons for not exhibiting the
item, see http://groups.google.com/group/alt.movies.
spielberg/browse_thread/thread/0f156b0680525de3.

p. 219 On the publication history of *Mein Kampf*, see http://
en.wikipedia.org/wiki/Mein_Kampf.

p. 220 On Erich Maria Remarque and Adolf Hitler in the
First World War, see http://greyfalcon.us/restored/
Hitler%20wwI.htm.

p. 221 On the arch-eccentric novelist M. P. Shiel, see http://
alangullette.com/lit/shiel/ and http://alangullette.com/
lit/shiel/mpsweb.htm. The full text of *The Lord of the Sea* is
available at www.gutenberg.org/etext/6993.

p. 223 On Mrs Thatcher's fears of England being
'swamped' by immigrants, see http://www.time.
com/time/magazine/article/0,9171,948011,00.
html?promoid=googlep.

p. 225 On Richard I's coronation and subsequent anti-
Semitism, see http://www.fordham.edu/halsall/source/
hoveden1189b.html. On the thirteenth-century 'Edict of
Expulsion' on England's Jews, see http://www.heretical.
com/British/jews1290.html.

p. 226 On Jules Verne's vindictive Captain Nemo,
see http://en.wikipedia.org/wiki/Twenty_
Thousand_Leagues_Under_the_Sea.

p. 226 On the social economist and would-be reformer
Henry George, see http://www.henrygeorgefoundation.
org/.

p. 227 On the British 'Aliens Act', of 1905, see http://
www.20thcenturylondon.org.uk/server.php?show=conIn
formationRecord.35.

p. 227 On Shiel's scare-novel *The Yellow Danger*, see http://
alangullette.com/lit/shiel/essays/academy_yellow.htm.

p. 228 For the full text of Shiel's apocalyptic fantasy *The
Purple Cloud*, see http://www.gutenberg.org/etext/11229.

p. 228 On John Gawsworth, heir to M. P. Shiel, see http://
www.lib.uiowa.edu/spec-coll/MSC/ToMsc550/MsC536_
gawsworth/GawsworthFA.html.

Chapter XXXI: The Resistible Rise of Arturo Ui

p. 230 On Bertolt Brecht, 'epic' theatre and the Berliner
Ensemble, see http://en.wikipedia.org/wiki/Theater_
am_Schiffbauerdamm and http://en.wikipedia.org/wiki/
Berliner_Ensemble.

p. 230 On Kenneth Tynan, the most influential drama
critic of his era, see http://arts.guardian.co.uk/critic/
feature/0,,567652,00.html.

p. 232 On Brechtian actor, Ekkehard Schall, see http://
en.wikipedia.org/wiki/Ekkehard_Schall.

p. 232 On the meaning of 'esemplastic', see http://
everything2.com/index.pl?node_id=234235.

List of Illustrations

Acknowledgements

THE PHOTOGRAPH OF Colchester Hippodrome on page 9 is reproduced by permission of the Colchester Museums, Museum Resource Centre. The photograph of the Hippodrome cartouche, on page 12, is reproduced by permission of the Theatres Trust. The illustrations from *The Wind in the Willows*, on pages 19 and 20, are reproduced by permission of the E. H. Shepard estate. The illustration from the film of *Great Expectations* on page 22 and the poster for the film of *On the Waterfront* on page 109 are reproduced by permission of MPTV-net. The photograph of George Ellery Hale on the Mount Wilson Toll Road is reproduced by courtesy of the Archives, California Institute of Technology. The photograph of Jack Gardner on page 50 is reproduced by courtesy of BritishBoxing.Net.

Verses from Alfred Noyes's 'The Highwayman' are reproduced by kind permission of Oxford University Press. Thanks too to Faber and Faber for kind permission to reproduce an extract from T. S. Eliot's, *The Waste Land*, Faber and Faber © The Eliot Estate, also lines from Philip Larkin's 'MCMXIV', taken from *Whitsun Weddings*, Faber and Faber © The Larkin Estate.

While every effort has been made to contact copyright-holders, the author and publishers would be grateful for information where they have been unable to trace them, and would be glad to make amendments in further editions.